The Legendary
Tugboat Captain Annie Brennan
of Puget Sound

Norman Reilly Raine (publicity photo,
Walters Studio,1959; Drew collection)

The Legendary Tugboat Captain Annie Brennan of Puget Sound

The Irascible Skipper of Deep-Sea Towing & Salvage's Narcissus Featured in Stories Related by Norman Reilly Raine in The Saturday Evening Post

Bernard A. Drew

BearManor Media

2025

The Legendary
Tugboat Captain Annie Brennan
of Puget Sound

Copyright © 2025 Bernard A. Drew

Published in the United States of America by:

BearManor Media

1317 Edgewater Dr. #110
Orlando, FL 32804

bearmanormedia.com

Printed in the United States.

Typesetting and layout by PKJ Passion Global

ISBN–979-8-88771-705-0

Minton, Balch published the first hardcover
collection of Tugboat Annie stories in 1934.

Contents

"Oh happy days is here some more ..."

— Tugboat Annie Brennan's version of
the Milton Ager/Jack Yellen standard from 1929

Foreword

I Was a Teenage Tugboat Annie Fan

I first encountered Tugboat Annie Brennan when my mother subscribed to *The Saturday Evening Post*. I was taken by the brash character, the Northwest setting, the striking artwork and the twisty plots in Norman Reilly Raine's stories. Over time, I collected actual magazines or over-sized photocopies of all of the *Narcissus* tales, also sea-going yarns of his Mr. Gallup and Dandy Man. It took several years lugging to a photocopying machine bound magazine volumes in either the Springfield City Library, the W.E.B. Du Bois Library at the University of Massachusetts, Amherst or the Smith College Library in Northampton, all in Massachusetts, to assemble them all.

The stories treaded water in my files. Once in a while I waded in and read one and smiled.

I acquired stills from the motion pictures and television show, also a handful of original movie studio contracts signed by Raine, a card with his signature and syndicated newspaper photos of the author.

I gathered the makings of a book, a dual bio-bibliography. But other projects intervened.

My interest re-sparked when our older daughter conveniently settled in Olympia, Wash., prime Tugboat Annie territory. My wife, Donna, and I visited in 2018 and Jessie M. Drew and her husband, Joshua Collins-Belden, took us to Budd Inlet in Olympia (we toured the *Sand Man*) and to Tugboat Annie's restaurant on Westbay Drive (for a hearty seafood meal). We walked around Tacoma (Thea Foss Waterway and Washington State History Museum) and Seattle (the *Arthur Foss* is docked at the Museum of History & Industry) and the Hiram M. Chittenden/Ballard Locks on the Lake Washington Ship Canal (as *Island Passage* and *Mudcat* floated through). We visited Woodard Bay (remnants of a railroad pier bridge from logging days is now home to thousands of bats) and Port Townsend (the Blue Moose Café in the shipyard is surrounded by tugboats and other vessels in drydock).

I read all of Annie's published adventures — some for the first time — and several other Raine stories, watched three films and one TV show, scoured for interviews and miscellaneous bits of information (surprises included three Annie pastiches, an unpublished story and an obituary notice) and began writing.

Here's the result: A double biography of a successful writer and his famous fictional character; a close look at a popular literature sub-genre; an acknowledgement of the hard work of tugboat men and women; an appreciation of a stellar fictional heroine; and an armchair tour of the Puget Sound, Juan de Fuca Strait and waterfront environs.

Step aboard.

— *Bernard A. Drew, Great Barrington, Massachusetts*

"The world is full of people who prospected in distant places while pay dirt was under their feet, and the origin of 'Tugboat Annie' was no exception."

" 'Tugboat Annie' Founded On Fact, Writer Reveals,"
Seattle Post-Intelligencer, 23 July 1933

Chapter 1

An Iconic Fictional Character

Norman Reilly Raine was often asked how he came up with his robust towboat character Tugboat Annie. It would have been immodest for him to say he just used his writer's smarts. But while he was adept at controlled, descriptive prose, made colorful use of dynamic world settings and conceived ingenious ways for a protagonist to turn around seemingly impossible situations, he really needed a hook.

The author had broken into leading periodical markets in Canada (*Maclean's*) and the United States (*Everybody's* and *The Saturday Evening Post*) specializing in seafaring stories, befitting his early wartime ambulance service and subsequent merchant marine career.

When he taught a writing course in Seattle in 1930, he told students: "I know and like the sea and sailors. That's the reason I use them almost exclusively for my stories. ... Whenever I try to inject feminine interest into my stories, the females invariably evolve into unsavory characters, so I decided it would be best to eliminate them almost entirely from my writings."[1]

Ironically, within a year he wrote the first of a string of 67 published stories about an enduring, quick-witted, verbal and at times physical brawler — a woman.

"The series came into being while I was a guest lecturer on the short story at the University of Washington in Seattle," Raine explained. "Edwin Wintermute, an instructor in journalism and one-time reporter on an eastern newspaper, told me of a woman who had inherited the job of her towboat skipper husband upon his death, and who had made a success of the job in competition with a lot of hard-boiled male opposition...."[2]

Wintermute (1898-1970), who got his writing start with *Film Daily*, later taught at Michigan State University and was arts and literary editor of the *Lansing State Journal*, loved maritime lore and wrote oceanic stories himself.[3]

Raine quoted Wintermute as telling him "a woman tugboat skipper should make a fine fictional character for you."[4]

His mentor had "a grand story idea, of course," Raine said, "but one which demanded, for its central character, a woman of more positive physical qualities than those possessed by an eastern woman. She, I was told, was middle-aged, gray-haired, quiet and ladylike and an exceedingly efficient business woman; but this did not present the human interest that was possible in a more rugged type in direct conflict with men."[5]

Providence's Kate Sutton

Raine investigated the East Coast tugboater suggested by Wintermute, Catherine "Kate" Brown Sutton (1877-1959).[6] He learned Sutton was "a warm, humorous and carefully groomed woman, able with ease to command the 30 crewmen of the old Providence Tow & Steamboat Co. of which she was president for 20 years.[7] She had succeeded her husband, N. Howard Sutton on his death in 1923,"[8] according to *The Boston Globe*.

New York-born and formerly a school teacher, Sutton oversaw a six-ship operation on Narragansett Bay and regularly hauled barges from Norfolk, Va.

Sutton resembled Tugboat Annie in physique. And in ingenuity. However, *The Boston Globe* said "she usually issues her orders through the port captain. She rarely sets foot aboard a tug and has never sailed on one. But ask her where her tugs are at a certain time of the day and she can tell you. She can figure out very quickly just about how much time will be required to complete a particular towing job."[9] She dismissed the idea a woman might command a tug;

the quarters were much too small for feminine comfort, even her small fleet's modern, $100,000, ocean-going *Maurania*.

Sutton's career, not necessarily her personality, suited Raine.

Thea Foss, who launched what became Foss Maritime in Tacoma with a fishing skiff in 1889, was one of author Norman Reilly Raine's inspirations in creating Tugboat Annie Brennan. (Foss Maritime)

Tacoma's Thea Foss

Closer to home, Thea Kristiansdatter Foss (1958-1927) was another Tugboat Annie prototype, and the one most often credited as having inspired Raine's short stories and novelettes.

A Norway native transplanted to Tacoma, she raised three children while living in a houseboat. Foss in 1889 saw opportunity in Commencement Bay and purchased a fishing skiff for $5. She sold it for more than she paid and bought two others, making sufficient profit that her husband, Andrew Oleson Fossen (1855-1937), shortened to Foss, gave up his carpentry and began to build boats, first rowboats then sailboats. From there grew a towing business and Foss Maritime, which is still active in the Puget Sound.[10]

As Thea's son Wedell Foss once pointed out, his "quiet, pious Norwegian mother" was quite different from the raucous Irish character that flew from Raine's typewriter; she had a "morbid fear of the water."[11]

"Unfortunately, I missed seeing Thea Foss, when I first visited the city in 1924, during her lifetime," Raine related in *The Oregonian*, in a slightly different telling of his fictional heroine's nascence. "I was then a forecastle hand and a malaria-ridden one at that.

"But I came back in 1930 as a writer of short stories. Mrs. Foss had died in 1927, but she was still a picturesque tradition of the waterfront. She came to my mind then, lecturing at the University of Washington. I decided to write a story of a woman tugboat captain.

"Knocking around to get tugboat atmosphere," Raine went on, "I met Thea's son, Wedell Foss, one of the heads of the great Foss Launch & Tugboat company. He turned out to be a great biographer. He explained that he not only wishes to honor his mother but to make the public tugboat-conscious. He succeeded in doing so through me, but I am sure that if I had not happened along some other writer would have dug into the gold of the Tugboat Annie tradition."[12]

Wedell Foss (1888-1955)[13] — he and his brothers Arthur and Henry had to endure being labeled "The Sons of Tugboat Annie," he said — downplayed his role in the fictional captain's legend. Foss told *Cleveland Plain Dealer* reporter George E. Griswold in 1941 he was disappointed Raine was so busy writing scenarios in Hollywood, new Tugboat Annie tales were becoming rare in print.

"I honestly believe Raine will be to our literature what Joseph Conrad was to England's. As I see it, he has both the red-blooded vigor of Jack London and the pathos and humor of Mark Twain. I'll be happy when he returns to writing fiction exclusively," he said.[14]

Raine said he learned of other women of the water, three of them in the Puget Sound region. "One was a woman who qualified as marine chief engineer and for many years followed that profession in the engine room of ships along the Northwest Coast;" he told the *Seattle Post Intelligencer*, "another was a woman owner — a very capable one, too — of a line of small freight packets that traded among the islands and inlets of that immense protected waterway bounded by Vancouver Island and the British Columbia coast; and still another was the skipper of a fishing and trading vessel along the Alaska coast."[15]

Raine also heard stories about Norway-born Captain Oystein "Mike" L. Tollaksen (1867-1928), a Port Townsend and Seattle tugboatman.[16] His wife, Myrtle Lucretia (Bliss), often accompanied him on his assignments.

There may have been an anonymous spur. "Once while waiting in the rain outside the old Star building on King St. [in Toronto] he thought up an idea. The rain and the fog and a view of a stout, purposeful woman scrubbing floors in the Star building gave him the idea. He worked on the idea that night. The result was a story called Tugboat Annie….," according to the *Lethbridge Herald*.[17]

From all these parts plus some intense research into maritime law and tradition Raine shaped a memorable character.

Where's Secoma on the Map?

For setting, Raine combined Seattle and Tacoma, arriving at the name Secoma.

Raine can't take credit for the merged name; Joseph Henry Jackson, the editor of San Francisco-based *Sunset: The Pacific Monthly*, in 1925[18] suggested, to calm trade competition between the two cities, consolidating the names of the seaports as either Seacoma ... or Tacomeattle.

There are other made-up locations in the stories, but Vancouver (older than its Canadian counterpart, founded in 1824; both were named for British Royal Navy Captain George Vancouver, the first to explore Puget Sound, in 1792); Port Townsend (named byVancouver for Marquis George Townsend); Everett (named for Everett Colby, whose father helped establish the community in 1892); Bellingham (William Bellingham was storekeeper to the Vancouver expedition); Port Angeles (short for Puerto de Nuestra Senora de Los Angeles, coined by explorer Francisco de Eliza in 1791); Juan de Fuca Strait (named for that early explorer); Cape Flattery (the northwesternmost point of land in the lower 48 states); and Olympia (named for Edmond Sylvester in 1853; previously called Smithter) all exist. And all and more are included in the Maritime Washington National Heritage Area, created in 2019 and encompassing the coastal areas of 14 Washington counties.

As he readied his first Tugboat Annie tale, Raine learned about Kate Sutton of Rhode Island, who succeeded her husband in operating Providence Tow & Steamboat in the 1920s. (Steamship Historical Society)

Connected to the Pacific Ocean by the Juan de Fuca Strait, Puget Sound stretches from Deception Pass (between Whidbey and Fidalgo Islands) to Olympia. British Royal Navy Lt. Peter Puget (1765-1822) explored the region aboard the *HMS Discovery*, part of Vancouver's 1792 expedition in search of a Northwest Passage.

And from the Movie House ...

Raine had the concept.

To round out his heroine's dynamic personality, he went to the movies.

"Some time before I had seen the talking picture, 'Anna Christie,' which, although starring Greta Garbo, had in it that grand old performer Marie Dressler. Miss Dressler's part was only a bit; but no one who saw her matchless performance as the broken-down drunken old waterfront harridan will ever forget it. She was definite, she was colorful, she could mask tenderness of heart behind a surface brusqueness that deceived no one but herself; therefore, deliberately, although not with any thought of writing for the films, I made 'Tugboat Annie' Marie Dressler, or, if you prefer, Marie Dressler 'Tugboat Annie.' Evidently the idea got across because the illustrator, Anton Otto Fischer, whose maritime paintings are widely admired, saw the character as Miss Dressler when he read the manuscript and so illustrates her....

"I tried to make Tugboat Annie do and say the things Miss Dressler, in such a role, would do and say," Raine told columnist Lee Shippey in 1932.[19] "*The Saturday Evening Post* bought the story and my agent asked for a copy of it to submit to Metro-Goldwyn-Mayer. They bought it for Miss Dressler. I've written seven Tugboat Annie stories now, and Metro-Goldwyn-Mayer have bought three of those magazine stories for the screen.

"It doesn't happen often — a story character inspired by a motion-picture actress which, after magazine publication, eventually becomes the logical vehicle for that same actress."

Tugboat Annie had a basic school education — grammar isn't her forte — but a master's degree in experience. She was well versed in maritime traditions and laws. Her bluster masks a kind heart. She is not above playing practical jokes but turns grumpy when jokes are played on her. She is the widow of a master towboat operator who taught her the Puget Sound from inlet to port, dry dock to cannery camp to logging outpost.

Raine made his heroine Irish, the survivor of a marriage to an alcoholic. He gave her a distinct pattern of chatter. As Charles Earle Funk explained in 1952, [20] "The speech of the character, 'Tugboat Annie,' popularized by her creator, Norman Reilly Raine, abounds in … instances of malapropisms. She speaks of 'a woman in Virginia who gave birth to "quadrupeds," ' instead of 'quadruplets' …; 'I'll "rumble" up to the office,' instead of 'ramble'; 'You want me "preposition," ' instead of 'proposition.' It may be thought that Mr. Raine somewhat overdoes the misapplied words that he has 'Annie' inject into her speech, but there are people in real life who are about as mixed up as 'Annie' is."

"Boom!" Raine exclaimed to a *Saturday Evening Post* editor. "I had the character to fit a tug."[21]

Finding a name proved easy.

The author's mother was Anne Reilly Raine. His sister was Anne Irene Raine (Saunders).

Thus was born Anna Maria Theresa Flynn, widow of Terry Brennan, best known as Tugboat Annie.[22]

"She was an easy character to write," he admitted to the *Buffalo Evening News* in 1939.[23]

And readers found her easy and pleasurable to read.

"The Puget Sound tugs are the comfort of yachtsmen, and almost none of our basic industries could do without them. They haul log rafts, and barges filled with sawdust or pulpwood chips. They are important to the fishing industry, and they help the big ships in and out of the fabled Strait of Juan de Fuca. They actually created a literature. … Through [Norman Reilly] Raine's stories in the Saturday Evening Post, Annie captured the hearts of Northwesterners particularly and became a myth-woman figure as indigenous to the region as Paul Bunyan. But former Saturdayevepost editor Ben Hibbs once told me that Tugboat Annie was one of the most popular characters ever brought to life by the magazine...."

Editor Nard Jones, *Northwest Today,*
Seattle Post-Intelligencer, 18 June 1967

Chapter 2

The Venerable Saturday Evening Post

Raine's fictional cargo ship captain Peter Trumpet and his tramp steamer third mate Belial Gallup were serviceable story characters, but traditional. Raine needed a fresh personality, a vibrant figure who would stand out among the *Saturday Evening Post's* stable of eccentrics that included a savvy barrister, an obnoxious tractor salesman and an urban hustler.[24]

The Saturday Evening Post was published under this name beginning in 1897. Its most prominent years were under editors George Horace Lorimer (1899-1937), Leslie Winans Stout (1937-1942) and Ben Hibbs (1942-1962). As Jeff Nilsson observed: "Editor George Horace Lorimer transformed the Post from a follower to a leader in the field of popular fiction."[25]

Tugboat Annie was not the first female series character in the *Post*. Mary Roberts Rinehart's small-town spinster Letitia "Tish" Carberry was two decades ahead of her, appearing in 23 *Post* stories from 1910-1937.

Tugboat Annie was not the most-often-appearing fictional character in the weekly. Arthur Train's lawyer, Ephraim Tutt, dug into the lawbooks in 88 appearances, from 1919-1951. Salesman Alexander Botts signed up bulldozer customers in 123 stories by William Hazlett Upson, from 1925-1974, nearly 50 years. Clarence Budington Kelland's country storekeeper Scattergood Baines appeared in four *Post* stories, failed the cut and relocated to appear 120 times elsewhere, mostly in *American*, from 1917-1954. And Florian Slappey wrangled his way out of difficulties in 165 Octavius Roy Cohen stories in the *Post* plus 158 stories in other publications, from 1919-1944.[26]

The Philadelphia-based *Saturday Evening* Post issued several story collections including these Bantam paperbacks from 1947 and 1948. Each contained a Tugboat Annie story.

Remarking on the Tugboat Annie and Botts stories, Stanley C. Hollander wrote, "These series exhibited nostalgia, old-fashioned rock-ribbed independence and suspicion of big business monopolization. They were appropriate to a magazine that put Norman Rockwell Americana paintings on its covers while serving as a major promotional engine for the growth of a mass production/mass marketing/mass consumption/mass culture society."[27]

Writers coveted acceptance by the better-paying periodicals. As a contributor to *Writing for the Quality Market* suggested: "Many of the quality publications favor stories in series, that is, groups of stories by one author centering about one main character. The 'Tugboat Annie' stories in the *Saturday Evening Post* are an excellent example of this sort of treatment."[28]

It was a lively age for fiction writers, obviously.

And many of them ended up in visual media.

"Hidden away somewhere in the television industry must be an enormously successful idea man whose entire career depends on a file of old Saturday Evening Posts," quipped syndicated These TV People columnist Bill Fiset.[29]

"A Buffalonian Who Was Gassed In France: Norman Reilly Raine … has been on the firing line for two years as a stretcher bearer in the Tenth Canadian Field Ambulance B.E.F. Though gassed, he was in the hospital only a short time and was not affected seriously."

— *Buffalo Morning Express*, 7 April 1918

Chapter 3

Norman Reilly Raine Born for Adventure

Norman Reilly Raine was born 23 June 1894, likely on Ross Street in the town of Ashley, though some sources suggest on Jackson Street in Wilkes-Barre, Penn.[30] As he said years later in a Camp-Fire column in *Adventure*, "I was born … on the same day in which Edward the Prince was born in London, from which point our mutual interests diverge. The acquirement of knowledge was interrupted — supplemented, perhaps — by several trips to the Old World between the ages of one and twelve years, to which early depravity I owe my present love of roaming."[31]

His father was John William Raine (1869-1937), a merchant born in Middleton-St. George, County Durham, England. His maternal grandfather was William Raine (b. 1838), a station agent with the Stockton & Darlington Railway. The surname was pronounced Ray-nee.

Raine's mother was Anna (or Anne or Annie) Theresa Reilly (1868-1925), a Pennsylvania native whose father was American and mother Scots.

The Raines had married in 1892.

In the late 1890s, the future author's parents moved to England, where William ran a department store and where Norman's education began. A 1901 English census indicates the family lived at 165 Saltwell Road, Gateshead, County Durham, near the border with Scotland. The family at the time included Norman and brother William Malcolm, born in 1893, also in Ashley/Wilkes-Barre. The family grew to welcome Anne Irene, born in 1898 in Gateshead, and James Bertram, also born in Gateshead in 1900.

Little is immediately known about the family. Anne married Charles Sanders in Burfurd, Ontario, in 1922. She died in 1947. James, who remained in England, married Elizabeth Potts; he died in 1987. Malcolm eventually migrated to North America, settling in Buffalo.

In 1906, William Raine Sr. brought the family back to Wilkes-Barre, living on West River Street and operating a mercantile business. Norman attended Ashley Borough public school.

The 1910 United States census shows the William Raines living on 7th St., Buffalo Ward 24 in Erie, N.Y.

After two years of technical high school,[32] Norman became successively a copy boy, cub reporter and police reporter for the *Buffalo Morning Express.* His address, per the 1912 Buffalo City Directory, was 501 78th St. His occupation was clerk.

In 1914, Norman began National Guard service in Buffalo with the 3rd Division 3rd Battalion. He resided at 414 Jersey St. By 1915, he was listed in the New York state census as a 25-year-old residing in Buffalo Ward 25, Erie.[33] He gave 316 Front St., Toronto, as his address when he applied to join the Canadian Over-Seas Expeditionary Force 28 October 1915. He listed his trade as reporter, his faith as Roman Catholic. He attested he was willing to be vaccinated. He claimed he had served four years with the U.S. Navy.[34] He became a stretcher bearer with the 10th Canadian Field Artillery Ambulance, No. 2 Field Ambulance Depot.

His military will handwritten in 1916 for the Army Medical Corps designated his mother as beneficiary, to receive "all money and personal effects which I have or are due me except two gold rings one plain, the other signet which I desire sent to Mrs. E.B. Sidas" of Buffalo.

In 1918, he re-enlisted with the Royal Canadian Over-Seas Expeditionary Force, again a member of the 10th Canadian Field Ambulance, B Section.

Ambulance Corpsman, Canadian Expeditionary Force

"For months [Raine] followed the [progress of the war through] the newspapers and the more he read the more the Irish in him 'got up' as the expression goes, and he could no longer resist the call of his fighting spirit. At the time there was not the remotest idea that the United States would get into the mixup, so he decided to try his luck over in Canada," according to the *Buffalo Evening News*.[35]

He crossed the border to Fort Erie. "After several attempts to enlist in various branches of the service Raine finally succeeded in becoming a stretcher bearer in the Tenth Canadian Field Ambulance, B.E.F. This was not just what he had expected, for they could not figure out how he was going to get into the thick of the fray picking up the wounded. But once over there he soon learned that the ambulance divisions are one of the most important units in the fighting forces and his corps has been continually in the foremost west area since the spring of 1916."[36]

He shipped abroad on the *S.S. Olympic*, 13 April 1916.[37]

Just before the Hindenburg offensive drive, Raine wrote home: "We have been hearing a lot of rumors of the wonderful offensive that Fritz is going to pull on us, and to tell the truth we find them rather amusing — not that we underestimate the beggar — far from it — but we feel confident of being able to hold anything that he puts across. Perhaps it is because we gave him such an excellent beating last year.

"I am rather glad that we are having a bit of a rest just now, for the last trip in the line was anything but pleasant. MUD! Tons of it, it seemed, distributed evenly over our uniforms — and it rained the whole of the time we were in. Still, when one gets out and shaves and scrapes the real estate away, one can even see a little humor in the silly tumbles and impromptu mud baths — but only in retrospect. They are far from funny at the time.

"Here is the latest trench yarn. The inevitable female nuisance, but who means all right maybe, was questioning the wounded soldier as to what was wrong with him, etc. The Tommy replied: 'Wounded? Nah! I were fellin' a bit sleepy an' so I leaned oop agin our barrage for a bit of a rest an' all of a suddint th' artillery lifted the barrage unexpected like an' I toombled into th' trench an' 'urt meself.'"

Raine was twice categorized as missing. "In both cases, my mother, a woman of simple faith, refused to believe, even though the probabilities were against her. Her womanish obstinacy was justified," he told columnist Shippey.[38]

Raine attained the rank of sergeant with the Canadian Expeditionary Force, 150th Regiment. He later transferred from the Army to the Royal Air Force. He saw actions at Ypres, the Somme, Vimy Ridge, Passchendacle, Amiens, Arras and other locations.

Though gassed on the front, he brushed it off as only a "whiff of the pineapple juice." The last entry on his "Casualty Form — Active Service" was treatment for shell shock was in September 1916, after which he returned to duty. He was hospitalized for a week in May 1917 for treatment of scabies, caused by biting mites.

Raine told *The Buffalo Evening News* in August 1918 of learning from his sergeant there were hometown soldiers with the 74th. He walked over to see: "The country hereabouts is the most picturesque of Northern France. All swelling hills, checkered with fields of green and yellowing crops, lovely little patch of woods, straight, tree-lined roads that fairly breathe romance and the quaint towers and crumbling walls of ancient chateaux. The white ribbon of highway tipped over a rise then down into a cool and shaded valley. In the valley was Buffalo in France — a long straggling street of white and yellow walls with red tiled roofs…

"Anyway, there were the boys, lots of them — hundreds of them swinging with long strides down the road, dashing along on motor cycles raising dust and curses in their wake; holding up the village walls with their broad young backs; chaffing, whistling, some busy drawing water from the wells, others carrying slops to the farmer's pigs or making advance to the farmer's daughters — doing all the healthy, hearty things a crowd of young fellows will do anywhere with an hour to spend."

It wasn't all relaxation, as Raine told of the routine British field drills and physical training in bayonet use. The British sergeant opined the fresh troops were " 'A likely lot o' chaps — aye, they are that! A bit Sankey, you know, but a trip in the line'll soon knock that out of 'em — and my, but you'd oughter see 'em with a bloody machine gun! They can learn a Lewis from backside to breakfast in five bloody days! They can do that!' His old army creed of iron discipline was rather shocked I imagine at the free and easy relation between commission and rank, but he was a wee bit tickled with it too, for your old soldier loves 'cheek' even though condemning it. So a slight smile lurked about the corners of his grim moustache as he watched his informal proteges at work."

Stretcher-bearer Raine provided several anecdotes and observed: "The Buffalo men are adept at picking up trench slang and are equally adept at French. It is surprising to note the rapidity with which they learn such phrases as 'Voulez vous promenade avec moi, cher Mademoisselle!' or 'Tu veux une bière, madame?' etc."[39]

He provided a gripping account to the *Buffalo Morning Express*: "Do you wish to come out in the trench with me and look at our surroundings? We are now in a concrete gunpit built and occupied for a considerable time by Herr Fritz. It affords very decent shelter against shells, etc., and we are quite attached to it..."

Inside a German bunker: "You see Heiny fitted these places with loot from French villages and made himself quite at home. When we first came in the main entry shaft was blown in and the stairway cluttered with German dead. They lay all about the place down below, too, where our bayonet men had run them down. They fled shrieking up the long galleries smashing the electric globes and the place rang with shots and screams and the acrid rifle smoke bit into the lungs and made the eyes smart. It was hard work carrying them all up those steps. There were more than 30 of them...."[40]

He left little to the imagination.

Raine (Regimental No. 527637) was discharged from the Canadian Expeditionary Force 3 August 1919, his final pay check for $119.83.[41] His medical examination found him of fair physic, weighing 115, 122 or 135 lbs., depending on the report. The red-haired, blue-eyed cadet stood 5 feet 7.5 inches. He had 30/20 vision and was capable of hearing conversations at 20 feet (right ear), 22 feet (left.) He evidence a scar from an appendectomy. He showed no evidence of hemorrhoids, varicose veins or hernia.[42] He had his tonsils removed at a Royal Air Force facility.[43]

He sailed to Halifax 17 February 1919 on the *Princess Juliana*.

In his last months in Europe, with war's resolution, Raine visited Monte Carlo and toured the Riviera before returning to the States, where, he told a newspaperman, "The sight of dirty old Exchange street after three and one-half years seemed just a little grander to me than anything I saw abroad. When I got as far as Main street I just stopped and looked at the smelly, smoky old section, trying to realize that at last I was actually home. I had a lot of remarkable experiences, and I can tell you there was many a time when I never expected to get back to Buffalo."[44]

Journalist for Maclean's in Toronto

"After demobilization at Toronto in March 1919," Raine told *Adventure*, "the seed of my youthful voyaging came into active germination and bore successful fruit, for since that time I have covered most of the globe.

"Turning the diamond of experience before your evening blaze, the facets flash with the blue of the skies of the world; the white of Canadian snows; the crimson gleam of the Western Front; the lambent green of terraced hillsides on the Inland Sea of Japan; the soft pink of blossom mist on the rugged heights of Manchuria; the yellow gleam of Nubian desert sands; the living turquoise of a Bengal sky; the cold jade of a distant Aleutian Island, tipped by the stormlight of a North Pacific winter day; a pool of vivid carnelian amid the purple shadows of Australian gum trees; the gold of a burnished idol in a temple of Hong-Kong; the russet stain of battering seas on the plate of a Danish tramp, the dreamy mauve of the Tasmanian dusk; the fluttering emerald pennant on the stern of an Arab dhow; the rainbow shimmer of tropic fish in the depths of a lost lagoon; the scarlet flow of a wastrel's life on the floor of a Brisbane 'pub'; the rippling beauty of an Eastern dawn in the Straits of Bab-el-Mandeb."[45]

Raine settled in Toronto for four years. He became an assistant editor with *Maclean's* magazine. The 1921 Census of Canada indicates Raine had been a legal immigrant since 1915. He lived at 78 Pembroke, Ward 2, Toronto, and later at 316 Lake Front and at 4 Balsam Ave.

Raine wrote several articles about the Canadian Government Merchant Marine for *Maclean's*, followed by sketches of Canadian mental hospitals.[46] *Maclean's* announced the series in newspaper advertisements.[47]

Raine generated a reputation for reliability. He gained the trust of the Ontario inspector of prisons and public charities sufficiently to allow him entry to the Ontario hospital system for a feature article for *Maclean's* in 1923. The inspector in his annual report reported: "Mr. Norman Reilly Raine presented his credentials to me and I was glad to arrange that he should have every facility to pursue his subject, and I advised him that the only way of understanding all sides of the work way to come and live here at the hospital for a week or two. Mr. Raine accepted the invitation...."[48]

By now, he also wrote fiction such as "Pearl of the South Seas" for *The Canadian Magazine*.

A footnote to Raine's military career: A Canadian Certificate of Military Qualification indicates Lt. Norman Reilly Raine attended Infantry School at Niagara Falls, Ont., 18 to 26 August 1926, and qualified to attain the rank of captain with the Canadian Army Reserve Regiment, Queen's York Rangers.

The Battalion noted the writer during the First World War "was in the Queen's Royal Fusiliers regiment in the Canadian Army. He has in his possession a solid silver cigarette case bearing the crest of this regiment."[49] Post-war Raine joined the Queen's Rangers, descendants of the American unit Rogers' Rangers of the 1750s. Raine was then working on the screenplay for *Northwest Passage*, a story of Robert Rogers and his guerilla unit of New England and Native American soldiers during the French & Indian War and a Loyalist unit during the American Revolution. Raine offered some relics of Rogers and his men for use during the filming.[50]

One of Norman Reilly Raine's bookplates.

Crewman in the Merchant Marine

His wartime experiences soured Raine's passion for investigative journalism. As a *Maclean's* editor explained: "Compared with the war, the newspaper business was a bit tame. Therefore he abandoned the newspaper business to its fate and made up his mind to be an author. Being an exceedingly practical person, it immediately occurred to him that it would be a sheer waste of time to write stories if he couldn't sell them. That being so, the logical thing to do was to find out why magazine editors bought some stories and didn't buy others. So he marched into the editorial chambers of Maclean's and convinced the then editor that in exchange for a small remuneration it would be a grand thing if he were added to the staff as a sort of part-time student of wheels going round. The rest of his time he spent writing."[51]

"He worked harder at his little portable typewriter than he ever did in his life before," the *Edmonton Journal* reported, "but he soon found he was using up a lot of time, energy and paper and that cheques were slow in coming.

"There came a time when unexpected expenses loomed in front of him, and Mr. Raine called at an editor's office, where he felt sure a cheque was waiting for him. The editor wasn't in his office and the secretary shook her head when he mentioned the cheque he anticipated. There wasn't to be any cheque for that story, but she didn't tell him that, for her information was unofficial. However she was a good friend of his and casually mentioned that it would be a good idea if one of his sea stories was waiting for the editor on his return in the morning. She had heard the editor say he needed a good sea yarn to complete the next issue, and it would go to press to-morrow.

"Mr. Raine didn't have any sea stories. He didn't even have the plot for one, but before the street car had carried him to his home he had a hazy one roughly formed. He couldn't get to his typewriter fast enough. Supper was ready, but he ate nothing. He sat writing,

writing while the hands of the clock crept round and round. Night came and went and when the dawn of a new day streaked the sky he was through. Gathering up his sheets he numbered them carefully and tacked them together. He reached the editor's office just as the secretary was unlocking the door. She noticed the young writer's red rimmed eyes and she accepted the manuscript he handed her, promising to bring it to the early attention of the editor. Raine went home to sleep and while he slept the story was read, accepted and the cheque with its bonus [25 percent more] made out.

"After that Mr. Raine paid no more attention to land stories. Also he gave up trying to make business hours for himself. A writer's imagination balks at punching a time clock."[52]

Raine's continued itch to roam was the result, he said, of the dozen years he had shuttled with his family back and forth from North America to England.[53]

"In 1923," *Maclean's* said, "he decided that what he needed was background — something to write about. So he sought out the Canadian Merchant Marine and sailed from Vancouver as an assistant purser of a C.G.M.M. tramp, and for two years wandered all over the world.

As ship's purser, he dealt with accounts and transactional matters.

"Returning to Toronto, he burst into *Maclean's* with a series of short stories so vividly done that the editors of some of the largest publications in the United States sat up and took notice...

"Luck? Luck nothing. Self-imposed training and years of good, hard slogging have put him where he is today."[54]

During his two years aboard the *S.S. Canadian Britisher,* Raine kept diaries of his activities. In 1923 he was listed among the crew of *Canadian Highlander* from Shanghai, arriving at San Francisco.

He used faraway locales for stories in *Maclean's* and in "And David Took Thence a Stone" in *Everybody's* in 1924, the former earning the praise of Editor Mackenzie (the story exhibits "exotic bits of workmanship … impregnated with the very dregs of actual experiences…"), the latter described by that magazine's editor as a magic carpet ride ala the Arabian Nights.[55]

Maclean's editor H. Napier Moore in 1926 wrote: "Of the younger Canadian writers none is more versatile than Norman Reilly Raine,"[56] one of whose stories, "Single Night," gave a fictional account of a military veteran's dark years confined to a mental health institution.

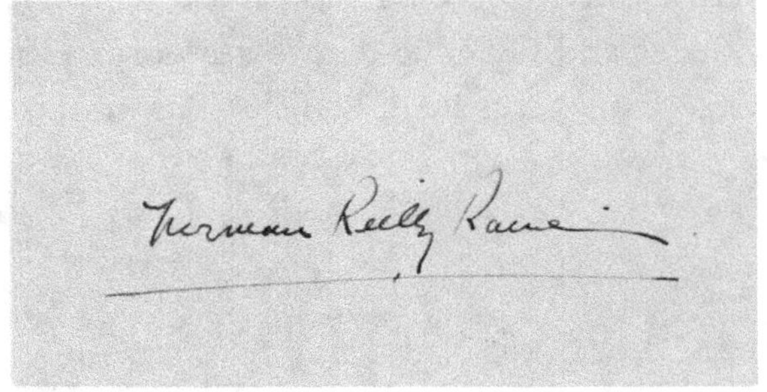

The author's signature, written on a
card at a fan's request. (Drew collection)

Raine once described his novice years. "I spent four years after the first war earning $7 a week white-washing barns and doing other jobs while I wrote on the side," he told a *Santa Barbara News Press* reporter, who added, "He finally wrote a story which he was sure would sell, and he sent it to the Saturday Evening Post. The story appeared during the same week as Colliers and Liberty published two other Raine works, but the author said 'it was a long, long time before I hit the Post again.'

"Raine said that he writes to sell. 'I happen to like to do it,' he added, 'but I wouldn't if it didn't pay.'"[57]

The author from 1927 to 1962 (omitting the war years, when he would be busy in Hollywood) would write 94 stories in three series and 17 free-standing stories for the magazine.

Raine described some of his challenges in working remotely in an article for *The Writer* in 1924, specifically a story, "And David

Took Thence a Stone." "My hardest moment, I believe, was when it became necessary mentally to reconstruct a scene of Montreal in winter when, at the moment of writing, I was steaming along the Red Sea coast of Abyssinia with the thermometer at 112 degrees in the shade, and the iron decks radiated waves of blinding, overpowering heat. I think writers generally will agree that it was a real test of the imaginative powers."[58]

Still on his Merchant Marine sojourn, Raine arrived in Vancouver, B.C., in 1924, fresh from seeing Australia, India, Soudan, the Federated Malay States and China and gave a report to the Vancouver Publicity Bureau on his estimate of British affairs in those regions.[59]

Joyce and Norman Reilly Raine find adventure on horseback in Jasper National Park in 1928. (Canadian National Railways/Drew collection)

Weds Joyce Pett, 1932

In 1927, Raine was again living in Toronto, at 4 Fernwood Park Ave. by Lake Ontario. The following year he married Marjorie Joyce Roberta Pett (1905-1989) in Gravenhurst at St. Anne's Anglican Church[60] in Toronto's west end.

Maclean's shared with readers an interesting fact about Raine: "Norman has an amazing passion for attending fires. No matter what hour of the day or night it may be, should the fire reels go by he will leave his typewriter or his bed and chase after them. We remember the day he was married and how all of us who knew his weakness sat, knelt and stood in watchfulness lest during the ceremony the fire engines should dash past the church."[61]

The bride was the daughter of James W. Pett and Jane Mary Ann Herrington. The Raines honeymooned on a motor tour of France and North Africa. They would partially raise her niece Nancy Joyce Pett and nephew Richard Pett.[62]

Among Raine's story sales in 1927-1928 were "Care to Lay a Little Wager" for *Elks* magazine[63] and "The Creed of the Desert" for *Boy's Life.*[64]

Enid Griffis, New York staff correspondent, wrote a profile of Raine, "The Making of a Short-Story Writer," for *The Passing Show* in February 1929.[65]

Just returned to Seattle from consulting on the filming of *Tugboat Annie*, Norman Reilly Raine proofreads copy in his apartment office in August 1932. *The Seattle Daily* Times ran the image with the headline "Back in Secoma." (Acme Newspictures/Drew collection)

Raine Breaks Out

Having abandoned his byline "N.R. Raine" in favor of "Norman Reilly Raine," the writer established a solid reputation for his prose.

British humorist P.G. Wodehouse in an essay for *Punch* in 1955 said he experienced a significant bump in sales when he gave his byline as Pelham Grenville Wodehouse: "Quite suddenly I spotted what was wrong … I had been labelling my stories 'by P.G. Wodehouse' and this at the time when a writer who went about without three names was practically going around naked. Those were the days of Richard Harding Davis, of Margaret Culkin Banning, of James Warner Bellah, of Earl Derr Biggers, of Charles Francis Coe, Norman Reilly Raine and Orison Swett — yes, really, I'm not kidding ,— Marden. And here was I, poor misguided fool, trying to crash the gate with a couple contemptible initials."[66]

The Raines spent 1928-1930 in England, with occasional returns to Canada such as a 1928 visit with Napier Moore in Vancouver.[67] Moore and his wife were on a cross-Canada jaunt and beyond a social get-together, the two men gathered material for *Maclean's* articles.[68]

Raine in his early Hollywood Days was clean-shaven.
(*Toronto Daily Star*, 23 March 1936)

Raine began his long-term relationship with *The Saturday Evening Post* when his first Mr. Gallup story appeared in the issue of 19 October 1929. His first Dandy Man story was published in the *Post* 13 March 1930.

The Raines were still on the move, returning to New York City from several months in Italy in 1930 on *Ile de France.*

"Joyce Raine and three guests were stranded when the 'Joyce Roberta' cruiser broke down at Bremerton, in May 1934, and a Coast Guard patrol boat towed it to a dock where it was moored behind the Washington Tug & Barge Company tug, the Wasp. Apparently the Narcissus, Pansy or other Deep-Sea tugs weren't available to help. But the Wasp's commander, Captain Horace True, learning of the Tugboat Annie connection, offered to give a tow, attached alongside a gravel barge. Later again visiting Mrs. Raine, True inquired: "Say, did your husband ever write a story about the captain who sold his boat to a farmer? ...."

— "Mrs. Raine Learns About Tugboats at
First-Hand," *Seattle Daily Times*, 28 May 1934

Chapter 4

Lure of the Puget Sound

Looking for a change, Raine ventured westward for a 10-week assignment as a writing instructor at the University of Washington in Seattle.

He stayed 15 months and left for even brighter prospects.

Maclean's editor J. Vernon Mackenzie, at that magazine's helm for five years[69] and responsible for bringing the publication to national prominence, had moved to *Cosmopolitan* in 1926 then became dean of the journalism department at the University of Washington.

He wired Raine, who with his wife was in Italy, to ask if he'd come lecture there in 1930.[70]

The writer was agreeable, though likely didn't anticipate the gushy reception. Instructing the ins and outs of short-story craft, Raine was recognized and appreciated by students. " 'Exhibit A — Norman Reilly Raine. 'Rare Species of Successful Author —Please Do not Feed (Except Cream Puffs).'

"Such a placard might well be hung outside the door of the School of Journalism at the University of Washington," suggested a *Seattle Daily Times* reporter. "For Mr. Raine, well known to readers of national magazines as the writer of rousing sea stories, has joined the faculty in the unofficial capacity of 'goldfish.'

"Yesterday he arrived. Today he is 'on display' for purposes of inspection and interrogation.

"Every would-be author in the state, whether enrolled in the University or not, is invited to visit Mr. Raine between the hours of 2 and 3 on Monday, Wednesday or Friday from now until the end of the spring quarter. He will answer any and all questions pertaining to fiction writing, his own or someone else's, to the best of his ability."[71]

"Vernon McKenzie … is responsible for this extraordinary scheme for putting an author in a glass cage. He sees in the project a double value — the writer will contact his readers and the readers, if they have a 'yen' for writing, will profit from the advice and self-analysis of one who 'has arrived.'

"Yes, Girls, He's Married. Mrs. Raine accompanied her husband on his exhibition tour and both are at present the house guests of Dean and Mrs. McKenzie."[72]

The Raines had previously been guests along with the Moores at the Calgary home of Elizabeth Bailey Price, president of the Calgary Women's Press Club and the Calgary branch of Canadian Authors,[73] where the men spoke to the group on editing and writing, respectively.

Raine was guest of the School of Journalism's Short Story Club in 1930.[74] When the Raines attended the Denny-Blaine Guild's Fashion Show — adding "a last touch of distinction"[75] — the author was asked his opinion about women's tastes in gifts. "The secret of woman's failures is that she selects a necktie as she would dress material," he said. "She completely disregards the man who's going to wear it and settles on 'something pretty.' Buy reading lamps."[76]

In between, they were passengers on the *Prince Henry*, traveling to Toronto and back.[77]

MacKenzie assembled several of his students' works for *These Stories Went to Market*. In one case he reproduced a student's first and final drafts (the story appeared in *Collier's*) paired with criticisms by Raine, who sat in on the seminars.[78]

Raine in spare hours roamed the waterfronts and haunted the library shelves, gathering background information for his stories. He did sufficiently well that he hired a secretary, June Pat Wetherell (Mrs. Daniel P. Frame) (1909-2010),[79] who was completing her graduate studies in journalism at U of W and who later wrote 31

Gothic novels.[80] He also briefly mentored Ruby Cannon (Mrs. Judge John A.) Frater, who had made non-fiction sales of cooking articles and wanted to venture into fiction.[81]

Raine was constantly on the lookout for ideas, and not just in Seattle. As he told a *Tacoma News Tribune* scribe in 1930, "There are a lot of old-time ships in Puget Sound and lot of shipping. Wherever there is shipping there is fiction material, and, since there is such vast shipping in Tacoma there must be equally vast story material. I hope to find it.

"I find the people of the Northwest more mentally alert than they are on the East coast. Their bodies don't do as much bustling, but they think faster. For this reason, I believe the stories I get here will be psychological rather than physical."[82]

From Tacoma he traveled to Alaska then east to the Great Lakes. There was a stopover in Vancouver, where the Raines stayed at the Evergreen Hotel.[83]

In 1931, he agreed to be a judge in Chi Omega House's preliminary judging for a Miss Tyee beauty contest in Seattle.[84]

He was a guest speaker at the interfraternity Conference of Mothers' Clubs of the University of Washington the same year.[85]

He found Seattle comfortable. As a reporter (who needed to do a little fact checking) put it in the *Seattle Sunday Times* in 1931, "The young short story writer, originator of the 'Steamboat Annie' [sic] series in a national magazine, has found safe haven in Seattle ... The love of the water remained [after his years on a tramp steamer] and he purchased a 30-foot yawl for sport on Lake Erie [succeeded by] a 32-foot cabin cruiser, the Joyce Roberta [named for his wife] ... Short cruises on Lake Washington, a venture into Puget Sound and a contemplated journey to Vancouver Island again make him feel the spray on his face and the salty tang in his nostrils.

" 'With such waters surrounding a person, he should find material plentiful to put in his stories. I have done so,' Raine says."[86]

LEE SIDE o' L.A.
BY Lee Shippey

Personal Glimpses of Famous Folks

NORMAN REILLY RAINE, creator of Tugboat Annie, is a medium-sized young man built like an ox — and exceptionally able—seaman. His hair is an uncompromising red and a pair of blue eyes are divided by a rather large and decided nose. Stick a friendly mouth under these features and you have the picture of a solid chunk of humanity you'd expect to go places, see things and make friends. And these are the things Norman has done.

Lucky Stars

Raine was a 30-year-old reporter on a Buffalo newspaper when the World War broke. But he was half English and all adventurous, so he at once went up into Canada and enlisted in the Canadian army, forfeiting his American citizenship by so doing. He got to the front in that very entertaining sector known as Vimy Ridge and the first time he went under fire he was in a gas attack. When the war ended he returned to Toronto where his parents had moved, and looked about for work. But the Canadian newspapers were holding their jobs for their own men, so he turned to fiction because he had to. And in his case there was no weary drizzle of rejection slips before the flowers began to bloom in the spring, tra-la. He not only sold his first story, but sold it to two magazines, McLain's in Toronto and Adventure in the United States.

Unquestionably, that boy was born under a whole Milky Way of lucky stars.

Living Material

"I wanted to write sea stories," explained Raine, with a quiet laugh, "and the only trouble was that I didn't know much about the sea. So I got me a job on a tramp steamer and spent three years knocking about all over the world. That helped a great deal in the writing of adventure stories. I did so well that by 1928 I was able to marry and go to Italy to live, for a while. When I returned to Toronto a friend who teaches journalism in the University of Washington got me to go there for some lectures on the short story. I'd visited the Pacific Coast on the tramp, but this time I fell in love with it. I bought a cabin-launch and do a lot of running about among the islands up there. My wife is as fond of it as I am and it's our way of spending a week-end.

Tugboat Annie

"One day up there a friend told me about a woman in Rhode Island who had inherited a towboat, and became its captain. I thought what a character that might make for a Puget Sound story. While I was mulling it, I went to see the motion picture, 'Anna Christie,' and was impressed by Marie Dressler's characterization of a waterfront termagant. I began to see the possibilities of such a character as captain of a tugboat. I'd never thought of writing for the screen and did not think of it then, but I kept Marie Dressler in my mind as I wrote of Tugboat Annie. I tried to make Tugboat Annie do and say the things Miss Dressler, in such a role, would do and say. The Saturday Evening Post bought the story and my agent asked for a copy of it to submit to Metro-Goldwyn-Mayer. They bought it for Miss Dressler. I've written seven Tugboat Annie stories now, and Metro-Goldwyn-Mayer have bought three of those magazine stories for the screen."

It doesn't happen often—a story character inspired by a motion-picture actress which, after magazine publication, eventually becomes the logical vehicle for that same actress.

Character

Tugboat Annie is the most striking feminine character that has loomed up in American fiction in at least ten years. She stands out as Harry Leon Wilson's Ma Pettingill stood out twenty years ago, a salty, humorous, hard-boiled philosopher. One can't help wondering why Ma Pettingill was never chosen for screen presentation by Miss Dressler, but Tugboat Annie certainly fits her like a well-worn sou'wester. Tugboat Annie has caught the imagination of the reading public almost as Charlie Chan has. The reader sees "another Tugboat Annie story" with delight, sure be s "I find a story by a man who kn[ows] and loves boats and boat peop[le]. Galsworthy says character is the only story, and Raine has created an outstanding character.

Raine is living in Hollywood.

When author Raine ported in Los Angeles to assist on the MGM motion picture *Tugboat Annie, Los Angeles Times'* "Lee Side o' LA" columnist Lee Shippey took an immediate shine. (11 December 1932 issue)

The Raines lived at East 43rd St. ME 4435, according to a 1931 street directory. The next year they resided in the 515 Brooklyn Building and the writer had an office at 1305.

That year, the first Tugboat Annie story ran in *The Saturday Evening Post* issue of 11 July. Almost immediately rights to the first three stories were sold to Metro-Goldwyn-Mayer studios[87] and a new chapter began in Raine's career.

•

As Raine expressed in a 1934 article in *Pacific Motor Boat*,[88] "My own return from the writing of the Tugboat Annie stories has included a reward that has nothing to do with money or a literary reputation. It embraces firm friendships of a large number of tugboat men. It includes an almost fanatical appreciation of what in my opinion is the greatest holiday ground on earth —, Puget Sound. It is sustained by the knowledge that through these stories I have done something to make better known to the rest of the United States the forthrightness of the peoples of the Northwest, as well as that country's incredible beauties."

Was Annie tempted to go elsewhere?

" 'Annie, I hear you've been asked to leave Puget Sound. What about it?' " Raine asked his heroine. " 'Who,— me? Hmmph! Not by a jugful, Red! I'm going to stick where me old friends and neighbors is. I'm just naturally nefarious!'"

After his initial stay in Hollywood, Raine made a whirlwind trip across Canada, arriving in Vancouver "minus hat now floating somewhere on the waves. Raine's first act was to replace same — then phone newspaper friends, whom he decidedly doesn't forget." He and Joyce were there for the Beaux-Arts Mayfair Ball at the Crystal Ballroom for a production of Noel Coward's *Hands Across the Sea*.[89]

In spring 1931, he was guest speaker at the Interfraternity Mothers' Club and the University of Washington Commons.[90] A week later, he was guest of the Free Lances at Blanc's Cafe.[91]

Besides his fiction, Raine in 1932 provided the text for a 24-page Canadian National Railways booklet, *Alaska and the Yukon*. It was published the next year, by which time Raine was hunkered in Hollywood to write film scripts. The writer was by no means through with the Puget Sound, however, making frequent visits over the next several years.

In August 1932, he was back in his office in the Brooklyn Building, examining proofs of his latest Tugboat Annie story. He told a reporter, "Seattle and the Puget Sound country have some of the best source material for fiction writing in the world...

The tugboat operations here have greater diversity than else-where and are a delight to the author who manipulates them in his stories…

" 'I don't believe in waiting for inspiration,' he said in talking about his art. 'I go to the office at 10 o'clock in the morning and work until 4 o'clock whether I feel like it or not. Having once been a newspaper reporter, I have learned to write at any time.'

"He has set himself the stint of two stories a month.

"He and Mrs. Raine are staying at the Edmond Meany Hotel."[92]

Raine returned to Hollywood in autumn 1932 to script additional dialogue for *Tugboat Annie*,[93] having been in Seattle "to seek color for a new series of sea stories.[94]

Columnist Shipley described the writer: "Norman Reilly Raine, creator of Tugboat Annie, is a medium-sized young man built like an able — and exceptionally able — seaman. His hair is an uncompromising red and a pair of blue eyes are divided by a rather large and decided nose. Stick a friendly mouth under those features and you have the picture of a solid chunk of humanity you'd expect to go places, see things and make friends. And those are the things Norman has done."[95]

Joyce Raine, wearing a white angora dress with bright colored plaited chiffon scarf, carved out a social life of her own, telling Collette, the *Seattle Daily Times* fashion editor, after having spent a year there, "Hollywood is an extremely well-dressed community — far more than ordinary… Women in all walks of life try to dress up to the movie actresses. It is probably the worst place in the world to be dowdy or homely."[96]

In March 1933, ricocheting from California to Broadway to Toronto, Raine passed through Winnipeg[97] and Edmonton, where he told a journalist, "The best and hardest workers writing fiction are to be found in the western field.[98] Then he was in Seattle, "catching up on correspondence and dashing off a couple of stories to pay I.O.U.s occasioned by the bank holiday.[99]

Raine "always works with a knitted cap on his head," columnist O.O. M'Intyre,[100] revealed in 1934. "When he mislaid it recently he astonished a casual visitor by appearing at the door with a substitute; a knitted stocking belonging to his wife."

That year, the Raines spent summer and fall in Seattle splitting time between an apartment at 4204 11th Ave. N.E, and "aboard their cruiser, voyaging about the Sound gathering new material for his salty sea tales."[101] Joyce Raine caught the attention of a Seattle newspaper, photographed wearing yachting togs before embarking on the 40-foot *Joyce Roberts*.[102]

While in Seattle, Joyce played hostess to a reception for Mrs. Frank Butler — who with her husband was visiting from California; he was a fellow scenarist. Among guests were Mrs. Wedell Foss and short story writer Janet (Mrs. W. Mahlon) Adams.[103]

Raine returned to the area in 1936, while working on a film adaptation of James Oliver Curwood's *God's Country and the Woman*. He and William Keighley, director, and W.L. Guthrie, Warner Brothers location manager, visit potential sites in and around Kelso, Cowlitz County, to find a locale to recreate a log jam.

Robert Lee, Raine's chauffeur, provided a testimonial to Triton motor oil in a newspaper advertisement.[104]

In 1938, the Raines — basking in the writer's winning an Academy Award — stayed at the Empress Hotel in Victoria and attended the Beaux-Arts Mayfair Ball.[105]

Raine with writers Frank Richardson Pierce and Alice Maxwell gathered at the latter's Seattle home to discuss their craft.[106]

Raine was back in California in time for a September sojourn to Lake Arrowhead in the San Bernardino Mountains to spend Labor Day weekend at a cottage with writers Frederick Hazlitt and F. Scott Fitzgerald. Chico Marx, their neighbor next door, entertaining them on the piano. McKenzie was another guest, visiting from Seattle.[107]

Joyce Raine was part of the cast in the Opera Reading Club of Hollywood musical presentation of *The Tales from Hoffman* during a Christmas program in 1939.[108] In 1942 she also took part in a musical sketch, "Juniors' Dream Christmas."[109]

"A salty widow, captain of the tugboat Narcissus, Annie is an exuberantly comic trickster, using her wits and her knowledge of maritime law to foil her underhanded rival, Horatio Bullwinkle… Tugboat Annie's serial adventures place her in the company of eighteenth- and nineteenth-century American tall tales, whose heroes' accomplishments would be recounted around the campfire or in town gatherings. She is a heroic figure, a big woman on a tiny tugboat, whose exploits are known for miles around … ."

— Victoria Sturtevant, *A Great Big Girl Like Me:*
The Films of Marie Dressler (2009)

Chapter 5

Tugboat Annie's 'Secoma'

Tugboat Annie yarns entertained readers from across the country and around the world. Besides being humorous and straight-out adventure tales, Raine's series, with its vernacular language, rustic characters and depiction of a specific geographic area, fit snugly into a regional or local color literature pioneered by Sarah Orne Jewett (1849-1909) with her stories set in a Maine coastal village; Joel Chandler Harris (1848-1908) with his Uncle Remus stories with an Atlanta background; and Rose Terry Cooke (1827-1892) with her small-town New England sketches.

Though disdained by many literary critics, local color writers pioneered in realism and were popular with readers.

Raine's Puget Sound setting could be considered what literary historians call "imagined frontiers"[110] — the westernmost great outdoors in the lower 48 states and its watery perimeters. Annie thus shares a sub-genre with another fictionist, James Fenimore Cooper, in whose Leatherstocking tales of Natty Bumppo and Chingachgook roamed a northeast frontier of the early 1800s (albeit in Leatherstocking Country in central New York state), to give only one example.

Consider Raine's tales examples of "edge culture," a phrase that evolved from Frederick Clement's 1904 ecological term "edge community." As applied to literature, Henry David Thoreau, for example, described his *Walden Pond* experiences of living apart from Concord villagers (many of them well-educated and famous) and comingling with scratch farmers, Native Americans and Blacks who survive and casually subsist on the outskirts of town.[111] Theirs was an edge community.

Likewise the sketchy river denizens Huck and Jim encounter in Mark Twain's *Adventures of Huckleberry* Finn live apart; the author wrote knowledgeably from his experiences as a Mississippi riverboat pilot.

Tom Joad and the desperate Okies huddling at the Weedpatch migrant camp in John Steinbeck's *The Grapes of Wrath* certainly clung to the verge. The writer traveled their roads and intensely researched the Farm Security Administration's migrant tent communities established during the Dust Bowl exodus in the depths of the Great Depression.

Annie Brennan has no home on land. She lives apart, in the master's cabin on the *Narcissus*. She knows her way around Secoma, Elliot, Bellingham and Vancouver, but is most comfortable on the Sound or Pacific, talking the language and expecting and meeting the expectations of mariners and harbor dwellers and lumbermen and canners. And Mother Nature. This edge is where cultures at times collide. Human power, jealousy and greed, however, can fall to the mercy of ocean gales and rocky shores. And Annie's out-of-the-wheelhouse ingenuity. Raine wrote with the experiences of his years with the Merchant Marine.

Raine rose to considerable popularity, in some part due to his ease in describing Puget Sound and environs communities real — Anacortes, Port Townsend, Everett, Olympia, Bellingham, Vancouver[112] — and made up — Secoma itself, as we know blends Seattle and Tacoma.

His descriptions of the shipping trade, the logging camps and sawmills, the fishing villages and canneries, the wharfs and fuel depots and shipyard drydocks are sometimes made up to convenience the story plots, but they come from the real thing.

Maclean's editor Moore, visiting Victoria, B.C, in 1931, said, "This is a very romantic Coast and there is ample material available for the short story writer."[113]

He singled out Raine as a successful author very aware of the possibilities of his environment. "I am amazed to find there are not more stories with the wonderful backgrounds that are to be found here."

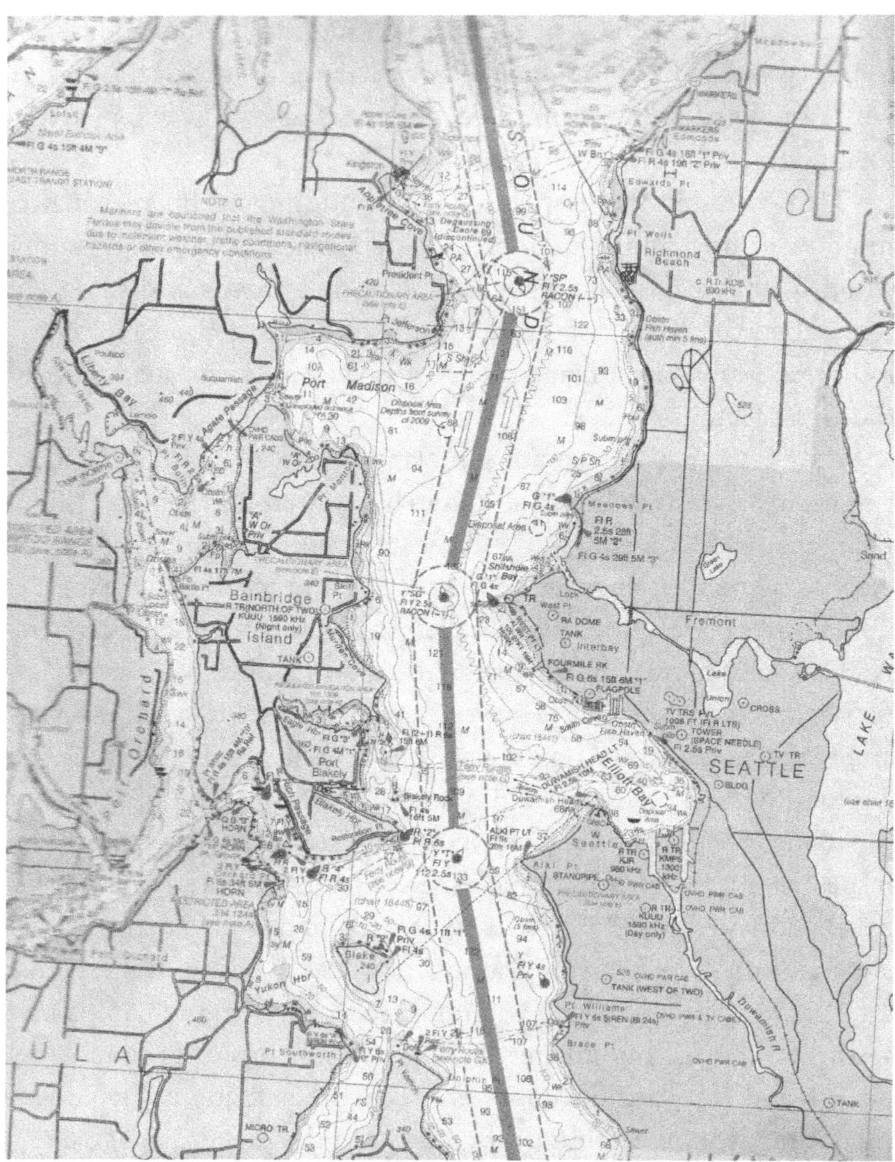

Seattle portion of the U.S. Department of Commerce National Oceanic and Atmospheric Administration (NOAA) soundings map. (2016)

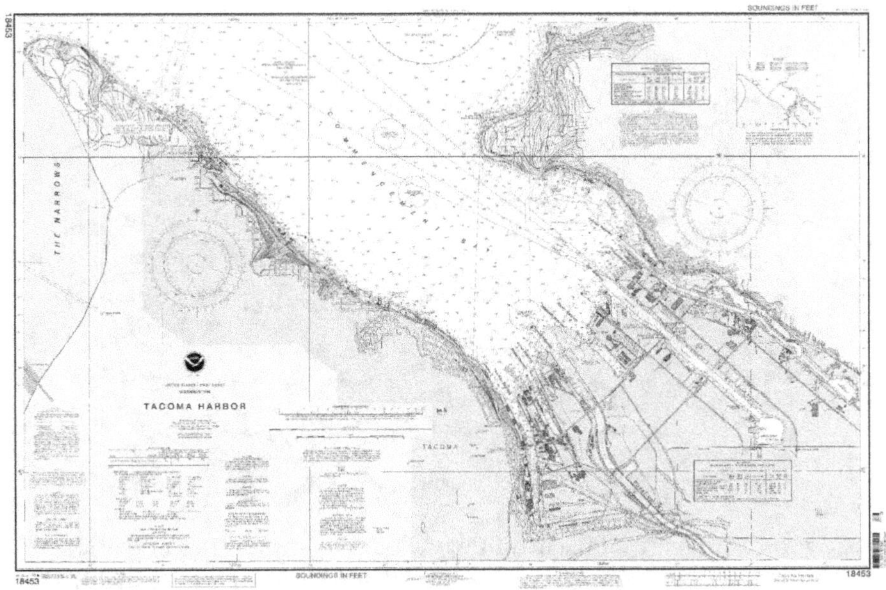

A NOAA map of Tacoma Harbor hints at the size of that seaport.

Seattle's waterfront was a busy place when this photo was snapped in 1910.
(Detroit Publishing/Library of Congress)

Tugboats are in evidence in all Puget Sound communities of any size. This is the *Island Venture* traversing Ballard Locks in Seattle in 2018. (Bernard A. Drew photo)

The *Sand Man* is maintained in Olympia as a public museum. (Bernard A. Drew photo)

The *Mudcat* navigates the Ballard Locks. (Bernard A. Drew photo)

The *Sharon Brusco* and *Ellis Brusco* are busy in Olympia.
(Bernard A. Drew photo)

The *Pacific Pioneer* is in drydock in Port Townsend in 2018.
(Bernard A. Drew photo)

A portion of a no-longer-used 528-foot pile railroad trestle across Woodard Bay, built for Thurston County in 1926 by C.C. Snyder Co. of Seattle, is a reminder of the vigorous logging that once went on in the vicinity.
(Bernard A. Drew photo)

Today one will find a handful of businesses that use the name Secoma. A Puget Sound steamer went by the variant name *Seatac*, frequently hauling lime, coconut oil and chemicals from Anacortes to Bellingham in 1928.[114]

Seattle-Tacoma International Airport is an old county airfield rebuilt into McChord Field. It served as Boeing Field for many years. When a new airport was under consideration in 1942, one suggestion was it be called Secoma airport "and that the big shipyards, under one management in Tacoma and Seattle, have a similar title first made popular by Norman Reilly Raine in his 'Tugboat Annie' stories. Certainly such a change would get the vote of headline writers who shudder at trying to squeeze Seat-tle-Tacoma' into a 10 count head," said a writer in the *Tacoma News Tribune*.[115]

The $5 million facility was built at Bow Lake, between Seattle and Tacoma, and became known as Sea-Tac — a name offered in 1943.[116]

The two city ports joined in 2015 under the Northwest Seaport Alliance, the first pact of its kind in the United States, acting jointly on major specified resource and logistics matters.[117]

•

"To know Seattle one must know its waterfront," suggests Murry Morgan in his classic *Skid Road* (1951).[118] "It is a good water-front, not as busy as New York's, not as self-consciously colorful as San Francisco's, not as exotic as New Orleans', but a good, honest, working waterfront with big gray warehouses and trim fishing boats and docks that smell of creosote, and sea gulls and rugs and seafood restaurants and beer joints and fish stores — a waterfront where you can hear foreign languages and buy shrunken heads and genuine stuffed mermaids, where you can watch the seamen follow the streetwalkers and the shore patrol follow the sailors, where you can stand at an open-air bar and drink clam nectar, or sit on a deadhead and watch the water, or go to an aquarium and look at an octopus."

In King County, Seattle — the state's largest city takes its name from Duwamish tribal leader Sealth — began as a lumbering center. Noted for its Space Needle and Pike Place Market, it is corporate home to Amazon.com, Microsoft and Pacific Market International, maker of Stanley all-steel refreshment containers. Needless to say, it has an active maritime trade and a seaport museum.

Tacoma in Pierce County is midway between Seattle and Olympia (30+ miles in either direction) and is home to the Washington State History Museum, the American Car Museum, the Museum of Glass and other cultural attractions. It has an active seaport.

"Tacoma spreads around the Puyallup River delta, encompassing all of Commencement Bay," is how Migael Scherer describes the port city: "Its residential and downtown areas on the southwest bluffs are not prominent from the water. What stands out instead are the broad industrial flats. The eight dredged commercial waterways of the Puyallup delta are lined with wharves, and as far as you can see upriver are manufacturing plants, warehouses, storage tanks and domes cargo loading cranes, ships, tugs and barges. Dwarfing all this industry is the astonishing mass of Mt. Rainier."[119]

Raine lived in Seattle and often explored Tacoma and environs by water. It was literary convenience to mix and match the wharves, shipyards and warehouses of the two.

This description of Secoma from the top of a steep hill is from "Tugboat Annie Gets the Works": "The smell of oil; tide flats, soot, locomotive smoke and salt air; the tooting of ferries, the high wild piping of gulls, the hoarse blare of deep-water craft, the rattle and hiss of winches and the clang and bang of freight trains running along the Water Street spur."

Seventy-Five Cents Change

"The New Yorker, Arthur J. Perry, sent $2 to Charles Pierce, supervisor of the Northwest District for the Coast and Geodetic Survey, to pay for two charts of Washington waters," we read in a 1954 newspaper story.[120]

" 'As these charts are for the purpose of following the nefarious activities of Horatio Bullwinkle (except when he crawls back under his wet log as Annie claims) and the delightful escapades of our beloved Tugboat Annie Brennan, it is not necessary to send me your latest editions,' Perry wrote...

"The staff of the Coast and Geodetic Survey, which normally deals with strictly scientific data but also follows the antics of Norman Reilly Raine's bellicose characters, found the map which Perry needed," plus two other charts for Grays Harbor and Olympia north to Victoria, B.C.

"Perry also got 75 cents change."[121]

"Her movements had an elephantine energy that galvanized everyone with whom she came in contact. When she passed through a room, dust and odd bits of paper danced in her wake."

— Norman Reilly Raine, "Tugboat Annie," 11 July 1931

Chapter 6

Crew & Fleet

Anna Maria Theresa Flynn Brennan, known to everyone as Tugboat Annie, is the widow of Captain Terry Brennan, a skilled tugboat operator but an alcoholic and overbearing husband. Her good-humored face has been likened to a bulldog or a mastiff. She is master of the *Narcissus*, flagship of the Deep-Sea Towing & Salvage fleet home-ported in Secoma, Wash. With 40 years of experience, she assumed Terry's command at his passing. She plies the Puget Sound from Olympia to Cape Flattery and along coastal Washington, Oregon and California, to Mexico, British Columbia and Alaska.

Usually wearing a rain slicker, boots, long skirt, tattered shirt and a dilapidated felt hat that once belong to Terry, she switches to a going-to-town dress and a bonnet of ancient vintage, crowned by a raffish feather, when venturing ashore. She greets friends as "old gafoozlers." In a good mood, she sings: "Happy days is here some more …."

Alexander "Alec" Severn is the chubby, harried Deep-Sea Towing & Salvage owner and president, often stressed by business matters. The company's office and storeroom are in a two-story, weathered building at wharf-front. Fred Dorr and Tom are office dispatchers. Olive Walker is office secretary.

On the *Narcissus*, Peter is first mate, Big Sam Dolittle is engineer and another Tom is second engineer. Shiftless and Henry[122] (aka Hank) are deck hands, Clem is radio operator and Pinto is boss of the cook stove. There are also unnamed coal shovelers before the tugboat's transition to diesel fuel in the 1940s.

Deep-Sea's fleet includes a dozen-plus vessels besides the *Narcissus* — not necessarily all at the same time: the *Pansy* and the

Daffodil are the most often mentioned. Other dockmates are the *Violet,* the *Asphodel,* the *Hyacinth,* the *Iris,* the *Lilac,* the *Orchid,* the *Cornflower,* the *Lily,* the *Rose,* the *Honeysuckle,* the *Buttercup,* the *Bluebell* and the *Daisy.* Annie named them all.

If we accept the wooden-hulled *Arthur Foss* — featured in the 1933 motion picture and now piered at a maritime museum — as a legitimate rendition of the fictional craft, the *Narcissus* was built in a Portland shipyard in 1897. The tug's standard colors in the stories are black hull, red deckhouse and yellow funnel. In "Horse of a Different Color," the tug is whitewashed. In "Tugboat Annie Wins Her Medal," the vessel still sports its wartime dazzle of "variegated warpaint of greens and browns and blue."

Bandy-legged, bullet-headed Horatio Bullwinkle, master of the other large tugboat based in Secoma, the *Salamander,* is Wiley Coyote to Annie's Speedy Roadrunner in frequently raucous rivalry. Jake is Bullwinkle's first mate and a willing co-conspirator. Shorty is a deck hand.

The *Salamander* has a black hull, white superstructure and canary-yellow funnel.

Noteworthy Secoma locations are the Greasy Spoon, a gathering place for sailors and maritime businessmen not far from the waterfront; the Waterfront Employees Association dance hall; and the Mount Rainier Hotel.

" 'I'm fired? Who says I'm fired?' Tugboat Annie Brennan leaned across the desk of the president of the Deep-Sea Towing and Salvage Company, and thrust her formidable jowls into his red, embarrassed face. She repeated, with husky emphasis: 'Who says so?' "

— Opening paragraph, "Tugboat Annie"
Saturday Evening Post, 11 July 1931

Chapter 7

Tugboat Annie Stories, 1931-1961

Annie Brennan, skipper of the *Narcissus* out of Secoma, makes her first appearance in print in the 11 July 1931 issue of *The Saturday Evening Post*. The artwork is by Anton Otto Fischer.

Tugboat Annie prose stories — and several non-story appearances — are summarized as to original publication and reprints, also illustration credits and full plots, with annotations as appropriate. First listed unless otherwise indicated are issue dates of the *Saturday Evening Post*.

The entries comprise Annie Brennan's biography and demonstrate the writer's skill at variations on a theme. Raine was selective with backstory, revealing her full name only in *The Glencannon-Tugboat Annie Affair*, two-thirds of the way through the canon, and mentioning a daughter only once, in the first story. (The son created for the 1933 motion picture doesn't count in the canon.)

Plot encapsulations often reveal solutions to Annie's impossible dilemmas.

Joining the short stories and novelettes are one brief conversation (1933), one vignette (1936), three letters to *Post* editors (1940, 1948 and 1951), one cookbook recipe (1951), one note to a media reporter (1957) and three letters to *Tow Line* (1955 and 1959).

1. Tugboat Annie

(*Saturday Evening Post* 11 July 1931) (Anton Otto Fischer begins illustrating stories) reprinted in *Tugboat Annie* (Minton, Balch, 1934) *Saturday Evening Post Treasury* (Simon & Schuster, 1954) *Post* (Summer 1971) *Tugboat Annie: Great Stories from the Saturday Evening Post* (Curtis, 1977) excerpted in *Saturday Evening Post Movie Book* (1977) excerpted as "The Genesis of Tugboat Annie" (*Sea History*, autumn 1982) reprinted *Alfred Hitchcock Mystery Magazine* (December 1994)

Tugboat Annie Brennan is about to lose her job. Alec Severn, owner of Deep-Sea Towing & Salvage, is bringing aboard a partner named Conroy. And old-fashioned Conroy can't comprehend a woman in a tugboat wheelhouse. Severn explains that Annie's late husband Terry was senior captain of the small fleet until his death a year before. "Terry was a drunken sot," Annie says, and he died of "Water poisonin'! Drank a glass o' water, thinkin' it was gin, and his stomach couldn't stand the shock." Still, she was fond of him, the cranky so-and-so, and often hatches solutions to impossible situations in thinking over his past deeds and misdeeds. With 20 years' experience on the Sound, Annie has ably taken over command of the *Narcissus*.

Conroy dismisses the flowery names of the Deep-Sea tugs. He'd prefer Titan or Atlas or Hercules.

To get a feel for tugboating, the would-be partner rides along on the *Narcissus* as they steam out with the *Pansy* to Juan de Fuca

Strait, near Neah Bay, where the *Barracuda* is beached and on fire. Competitors *Firefly* and *General Mason* are heading that way, too, hoping to be first and gain the tow contract. Conroy is reluctant to join the crew in the mess, but he has no choice.

Captain Crabtree of the *Barracuda* directs the three tugs to position abreast the gangway. He insists this will just be a tow, as the ship could float off at high tide. It simply has water in No. 1 hold and the steering gear is jammed. Conroy doesn't like the way the bidding goes, dropping to $300 once the ship restarts. Annie asks Crabtree if there's any other damage to the ship and he replies no. She takes the job, to Conroy's dismay.

On the way back to Secoma, Annie puts Conroy to work shoveling coal into the boiler firebox. At a meeting afterward, Annie announces Crabtree doesn't owe a cent on the tow. Annie had tumbled to Crabtree's game. She quotes maritime law that if a client conceals any material facts from a tug operator, "the towage may cease to be towage and become, in effect, salvage." Crabtree didn't say the *Barracuda* had a stripped propeller and could have been pounded to pieces if not taken off the rocks. So she claims a third of the value of the ship and cargo.

We learn in passing that Annie has a close relative when she tells Severn: "And now, if ye can see clear to lend me sixty cents till payday, Alec, I'd like to go ashore and telegraph me daughter."

The offspring is never mentioned again.

• Raine hoped to generate more sales to the *Post*. He may have considered another new character, Master William H. Fisher, known to all as Captain Windy Bill, skipper of the four-masted schooner *Tamerlane*. He's described as having an "elephantine body" in the story "Windy Bill. " In the tale, the ship faces a fierce storm: "Windy Bill was on the edge of a hurrah's nest of tangled limbs about the wheel and binnacle, as the Tamerlane commenced to capsize. Grasping at arms and legs, he heaved and by sheer bull power managed to save some of the men from catapulting down the sharp slope into the sea. With uncanny skill he crab-walked up the deck to the windward side of the low after-house and, assisted by another of the hands, dragged the rest of the men, including the second mate, to comparative safety." The story, though, may have been rejected by the *Post*. It appeared in *Collier's* for 26 December 1931, his only sale to that periodical. It turned out Annie had a permanent home with the *Post*.

2. Passage to Secoma

(12 March 1932) *Tugboat Annie* (Minton, Balch, 1934) *Tugboat Annie: Great Stories ...* (Curtis, 1977)

Annie and Big Sam the first engineer have just delivered the *Lilac* in California — Deep-Sea sold the vessel — and Annie attempts to book passage back to Secoma via the Pacific Cargo Carriers' *Mercurio*. But Captain Nelsson refuses to take her and instead the two travel on the Green Stripe Line's *Bandora*, a cargo carrier taking citrus fruit to British Columbia. Captain Hannibal Neap decides not to go to Secoma as he won't be able to pick up a return cargo. His consignees, as allowed by their contract, instead want delivery to San Diego, and thus the *Mercurio* will pick up the citrus fruit. Annie asks if any of the present cargo had been unloaded, and Neap confirms two crates had been checked in and accepted by the agent. Annie says that constitutes legal delivery, and the rest of the cargo should be unloaded.

When on route through heavy fog, Neap stops his ship and blows his whistle, despite which, the *Ajaxia* out of Melbourne smashes into the *Bandora's* port bow. Neap signals for assistance and Nelsson, with several jibes, throws a line and takes Annie and Neap aboard. When he sends Annie and Neap back to the *Bandora*, the *Mercurio's* second mate claims to be in charge, Nellson having claimed salvage. Annie and Sam work with some of Neap's crewmen and stage an alarm: the ship is sinking, abandon ship. The *Mercurio* mate and his men leap into rowboats, leaving Neap to again take charge. Annie wires for the *Narcissus* for a tow.

• President Franklin D. Roosevelt took some 300 books with him when he went on vacation in 1934 including 50 detective mysteries, a work on the "Old China Trade," a handbook on Alaska and "a work entitled 'Tugboat Annie.' "[123]

3. Nickel-or-Million

(9 April 1932) *Tugboat Annie* (Minton, Balch, 1934)

Deep-Sea Towing and Salvage is going through slow times, Alec Severn admits, and Annie offers to approach an old drinking buddy of her late husband Terry, Tyburn "Nickel-or-Million" Connor (both men courted Millie Fleming in their day, but Connor won her hand), a well-to-do businessman. The meeting doesn't go well — Annie is splattered in mud when crossing the street, courtesy an arrogant war hero, Ashburn Knoblee, who is engaged to Connor's daughter Patricia. The towing business picks up the next week, with the *Narcissus* assigned to escort logs past Kidney Island to a Secoma sawmill. It's still wet weather and Annie makes a hasty decision to take a shortcut through Hook Narrows.

As they begin passage, a fancy cruise ship races past. Despite shouts and waves of Annie and Peter the mate, the skipper, Knoblee, thumbs his nose. As Annie predicts, his craft is blown sideways into Dog Rock and crew and passengers — including Patricia and her father, Ty Connor — are in the water. Annie drops the log tow to rescue the swimmers. Ashburn and Pat chaff at menial tasks given them by Annie, and Ty Connor doesn't calm down until he and Annie share Annie's concoction of "carbolic acid and juniper drops."

Connor admits he had been unkind in holding an old grudge against Annie, and said he'd arranged the log tow — now in ruins — and would continue to send work Deep-Sea's way. Annie saw promise in Patricia's grit, and Connor said she had seen the light regarding Ashburn's arrogance and would never marry the suitor.

• Longtime friend Connor, a shipping and lumbering magnate, is grateful to Annie for a past favor. He shows up in four more tales.

Other crew members mentioned include Shiftless and Pinto. Except for Severn's secretary, few other women appear in the stories.

4. Spareribs and Sauerkraut

(9 July 1932) *Tugboat Annie* (Minton, Balch, 1934) *Tugboat Annie: Great Stories …* (Curtis, 1977)

Ty Connor bemoans his inability to get his nephew, Dick Simmonds, to settle down and take a job in his office. Simmonds is of independent means and prefers partying. Annie invites Connor to join the crew in the mess for a meal of spareribs and sauerkraut as cooked by Pinto. Unfortunately, Shiftless has dropped a bar of soap into the mix, and it's inedible.

Later that evening, Annie accompanies Big Sam and Shiftless to Secoma's theater district to see a gangster movie. After, they go to a nightclub, where Annie orders spareribs. As food is about to arrive at her table, a fistfight begins between gun-wielding, would-be bad guys. The waiter's tray files to the floor. In disgust, Annie takes charge of one of the "bandits" and hustles him to the *Narcissus*, departing at midnight. The nameless young man refuses to give his name, answer questions or do any work for Sam.

The tugboat encounters a four-masted schooner, *William Chapman*, the worse for wear because of a storm. The tow to shelter is made difficult by a boiler leak. The prisoner has a change of heart as he watches the crew pull together to keep the tugboat going, and is himself rescued from a hot boiler. At the last, Annie and Sam shovel coal into the two fire chambers.

Back on shore, Annie sees a newspaper and recognizes her captive as Dick Simonds. Dinner that day is spareribs and sauerkraut.

5. No Cure, No Pay

(3 September 1932) *Tugboat Annie* (Minton, Balch, 1934) *Tugboat Annie* (Dell, 1947)

The *Narcissus* has new pumps, towing winches and lines, but the same tired engines and Annie pleads with Severn for a refit — especially since the arrival in Secoma of Horatio Bullwinkle and his big tug *Salamander*, out of San Francisco. The *Narcissus's* top speed of 9.5 knots can't keep up with the *Salamander's* pace, and Deep-Sea begins to lose out on assignments. Annie arranges for a comfortable payment schedule with one overhauler, and the tug is dry-docked for six weeks. With new engines, it can achieve 11.25 knots.

Mackay's White Funnel Line contacts Bullwinkle about a client, a Brazilian hauler, whose *Amazonas* has piled up near Destruction Island and needs to be dragged off. It's a no cure, no pay $60,000 salvage. And, Mackay says, tell Tugboat Annie so both have a fair shot at the haul. Bullwinkle sends a written message to his rival, delivered an hour after he's left Secoma. Annie despairs of catching up until she spots the 20-knot *Haligonian* passenger packet arrive in Secoma. She charters the *Haligonian* for $2,000 and its speed plus the *Narcissus'* makes an average of 16 knots, enough to pass the *Salamander* and get the job.

Annie offers to split the job with Bullwinkle, she'll take the pay, he can have the cure.

• This was the first of 57 appearances by Horatio Bullwinkle in the Secoma tales: 85 percent.

"Annie's a lovable foghorn-shouting old girl," proclaimed a later newspaper scribe, Captain Barnacle, "broad of beam and solid in the middle, as Raine writes her up but Bullwinkle the villain, must have a few fellows on the water front, too.

"Says Raine: "You wouldn't believe the calls and mail I got the week Bullwinkle first appeared, trying to scheme Annie out of a tow job. From all over the country and everyone saying the same thing: 'I know that dirty so-and-so.'"[124]

The soap in the sauerkraut and the hot boiler episodes were worked into the 1933 motion picture *Tugboat Annie*.

6. An Old Alaska Custom

(12 November 1932) *Tugboat Annie* (Minton, Balch, 1934)

Annie feels spent after bringing a tramp ship with broken propeller, 200 miles off Cape Flattery, to drydock, narrowing avoiding the cruise ship *Taku Mount*, whose master "Split-Second" Wilton pulls speedily in front of the *Narcissus*. She's feeling "la-de-da," she tells Ty "Nickel-or-Million" Connor, who sends her to see a doctor. The doctor prescribes a vacation.

Connor books her on a trip to Alaska on the *Taku Mount*, which is part of his Glacier Steamship line. She takes along a macaw named Elmer, a gift of her towboat crew. She makes friends with chief officer Jack Bushell — he plays fiddle and Annie's father was an amateur musician — and takes his side in a confrontation with Wilton. The ship hops from port to port in British Columbia[125] and Alaska. Wilton cuts off a fishing trawler's nets at one point, and sideswipes a cannery ship another time, insisting nothing happened. Bushell disagrees, Annie intervenes, Wilton lunges at Annie, trips and falls down a stairway. The *Taku Mount* crew rescues the bobbing seamen of the cannery ship. Annie helps navigate the cruise ship into Skagway, Bushell now given full command.

• East of Cape Flattery is where the Strait of Juan de Fuca meets the Pacific Ocean. It is the northern boundary of the Olympic Coast National Marine Sanctuary. Captain James Cook gave the rugged, storm-battered coastline this name.[126]

7. Old Mefoozelem

(10 December 1932) *Tugboat Annie* (Minton, Balch, 1934) *Tugboat Annie* (Dell, 1947)

Captain Nat Gumble, with 60 years of sea experience, has been relegated to the job of watchman for coal bunkers. He lives humbly on the wharf premises. Annie sometimes mocks "Old Mefoozelem," as she calls him, but later sympathizes when Bullwinkle mistreats the man. Gumble after a while admits to Annie he's in trouble. He'd allows Charlie Bagshaw to store "coal" that's full of slate and slag, not fit for any use. No one would buy it, and now the yard owners are bringing a shipment of real coal and will need the bins.

After Bullwinkle cheats another tow from Deep-Sea Salvage, Annie works up a plan. She enlists Gumble to hire Bullwinkle, on the pretext Annie wants the work, to rent four barge and load the "coal" in anticipation of a sale. The only barges available are through Deep-Sea, which Bullwinkle hires for $12 a day each for as long as they are needed. When Annie reveals things to Bullwinkle, he shrugs that he will attach a lien and get paid by Bagshaw. Bagshaw, of course, could never find a buyer for the "coal" and Bullwinkle was stuck with it — and a mounting bill.

• The reference to Cap'n Nat points to Captain Nathaniel W.H. Sutton (1834-1915),[127] one-time president of Providence Tow & Steamboat and father of N. Howard Sutton, Kate Sutton's husband. The senior Sutton began his career as pilot of a schooner on the Seekonk River and became master of the steamer *American Union*. He switched to tugboating in 1882.

8. A Man of Few Words

(7 January 1933) *Tugboat Annie* (Minton, Balch, 1934) *Tugboat Annie* (Dell, 1947)

Murdoch McArdle owes Severn $2,500 for five tows and refuses to pay. Annie confronts McArdle, who takes his business elsewhere.

Severn reveals he had planned to take the tow without payment, and place a lien on it. Annie figures to do the same through a front, Red Halloran of the *Firefly*. Bullwinkle overhears the plan and alerts McArdle, who give the tow to another crew.

Annie notices that barges stored at the dock are numbered by Roman numerals. She witnesses Shiftless wash coal dust from a barge's numbers, revealing a digit she hadn't noticed. She schemes to disguise Barge 15, loaded with a McArdle tow of lumber, as Barge 5, and hires Halloran to tow it out of storage. She "discusses" the error after Halloran delivers it to her, and calls McArdle to inform him — after she's placed a lien on it. As the lumber is due in a couple of days at the client's, McArdle has to pay.

• Semi-regular Secoma tugboatman Red Halloran of the *Firefly* will show up in four more stories.

Frequent nemesis Morton McArdle, a taciturn, parsimonious and at-times unscrupulous commercial operator, appears in a dozen stories. This is the first.

Tugboat Annie by Constance Brighton
(*Movie Mirror,* pastiche, August 1933)

"It was a clear, sunny day. In the busy harbor of Secoma, tugs and scows ploughed puffingly through the blue-gray waters of the Pacific. A medley of whistles split through air at intervals. Aboard the tug 'Narcissus,' excitement ran high. It touched Sam, the grimy, slouching engineer and Shif'less, the squatty, good-natured deck hand. It touched even more the bulky, baggily clad figures and the bronzed, lined faces of Tugboat Annie Brennan and her husband, Captain Terry Brennan," begins the tale.

The Brennans are awaiting arrival in Secoma of the *Glacier Queen*, owned by Red Severn and on her maiden voyage. Their son Alec Brennan is at the helm. Alec is courting Severn's daughter, Patricia. Annie doesn't know her son has retirement plans for her.

Terry Brennan says he's sworn off liquor — then discovers the hair tonic in his cabin. The result is, he puts on a drunken show on the wharf. There's a disruptive scene in the messroom as the Brennans entertain their son and his girlfriend — including soap in the sauerkraut. Annie refuses son Alec's urging her to leave Terry. Alec sails off without saying goodbye. Engineer Sam informs Annie of the dangerous condition of the *Narcissus's* boiler tubes. A report comes in. The *Glacier Queen* has a broken tail shaft. Terry and Annie race to help. The tug throws a line to the ship, but the boilers fail. Terry goes behind the boilers to make repairs and is nearly overcome by fumes. He dies a hero, in Annie's arms.

• This non-canonical, 6½-page story with eight images from the movie, somewhat follows the motion picture scenario, but ignores large parts. The storyline is choppy. The actual movie plot is derived, according to the magazine, from Raine's *Post* stories "Tugboat Annie," "Hallelujah I'm a Bum" or "A Nickel or a Million" [sic] and "Spareribs and Sauerkraut." Constance Brighton also fictionalized Sax Rohmer's "The Mask of Fu Manchu" for *Movie Mirror's* March 1933 issue.

9. When Greek Meets Greek

(7 October 1933) *Tugboat Annie* (Minton, Balch, 1934) *Tugboat Annie* (Dell, 1947)

The *Narcissus* steers out of Everett with a tow and spots familiar boats along the way, including the *Wedell Foss*. Annie's counting on her friendship with Esau Leroy, master of the *Port Ludlow*, to favor her for the contract over Bullwinkle, but is dismayed when it's the First Mate Willie Levanway in charge. And he's a friend of Bullwinkle. Leroy has spent the night in jail for a bar brawl, and is under order from owner C.J.T. Boys to behave or lose his command. Bullwinkle catches up with Leroy and Annie in Secoma and provokes a fight, then files a complaint, and Leroy is a wanted man.

Annie has a solution and they visit Leroy's friend, Manuel Gonsales, consul for Coloragua, where the Boys ships are registered. Gonzales agrees to name Leroy a consul emissary, with immunity. There's considerable discussion at the dock when police are foiled in their attempt to arrest Leroy, though Levanway cites seafaring code that an emissary can't simultaneously serve on a ship and act in official duties. Annie plots a way for Leroy to board the ship via a swing from a dock boom and the *Port Ludlow* steams off — leaving the mate Levanway behind.

• In Snohomish County, Everett was first settled as a lumbering center. Twenty-five miles north of Seattle, it was home to several fish canneries. [128]

10. The Last Laugh

(16 December 1933) *Tugboat Annie* (Minton, Balch, 1934) *Sea Captains' Tales*, Douglas Reeman ed. (London: Century Publishing, 1986) excerpt, "Tug-boat Annie and Horatio Bullwinkle," J.O. Coote, ed., *The Norton Book of the Sea* (1989) excerpt, *The Faber Book of Tales of the Sea: An Anthology* (Faber and Faber, 1991)

Travel through a blizzard exhausts the *Narcissus* crew members, who welcome sight of Secoma's "hilly streets." There's immediate action, however, as Alec Severn says the *Narcissus* has to go to Cape Flattery where the big steamer *Utgard* has run aground near the coastal Indian fishing hamlet of LaPush. A second large tug is needed. The *Salvage Prince* at Victoria is in drydock. That means the *Salamander*. Bullwinkle insists on a 60-40 split of the salvage fee, in his favor. Annie has little choice but to accept. Through stormy weather, they locate the *Utgard*, where Captain Hall immediately disrespects Annie as "cookee." She sets him straight.

It's not an easy chore, but the veteran tugboat skippers work together, "animosity submerged in the stress of a common task." Annie has Hall sign a receipt for services. Hall then wants to continue to Secoma on his own power. But Annie, concerned about the condition of the ship's bottom plates, wants to make it a tow. Bullwinkle underbids her and gets the job. Before returning to port, Annie risks a rowboat visit to LaPush to use the telephone.

Powering home, she learns the *Utgard* has piled up again near Coullan Bay and may be a total loss. She goes to the scene. Hall had cast off his line once they reached the Juan de Fuca Strait, Bullwinkle says. Hall asserts Bullwinkle wanted an additional fee due to the weather. Hall claims since Bullwinkle was in Deep-Sea's employ, it was all one big salvage operation and Annie's company is responsible. She therefore forfeits a $110,000 salvage fee on the $1 million value of the ship and cargo. He wants the receipt returned, and over Bullwinkle's objections, she tears it up. She tells Bullwinkle Deep-Sea will pay the $5,000 tow he had negotiated with Hall and Bullwinkle gives her his contract. Bullwinkle is puzzled until Annie reveals that the reason for her LaPush phone call was to direct Severn to take out insurance guaranteeing the salvage fee — the entire amount, as Bullwinkle having given over his paperwork.

• Beach-blessed LaPush is a hamlet in Clallam County at the mouth of the Quillayute River, surrounded by Olympic National Park. It is a community of Quileute, a federally recognized tribe.

Puget Sound communities were originally occupied by Aboriginal tribes: The Duwamish and Suquamish in Seattle, the Snohomish in Everett, the S'Klallam in Bremerton, the L'haq'tem-ish in Bellingham, the Samish in Anacortes, the Puyallup and Ste-lacoom in Taconic. Also the Nisqually in Olympia, Klallan in Port Townsend and Port Angeles, Makah in Neah Bay and Chinook in Vancouver.[129]

The Saturday Evening Post advertises the 11th Tugboat Annie story in the *Chicago Daily Tribune* for 16 January 1934.

11. Iron John

(20 January 1934) *Tugboat Annie* (Minton, Balch, 1934) *Tugboat Annie* (Dell, 1947) *Tugboat Annie: Great Stories …* (Curtis, 1977)

"Oh, happy days is here some more…" for Tugboat Annie, whose friend "Iron John," a veteran towboatman and a crony of her late husband Terry, is coming from Portland for a visit. Bullwinkle catches wind and wonders who Iron John is. The more he inquires, the greater the legend grows, until Bullwinkle expects a Paul Bunyan of a character to arrive. He's surprised when a thin, short, bandy-legged man appears wharfside, inquiring about Annie. Bullwinkle picks on him and gets into a scuffle. When Annie tries to intervene, she twists her ankle. This is Iron John, she tells Bullwinkle. The rival tugboater is briefly chastened, then determined to show up "the runt." Iron John gets mad, and tells Bullwinkle he going to have to get even. Bullwinkle scoffs.

Iron John pilots the *Narcissus* to meet the schooner *George Cary* at Cape Flattery. Bullwinkle in dark of night sabotages the *Narcissus'* anchor. The *Salamander* negotiates for the tow. But while Bullwinkle is discussing price, Iron John manipulates the tossed wires, so when a hawser is drawn aboard, it's the *Narcissus*', not the *Salamander's*. Bullwinkle loses a big wager to Iron John, who wins Annie's praise.

• This was the last of the stories collected by a New York book publisher. A first edition copy hardcover copy of *Tugboat Annie* with dustjacket, published by Minton Balch & Co. in 1934 with a retail price of $2, sold for $5,500 through Abebooks in 2009.

12. The Other Cheek

(5 May 1934) as "By the Luck of the Brennans" (*Pearson's Magazine*, March 1934)

The *Narcissus* returns to Secoma, the captain and crew weary with boredom. A call to Port Ludlow proved a dud — only a dead whale on the beach. Annie mends one of First Mate Peter's shirts. Peter plays string with a kitten. Deck hand Shiftless reads a pulp magazine.

Annie is convinced rival Bullwinkle was behind the apparently false call for a tow, but Severn says she was supposed to go to Port Townsend, not Port Ludlow. Annie chaffs as Bullwinkle cruises by, taking the tow to Olympia, bragging about all his business. Severn warns her to play nice.

There's a new garbled radio message: Was the barkentine *William Groundwater* arriving from Honolulu to be met north or south of the lightship? She sets off, arranging to get the details later. Bullwinkle shadows her. She's tempted to try a shortcut through the mud flats behind Crowley Island, but Peter points out the danger in the tide tables. Bullwinkle is heedless and shoots into the flats and becomes mired.

Annie backtracks and offers him advice on how to get out without high tides damaging the *Salamander*. Hardly thankful, Bullwinkle quickly catches up. Annie has Peter set a false course, which Bullwinkle thinks is the real one. Big Sam stages a fake engine room fire and the tug drops back. When Bullwinkle gleefully charges off on what he thinks is the correct course, Annie veers away and connects with her tow.

"Luck of the Brennans," she chortles.

• The *William Groundwater* was a real ship, named for the director of transportation for Union Oil and well-known to marine and refinery men in the Harbor District. Raine and Groundwater were friends.[130]

Puget Sound extends from Point Wilson near Port Townsend[131] southerly to Budd Inlet in Olympia. Olympia, Washington's state capitol, is in Thurston County. It boasts numerous natural attractions including Nisqually National Wildlife Refuge. Its legislative buildings are on a hill; Percival Landing Park is near the water.[132]

Crowley Island, today known as Fortress Island, is at the entrance to Mud Bay on the south tip of Lopez Sound in San Juan County.[133] Port Ludlow is on the northeastern shore of Admiralty Inlet.

13. Mr. Bullwinkle Earns His Pay

(26 May 1934) *Tugboat Annie: Great Stories ...* (Curtis, 1977)

Annie returns from a shopping excursion in anticipation of feasting on steak, baked murphies, stewed corn, fried onions, a growler of beer and a chunk of hot mince pie in the *Narcissus* messroom.

Bullwinkle, meanwhile, has learned the *Snoqualmie*, a cargo steamer, has been rammed at sea by the Swedish tanker *Hudiksvall*. The former, under Captain J.C. Millward of Eugene, Ore., and owned by McArdle of Secoma, is taking water. McArdle tells Bullwinkle to alert Annie of the need for a tugboat to stand by, the first one there gets the job, no cure, no pay. Bullwinkle quickly passes off to Annie a short tow for Marine Contracting — a barge to Everett.

A few days pass, and Bullwinkle sends a radio call for help. He's 150 miles off the cape. When Annie arrives, Bullwinkle tells her the *Snoqualmie* is taking water faster than it can be pumped out. Two tugs can more quickly tow the ship toward land to be beached. Before taking the job, Annie and Big Sam inspect the damaged ship. Millward is critical of McArdle for buying cheap equipment and paying little to the crew. In the engine room, Chief Engineer Andrew Bogle proves to be as stingy as McArdle. He'll only burn poor-quality coal, mostly slag. Annie tells Bullwinkle she'll take nothing of the salvage if he pays her $3,000.

The ship sinks 4 miles from the cape. The crew is safely removed. Bullwinkle is rebuffed by McArdle — no pay. Annie steps in, chides McArdle for blaspheming all tugboatmen and tells him he's vulnerable for an accusation of barratry — when an owner willfully takes action that endangers a craft. Specifically he used the trash coal when there was perfectly good coal on board. If Bogle had used that fuel, the crew could have pumped out more water and saved the ship. She settles for $30,000, which she shares with Bullwinkle, less the $3,000 he'd agree to pay her.

14. A Matter of Business

(7 July 1934) *Tugboat Annie: Great Stories ...* (Curtis, 1977)

Leaving town, Severn asks Annie to meet Jim Henneberger, who is arriving by train with plans to start a Boston-to-Northwest maritime service. His *Minute Man* is due from the Panama Canal within a day. Bullwinkle corners Henneberger first, but Big Sam tinkers with the *Salamander*'s engine and a tour of the harbor falls short.

Bullwinkle has one of his men tinker with the *Narcissus's* air starting valve lever and Bullwinkle heads for the *Minute Man*, which needs assistance off Destruction Island.

Annie arrives first but the ship's master won't take her line. She pleads and yells advice, but the captain takes no action until Bullwinkle arrives. Henneberger pays Bullwinkle $750. Annie says she will file for salvage, explaining that under marine law, when a vessel is in distress and unsolicited advice is accepted that saves the ship from damage, the advisor has a legitimate claim for salvage. Maritime court would likely award her $5,000, Annie says. But if Henneberger would care to sign a contract….

• Destruction Island in Jefferson County, part of the Quillayute Needles National Wildlife Refuge, is home to numerous species of migratory birds.

15. Captain Terry Comes Through
(22 September 1934) (artwork by Dan Sweeney)

Whether she's joyous, brooding, tired or peppy, Annie takes one look at the plush-and-gold oval-framed portrait of her late husband, at times abrasive Terry, and becomes nostalgic. This is one of those days. She's slept late, her morning brightened by the prospect of afternoon tows — a couple of scows to Manchester, later meeting the *Galatea*, a Pine-Star Line tanker, to be escorted to Secoma Tar Products' wharf.

As she's about so set off, old nemesis Murdoch McArdle shows up. Annie calls him McGargle. He owns the Tar Works and isn't ready to offload the *Galatea*. He offers her $100 to $200 to delay the tanker for a day or two. He suggests she ground it temporarily, maybe tow it off for salvage later. Acting as the ship's pilot, she wouldn't be liable. Annie bristles and refuses and propels him off the *Narcissus*.

She greets the *Galatea* and its Captain Thomas White, who shows her a telegraph from the ship's owners warning the price of creosote is fluctuating and the consignee may attempt to refuse delivery. Annie suspects McArdle is up to something, but the delivery goes as scheduled. McArdle's chemist finds a sample to be below standard and he won't accept it. White agrees to shut off his pumps — and presses Annie for a quick solution.

Next morning, Abel Child of Pine-Star sends a wire appointing Deep Sea Towing agent for the Port of Secoma — a permanent designation, if she can solve the McArdle problem, which is costing Pine-Star $1,200 a day. Severn is away. Annie has to decide and quick. She pores over books on maritime law. In her cabin aft of the wheelhouse, she chides the "old bar beetle" Terry (at least, his photo). "The only smart trick you ever done was to suck the bottle and then fill it up wid water so's I wouldn't miss none. I —." And she has her answer.

She rushes to the *Galatea* and tells White to begin the discharge again (the pipes had never been disconnected) and lower a hose to siphon water from below the wharf. McArdle's man on watch has an eye on the *Galatea's* draft marks and sees no change. Her tanks emptied, the *Galatea* is disconnected and leaves the Tar Products wharf. There's no time to gloat — Annie learns the price of creosote has gone back up.

She sends for the *Galatea* and makes a deal with McArdle to buy back the creosote at that day's price. Annie had just read a news item that Powder River Lumber of Vancouver, B.C., had immediate need for 2 million creosoted railway ties. It would need the creosote. It means a profit for Pine-Star and Severn, who had paid for the creosote from McArdle.

• There are two Vancouvers. The one in Clark County, Wash., "The Couve," is on the Columbia River. It was established around a fur-trading outpost. The one in Canada, bordering the Fraser River, is the largest city in British Columbia. It grew from indigenous settlements, traditional territories of the Squamish Nation, Musqueam Indian Band and Tsleil-Waututh Nation. It was called Gastown, then Granville, then, in 1886, Vancouver, after explorer George Vancouver. It has the largest natural seaport accessible to the Pacific Ocean. It is served by the Canadian Pacific Railway.

Dell paperback No. 192 collects a half-dozen Tugboat Annie yarns. A map of Puget Sound Country — noting real communities but not Secoma — appeared on the back cover.

16. A Great Day for Mahoney

(22 December 1934)

"The bright Puget Sound sunlight laced with the fragrance of giant pines and the sharp salt tang of the sea, pored its golden beneficence over the blue waters of Puget Sound, and more specifically upon the broad back of Tugboat Annie Brennan, master of the deep-water tug *Narcissus*, of Secoma, as she leaned over the rail outside the pilot house, holding forth with her usual bonhomie to a reluctant audience of Shiftless, the deck hand, and paunchy Peter, the mate who was at the wheel. The water was flecked still with foam and whitecap, reminder of the previous day's vicious gale, but the air was clear and bracing, and the clean-washed sky presaged good weather."

The *Narcissus* is escorting a Portland steamer destined for Secoma. Aboard the *Worcester* is Tim Mahoney, a veteran pilot who a decade earlier had given his expert testimony at a trial, the upshot of which cost Captain Terry Brennan $6,000. Annie never got over it, and let Mahoney know it. She learns he has been scheduled to pilot a military cruiser up the Columbia River from Astoria to the Rose Festival in Portland. Joseph Wright is captain — a young man who Annie had once given work as a deck hand and helped secure an appointment to Annapolis.

She goes to Portland and has a reunion with Wright. Turns out, Mahoney has long had his heart set on piloting the ship — in all his years, he'd never navigated a naval battleship. After some rumination, and learning that Mahoney is slipping into alcoholism, Annie relents and fakes an injured leg, enabling Mahoney to take the job. Annie is optimistic Mahoney's joy for the day may curb his enthusiasm for drink.

• Puget Sound, a complex network of interconnected waterways, stretches about 100 miles between Deception Pass and Olympia, It has an average depth of 450 feet.[134]

The 1,243-mile Columbia River rises in Columbia Lake in British Columbia's Rocky Mountains, flows through the province into the Pacific Ocean near Astoria, supporting 19 hydroelectric dams along the way. It serves as a boundary between the U.S. and Canada.

Captain Mahoney is a character in the motion picture *Tugboat Annie Sails Again,* a tired skipper recruited by Annie to substitute for her in a drydock tow. Echoing Wallace Beery's scene in the first Tugboat Annie picture, Mahoney become intoxicated from drinking bay rum and can't take command.

17. Welcome Home

(2 March 1935)

Stopping in Port Angeles on her return from a towing commission at West Vancouver Island, Annie learns of a new assignment: escort the lumber schooner *Roberta Pett*, 20 miles off Cape Elizabeth. The vessel has a broken tiller stock but is not salvage. She encounters the ship sooner than she expected, being towed by Bullwinkle, who was returning from a trip to Panama. She argues with the *Pett's* master, to no avail, so decides to tag along and see what happens. Near Tatoosh Island Light at Cape Flattery, the *Salamander* pump breaks and the fire pump is insufficient to handle the work. Bullwinkle toots Annie to take over the schooner, which she does, having watched the ship gusting very close to shore.

At the wharf, the schooner's master serves Annie with papers; the owners are suing for $2,000 for the loss of two anchors and chains. Severn is annoyed, and suggests Annie take a vacation. Bullwinkle doesn't want to pay Annie a fee, but the two work out a contract, stating the *Narcissus* was hired by Bullwinkle. He pays $2,000, then gloats that he will collect a tidy $25,000 savage fee. Annie, consulting the Admiralty books, advises Bullwinkle that the law changed during the time he was away on his voyage to Panama, and it was illegal for one tugboat to misrepresent itself and take over another's tow, and as the ship could still have maneuvered (in a limited way) on its own. It was not a salvage. Plus, since the *Narcissus* was hired to Bullwinkle, he was liable for the schooner lawsuit as well.

• *Roberta Pett* shares its name with Raine's wife, Joyce Roberta Pett.

On Washington's northern edge, Port Angeles is in Clallam County. Its ferry service crosses the Strait of Juan de Fuca to Victoria, B.C.

Cape Elizabeth in Taholah, Grays Harbor County, is home to the Quinault Tribal Nation. The National Data Buoy Center is located here.

18. A Horse of a Different Color

(4 May 1935) *Post Stories of 1935*, Wesley Winans Stout, ed. (Little, Brown, 1936)

The *Chehalis,* a freighter of the Cliff Stewart Line, has lost one propeller near Cape Blanco and will need a tug after it reaches Cape Flattery. Annie and Bullwinkle compete for the tow. Bullwinkle wants them to agree on a figure — $200 a day — in a meeting with Ellis, the shipping agent. Ellis won't assign a tug until morning. Mate Jake urges Bullwinkle to sneak out of Secoma after dark, but Bullwinkle wants to keep a promise to Annie.

The two *Salamander* men visit the Forepeak bar and get sloshed. They knock out the bartender Fantail, stash him in a closet and take off in the *Salamander* on a 12-hour trek to wait for the *Chehalis.* Fantail alerts Annie, who decides not to go in pursuit of the tow, being two hours behind Bullwinkle. Returning to her cabin, she trip over a bucket of whitewash that Shiftless hasn't put away, and is coated with a ghostly sheen. This giver her an idea. The *Narcissus* is a snub-nosed craft with a bleached bow fender of woven hemp, red housing and tall yellow funnel — colors that stand out even in fog.

Soon at Neah Bay, Bullwinkle is surprised to see the *Chehalis* sailing his way, towed by a white phantom — the *Narcissus,* white-coated so as to be invisible and sneak past Bullwinkle and Jake in the dark. And, Annie's getting $300 a day, a bonus from Ellis for one-upping Bullwinkle.

• Neah Bay, a fishing village on the Makah Reservation in Clallam County, is a popular destination for hikers and campers. The name came from Chief Dee-ah (pronounced Neah). The bay itself has had several names. Described by the British Captain James Cook in 1778, it was site of a Spanish fort in the 18th century. A U.S. Coast Guard base is maintained here.

19. Tat for Tat
(30 November 1935)

Annie visits her friend Henry Ramon and his fellow woodsmen who have a summer's worth of logs in a boom but the only closest tug, *Ruby B,* is available from owner Ed Blackmore only at an extravagant price. Since it's on her way south, Annie agrees to tow it to Millport, 120 miles, not anticipating very rough seas near Blind Man's Bay.

The *Narcissus* needs to tank up and Annie informs a man she thinks runs the fuel station. She doesn't recognize it's Blackmore himself, who switches hoses so Big Sam fills one fuel tank with water, not oil. Sam discovers this before it damages the engine, but nevertheless the tow and tug are in a predicament. Blackmore shadows them, waiting for Annie to release the boom. He plans to collect the logs for himself as salvage. Annie, however, has the crew jettison the water and anything they don't need, to lighten the tug so it will ride above mud flats. She then tows through Breakneck Passage, luring the *Ruby B.* behind. The *Ruby B.* hangs up. Annie responds to a demanding whistle for help.[135] She quotes $3,000 to tow Blackmore to port, plus $2,000 when he lets on he was responsible for the water in the tank. She threatens to leave him behind. He signs a contract.

She takes fuel from his tank for the *Narcissus* — tat for tat, as she says.

Who's Who — And Why
(11 January 1936)

The Jaipur Prince is in Secoma and Mr. Gallup finds Tugboat Annie on the *Narcissus*. Gallup recalls the time they served together on a ship out of Vancouver. They reminisce "that writer feller used to come around asking questions by the dozen." Annie, noting the scribbler — red-headed with a long nose and "ginger fuzz" under his nose — now visits from Hollywood and often cruises around the Sound. Speak of the devil, almost immediately Raine shows up on his cabin cruiser to talk with them.

" 'Oh, oh! It's the pest sure enough!' said Annie resignedly to Mr. Gallup. She waddled to the rail. 'Go home, ye prattle trap!' she bellowed. 'I don't know ye!'

" 'All right with me, Annie,' he retorted. 'Only, Bullwinkle was telling me awhile back how he and his Salamander put it over on you yesterday across at Port Orchard. It's a pretty good story — '

" 'Sa-ay!' cried Annie, alarmed. 'Don't you believe nothin' that big lumbago tells ye! He's lyin'!'

" 'What did happen, then?'

" 'Come over to the dock when we git in. I'll tell ye!' …'"

She promises to bring Gallup.

" 'Okay, meal tickets!' the man in the cruiser grinned. 'I'll be seeing you!'"

• This whimsical piece filled two *Post* columns.

20. If the Cap Fits

(25 January 1936) *Tugboat Annie: Great Stories …* (Curtis, 1977)

"Darkness had fallen over the harbor of Secoma, and the rumble of trucks, the clatter of ships' winches, the pious ejaculations of stevedores were stilled, and the only sounds were the merry voices, deep laughter and the music of a fiddle and harmonica issuing from one of a line of moored tugs tied up at the Deep-Sea Towing & Salvage Company dock. Tugboat Annie Brennan, master of the deep-water tug *Narcissus,* was giving a party."

It's her birthday. Bullwinkle leaves a gift: a straw hat with holes cut for a horse's ears.

Annie and Bullwinkle are rivals for Tom Keane's drydock towing job. Bullwinkle has recruited Red Halloran of the *Firefly* and Clay Kniss of the *Sea Scout* to make a joint bid. But Severn gets the job when Keane is impressed with Annie's quick thinking in beating Bullwinkle to a taxicab.

Annie nearly completes her tow when the drydock scow is struck in the fog by a passing steamer, beaching it on Whip Island. The *Narcissus* and the *Knight of Malta* blew their whistles at the same time, neither hearing the other. Thus the collision. Equipment is needed to make repairs before the drydock scow can be recovered. Bullwinkle reaches the scene and claims salvage. Keane is sore and cancels the Deep-Sea contract. Annie advises Keane to let Bullwinkle make the repairs and remove the dredge. And she lectures him on his attitude toward women in the wheelhouse. She explains that everything that floats is not necessarily a vessel. There is no salvage, she says, as the drydock is incapable of navigating on its own.

She sends the horse hat back to Bullwinkle: "If the cap fits, wear it."

• This is the last story for a while. The next year, Raine wrote from his Warner Brothers' office: "It's pretty warm here today, so I've got the window open, but it would really be better if the window were closed, because the odor of the flowers in the garden below is sort of overpowering and in addition there is the too-audible conversation of two sun-tanned girls in shorts standing in the shade of the building. Ah, well … What do you think about some more yarns on Annie? I get, at times, a positive craving to turn her loose on Bullwinkle and the old gang once more. I figure on taking my layoff period of three months somewhere around February, and would like to know if Annie could once more stick her battered old face into the pages of the Post? ...."[136]

Would they say no?

One reader complained that Annie and Glencannon don't belong in the magazine as "your subscribers do not associate with that class of people." Other readers gave an outstanding contrary opinion in their responding letters, including one who wrote:

If I may, allow me to say
Concerning Reader No. 1's protest
'Gainst Tugboat Ann and Colin Glencann'
Their stories are some of your best.[137]

The film *Tugboat Annie Sails Again* incorporates Raine's straw hat with ear-holes cut for a mule, from this story. Also Annie's underbidding of Bullwinkle and his loose consortium of tugboat-men. Also the kicker — drydocks aren't vessels, and therefore are not subject to salvage.

• Keeping Posted notes in June 1938 that Raine had three new tales in preparation, "and that he was prepared to take time off from his movie job and write them, if the Post was interested. After cold compresses and wrist-rubbing had brought our associate around, Mr. Raine further confessed that his heart was always where Annie was. We've been wondering about that heart, together with a number of thousands of Post readers. Where is Annie, eh? Well, where is Annie?"[138]

21. Tugboat Annie Sails Again

(1 October 1938) *Post Stories of 1938*, Stout, ed. (Random House, 1939) *Tugboat Annie: Great Stories...* (Curtis, 1977)

Work is slow and only the *Narcissus* and *Daffodil* have tows. The other four tugs in the current Deep-Sea fleet are idle. Annie delivers an oil barge, tussling with Bullwinkle along the way. She is sent to help retrieve a Transcontinental & West Coast Railroad craft, the *Justine*, loaded with boxcars. It is stranded at Foss Island. Red Halloran of the *Firefly* needs assistance. When Bullwinkle blocks the way with an oil line, Annie rams it. She repeats the maneuver on her return, only Bullwinkle has rigged it to pump seawater, which saturates the *Narcissus*. Severn, not for the first or last time, is fed up with her constant brawling and gives Annie her notice.

The sinking car barge is blocking rail traffic. J.J. Pendleton, T&WCRR vice president, calls for bids, which come in at the $20,000 to $23,000 range and 10 work days. Severn at Annie's suggestion bids $14,500 and 10 days. Bullwinkle, who has rifled Severn's trash, underbids him by $100. Annie counters with an offer of $14,500 and a 24-hour turnaround, plus $1,000 per day shaved off the 10. She takes her command and the *Daffodil* and two scows full of sawdust, and with one tug pumping in, the other pumping out, fills the cracks in the barge with sawdust. The sawdust swells and refloats the barge.

• Raine advised *Post* editors in June that he "had three Tugboat Annie stories ready for the typewriter, and that he was prepared to take time off from his movie job and write them, if the Post was interested. After cold compresses and wrist-rubbing had brought our associate around, Mr. Raine further confessed that his heart was always where Annie was."[139]

This story, or at least its title, was used for a movie sequel and radio dramatizations.

22. Tugboat Annie Saws Off a Leg

(22 October 1938) *Tugboat Annie: Great Stories …* (Curtis, 1977)

Severn needs to put the *Pansy* and *Hyacinth* back in operation and make repairs to the *Narcissus* but is short of funds. Annie visits Ole Oleson at Deep Sea Logging's Camp No. 2 to see about the $2,200 he owes. Oleson says he can't pay unless his regular client Bob Anderson buys his 20 million board feet of cut logs at $22 a thousand feet. Anderson has refused the price, saying he already has too many logs. Puzzled, Oleson says Anderson typically saws 200,000 feet a day.

Annie goes to Anderson's mill to check his ponds and finds they are depleted. Anderson says he needs Oleson's logs, but not at his price. Annie tells Anderson to invite Oleson to the mill, and when the latter shows up, the ponds are full of logs. A new contract is ironed out at $19 per thousand feet. When the papers are signed, the *Narcissus, Pansy* and *Daffodil* return the log tows to the sawyers who loaned them for the day.

• The magazine advertised the story as "First of a New Series."[140]

Oleson is a tribute to Andrew Oleason Fossen/Foss, husband of Thea Foss.[141]

The *Post's* editor advised readers of Raine's receipt of an Academy Award and shared a letter from the writer: "It is two years and some months since I wrote a short story, and in that time I have learned something of the trade of a screen-play writer — a trade that differs in many respects, of course, from that of a fiction writer. But somehow I always felt that the two kinds of writing were in two separate mind compartments. And it seems I was right — in my own particular case, at any rate — for I had no difficulty in turning to Annie again. There the old girl was, waiting; saying, 'Come on, Red … what are ye foolin' around wid that Hollywood floozie fer? Let's cast off afore Bullwinkle beats us to it!' So I stepped aboard, Annie jingled Big Sam and away we surged, not to stop until we made fast again in the pages of the Post."[142]

23. Tugboat Annie Blows the Man Down
(26 November 1938)

Back from a tow outside Vancouver Island, Annie looks forward to three days' leave as she consumes spareribs, potatoes, sauerkraut and apple pie at the Greasy Spoon. Severn, however, wants her to help pull the *Baronga* — chartered by McArdle — off a sandbar at Sand Spit.

Bullwinkle is McArdle's regular tugboat hire, and the ship's captain, Chipman, won't allow Annie to board. Annie takes depth measurements around the stranded refrigeration ship and returns home. She's puzzled why a ship showing 28 feet 6 inches depth should mire in water nearly 31 feet deep. Insurances underwriters want to hire both the *Narcissus* and the *Salamander* to pull off the ship, then accept Severn's offer of a no cure, no pay salvage arrangement. There's a momentarily scuffle. Annie's boat brushes against Bullwinkle's, with minor damage. Bullwinkle rushes off to Secoma to fill out a complaint and the *Narcissus* is confined to port. Nothing can be done on a Saturday afternoon, the matter will have to be resolved Monday.

Annie takes the *Daffodil* (Dogface Jackson, skipper, Pat Mulligan, first mate) to Kettle Creek with a handful of experts and boxes of dynamite, fuses, batteries and detonators. She blows a chunk of mountainside into the river, blocking its flow. The tide, as she expects, eats the silt holding the *Baronga*. Come morning, however, Bullwinkle has pulled the ship off and it is merrily on its way to India. Annie alerts Revenue agents, who stop it at Port Angeles. Chipman is under arrest for altering the depth margins painted on his ship. Bullwinkle could be considered an accessory after the fact, Annie speculates, but her rival signs a quitclaim to the salvage.

In Secoma, Annie thinks she might go to a movie, "Snowdrop and the Seven Little Warts."

• Sand Spit is likely Peacock Spit near where the Columbia River empties into the Pacific Ocean, known, according to the Tacoma Public Library digital Place Name archive as the "Graveyard of the Pacific for the many ships that have been wrecked there."

Kettle Creek may be Quillascut Creek in Stevens County — south of Kettle Falls — which drains into the Columbia River.[143]

24. Tugboat Annie Borrows Six Bits

(13 May 1939) (last of 23 stories illustrated by Fischer)

Tugboat Annie gallops and prances and sashays up a storm with Big Sam at a Waterfront Employees Association Hall dance until she gets word from Fred, the night dispatch, that Bullwinkle's *Sala-*

mander, towing Murdoch McArdle's lumber transport *Chinook*, has broadsided and sunk the *Pansy* at its wharf mooring.

With Severn in Europe, Annie is in charge of business. She tells McArdle that Bullwinkle was his agent and therefore he's liable for $20,000 value of the *Pansy* plus lost business. McArdle sputters the *Pansy* is 20 years old, built in wartime as was the *Violet*. It's several days before the case will be heard and deliberated by officials. Meanwhile, "One-No-Trump" Parsons, master of the *Violet*, hitting the bottle, comes to a near miss racing to port. She replaces him on the *Violet*, and takes over towing a dredge.

Reaching Sound City, Annie sees three tugs and a derrick barge trying to right the cargo ship *Odessa* from a sandbar. Annie plays it too loose in steering close to the *Salamander* and a wave tosses her tow into the barge, upsetting the derrick. Bullwinkle claims Annie was drunk and was known as "Rumpot Annie." She's in a spot, the *Odessa's* owners demanding $25,000 in damages. She sputters the *Violet* is only worth $8,000. She's frozen in port until posting a bond. In a reverie about her late husband, she hatches a quick fix for the *Odessa* and persuades the owner and captain to sign a no-risk contract if she can refloat the ship in a few hours. They have nothing to lose and agree. She works with the *Odessa's* engineer, first filling the ballasts to sink it lower into the sandbar, then emptying them, freeing the vessel to rise like a cork. She earns a $5,000 bonus.

Rushing to Secoma for the earlier case, she provides the contract indicating the *Violet* is worth $20,000, and thus McArdle is due costs. Severn has returned for the hearing, shakes his head at Annie's rabbit-from-a-hat trick and agrees to pay a bonus: six bits, so she and Big Sam can go to the next dance.

• The fill-drain ballast tanks solution is used in the second movie, *Tugboat Annie Sails Again.*

Tugboat Annie Sails Again came out in autumn 1940. Raine told the *Montreal Gazette* he was pleased with the casting. "Miss Rambeau is playing 'Annie' so well that she not only makes me want to write another tugboat story — she also shows me a possible facet of Annie's character that might go well in fiction. She is putting into the film portrait a certain spiritual quality, along with bluff good humor, and I think that must have been characteristic of Annie's prototype, too."[144]

A magazine reader from Rio de Janeiro advised that his agency sells diesel motors and subscribes to the *Post*. "The motores are for marinha, and for this the management makes each vendor of the motores read about Tugboat Annie, so to receive the Spiritual feelings of the ocean and also to tell the buyers the stories of the old times in Puget Sound — not the undersigned writer who is only used to make into Portugues the matters who come to Brasil in English."[145]

Annie Rides Again

A letter from the *Narcissus'* master to the *Post* in 1940 explained the lapse in new stories:

"I just seen the piece what you wrote about me in your paper where I was in Hollywood makin' a pitcher. Sure, I was down there all right and it was hotter'n seven hells, but it's some place. All them. Beautiful Australian erysipelas trees, and callous lilies growin wild. And that ain't all what's while, wid hundreds of little painted flippets all dolled up like a monkey-grinder but they're so pretty it made me feel kinda skittenish meself. Yea, Hollywood's a funny place, only they don't speak good English here. I was sittin at a counter in a eatin place one night, it was shaped like a towin' bitt and they called it the Toadstool, and I says to the feller on the next stool I says, 'Hey Pal,' I says, 'give the sugar a fair wind, will ye,' and he stares at me like I was the buccolic plague and he says, 'What,' and I telled him again, and he says, 'Madam, I ain't the weather man,' and I says 'Don't you call me a madam, ye horse's tail,' I says, 'or I'll kick ye clear back where the weather comes from,' and I sashayed over and salvaged the sugar meself.

"Well anyways about the piece ye wrote. I ain't seed Raine neither lately although I did get a peek of the red-headed scut or his splittin imige one day, as he tacked around a corner towin' a little fly-terrier on the end of a string. He's probly went Hollywood wid a bang and three short blasts and lies around wearin plushfour pants and livin off the flat of the land. Ye'd think he'd have gave me a mail, but I should worry, he don't draw enough water at any time to bother me. Anyways, when they made the pitcher outa a story Raine write about me called Tugboat Annie Sails Again I got enough dough to buy a new winch for the Narcissus, so to heck wid Raine and I advise you to do the same. Here's mud in yer face, pal, yours respeckfully, Tugboat Annie Brennan (signature)."[146]

•

Raine told a *Philadelphia Inquirer* reporter he had "only scratched the surface of the material left him by 'Annie's' prototype the late Thea Foss, of Tacoma, Wash.

"Annie's adventures could sail on indefinitely. If I haven't the time and endurance to finish them, I may bequeath them to some other writer to carry on for me."

He still had 40-plus tales in him, though — just don't expect them right away.[147]

•

Raine came in for both support and criticism for a telegram he sent to *Time Magazine* in December 1940 taking exception to the views of an Irish spokesman: "AS AN AMERICAN OF IRISH DESCENT I DEPLORE THE LACK OF LOGIC AND REALISM DISPLAYED IN THE LETTER OF HIS EXCELLENCY THE IRISH [FREE STATE] MINISTER TO THE U.S. (*Time*, Dec. 2). THAT IRISH PORTS WOULD BE USEFUL TO GERMANY IS SELF-EVIDENT TO AVERAGE INTELLIGENCE AND IF

Mr. [Robert] Brennan supposes Eire's policy of neutrality will prevent Nazis occupying it when and if possible he has quickly forgotten Denmark, Norway, Holland, Belgium ... We have long lost patience with the small vociferous group of fanatics and professional Irishmen with the smell of synthetic peat about them who have worked for so long and so viciously against better understanding between this country and Great Britain."[148]

Raine's response drew praise from the editor of the Kingston, Ont., *Whig-Standard,* which reprinted it entirely.[149]

•

Raine's Hollywood commitments delayed a new story. The *Post* told readers in March 1942: "We've tracked down the Narcissus, Tugboat Annie's pride. She (the Narcissus) is doing war work now and we'll have pictures for you in a week or so."[150]

Raine wrote in 1943: "I have an Annie story on the ways, in case you'd be interested. About time she got into the war effort."[151]

Tugboat Annie Sails Again

(*Movie Story,* November 1940, pastiche, author not identified)

To secure a contract with J.S Armstrong, Annie agrees someone else will helm the *Narcissus.* But when Mike Mahoney shows up dead drunk, she has no recourse but to pilot the ship herself. Severe weather. Armstrong's dry dock is damaged. She parks it at Whip Island for repair. Bullwinkle claims it as salvage. Severn fires Annie.

A side story is the growing romance between Armstrong's daughter Peggy and Annie's protégé Eddie Kent.

All is not lost. Annie locates a pertinent passage in marine law: dry docks can't be used for navigation and therefore cannot be considered salvage.

Severn to patch things up tells Annie she has her job back.

"But Tugboat Annie had other plans. There was the gleam of far horizons in her eyes. She was sailing out to charter new seas. Proudly she walked to the door, her chest out, her shoulders erect. She paused then, her hands on the knob, gave her wide-brimmed hat a little tug, then drew a yellow telegram from her bag. Happily she waved it in their direction.

" 'You see, gentlemen, I've had an offer from Hollywood. I'm going into the movies!'"

• Fawcett's *Movie Story* specialized in "New films in story form." A full-page advertisement for the new movie appeared in this issue.

The reading public thirsted for new Raine stories about Annie; the last was in May 1939 and the next wouldn't appear until June 1946. The 21/8-page non-canonical account, with two images from the motion picture, and another pastiche in 1945, attempt to bridge the seven-year gap though its audience wasn't necessarily regular *Saturday Evening Post* readers.

Tugboat Annie's Son

(*Movie Story*, pastiche, 1945, author not identified)

"It was as close as she would ever come to heaven on earth," begins the story, "feeling the planks of the Narcissus under her feet again, tasting the salt of the spray flung against her weather-beaten face, knowing herself secure and confident again in this fog-misted world she loved.

"Gone were the long, dreary days on land where she had scuttled around like a flea looking for something to hold fast to. No one knew what these months away from the harbor meant to her, no one. Not even Alec Severn, whose ace captain she had been before the Coast Guard had taken over his fleet of tug boats at the start of the war, and whose ace captain she was again, now that all harbor craft had been returned to their owners. Never had a woman been so happy as Tugboat Annie, now that she had come home at last...."

She rehires her old crew — the ones still available — and Johnny Webb, after she learns he has a prosthetic lower leg. " 'Knowed I was hirin' myself a real man,' her great, warm voice had boomed. And then, looking defiantly at the others, smiling because they'd caught her in one of those sentimental moods she tried so hard to hide from them, her voice sharpened. 'What ya clunkheads grinnin' like baboons for? C'mon, an put yer things aboard, then we'll get a bite to eat.' "

Webb is unsociable and shunned by most of the crew — but then shows the ultimate heroism when a tanker catches fire.

• The longest of the pastiches, the narration uses the film's working title and is illustrated with images from *Captain Tugboat Annie*. It takes up 11 columns spread across eight pages. There's one still from the film, plus three closeups of the actresses who portrayed Annie on film.

25. Tugboat Annie Wins Her Medal

(15 June 1946) (first of 32 stories illustrated by Harold Von Schmidt) *Post Stories of 1946*, Ben Hibbs ed. (Random House, 1947) *Tugboat Annie: Great Stories…* (Curtis, 1977)

Annie regrets her lack of wartime service, having been rejected by the Navy and Coast Guard and relegated to mundane to her — but vital — tows. Peter served in Japan. Pinto cooked on a corvette. Hank became a gunner's mate. Even Bullwinkle wrangled a commission with the Coast Guard — though he lost his *Salamander* at the Battle of Wake Island (replaced by the government with *Salamander II*).

Annie had taken the *Narcissus* to Boston and run the German blockade at the time of the Battle of the Atlantic. Now she's towing a steel barge carrying 300,000 gallons of fuel. She keeps abreast of the latest news: Even though war has been declared over, a renegade Japanese submarine menacing the waters off Los Angeles, Calif., sinks a troops ship. A state of emergency has been re-declared. The *Narcissus* still sports its dazzle colors. An idea percolates in Annie's head. Despite mandated radio silence, she shortwaves the Coast Guard. Bullwinkle answers the call. She announces she has had trouble and dropped an oil barge carrying 8,000 barrels of fuel. She's left an oil slick as marker and gives a location. Bullwinkle hears the radio chatter, catches on to what Annie is up to (making herself bait) and alerts the proper forces.

Annie has not abandoned the barge, and is nowhere near the slick or fake coordinates. Dive bombers take out the submarine when it surfaces. A Coast Guard vessel overtakes the *Narcissus* to relate the success.

Annie earns her medal.

• The Foss family for many years owned the Harold Von Schmidt painting that illustrated this *Post* story, selling it at auction in 1986.[152]

Post editors explained how, even with near-annual pleas, they had not been able to coax a new Tugboat Annie story from Raine until now. "Then, one fine April day, Annie suddenly barged in here. She came, as of old, all dressed up in a clean manuscript — still cussin' and stompin' and telling people off. We opened our arms, asking no questions. So here she is — from us to you. And now will you quit abusing us for a while?"[153]

26. Tugboat Annie and the Prodigal Calf
(13 July 1946)

Bullwinkle is given a hero's welcome when discharged from Coast Guard service, and is presented with a replacement *Salamander II* — the old one was destroyed at Wake. This vessel is the powerful former *Atlas*.

Deep-Sea, Alec Severn reports, has very war-tired tugboats, all, according to surveyors, needing engines, planking, pumps, windlasses, bitts or towing gear. He can't afford repairs.

Severn made money during the war, but also lost seven various crewmen, prompting him to establish trust funds for the families. Now Bullwinkle is back on the scene. Annie still has mixed feelings, but downing a drink or few reminisces some about Terry and his playing a harp in a small band. Bullwinkle as a goodwill gesture offers Annie one of his jobs, bringing the *Blue Star* from a Bellingham lumber yard to Secoma to drydock.

An old friend of Terry's, calling himself Tom Ferris, visits the *Narcissus* and rides to Bellingham. Along the way, Annie is dismayed at a near miss at Marrow-Bone Ledge and lucky avoidance of a cargo ship in the fog. Something's wrong with her compass. Chatty Ferris says he played cornet in a pick-up band with Terry, who played harp. Annie catches on. Terry never played harp, that's just a lie Annie had told Bullwinkle. Turns out, Bullwinkle put Ferris up to waving a magnetized iron bar at the compass, throwing its directions askew. Bullwinkle wanted her away so he could bid exclusively on a profitable tow. A new bridge has gone up at Watchikan and the contractor to remove the White Sand Inlet drawbridge, McArdle, needs to remove the old one. There are deadline and traffic specifics to the contract.

Annie barges in at the last minute, and whittles Bullwinkle down to $32,500, forcing Bullwinkle's assemblage of independent towmen to back out of a consortium. Annie later reveals to Severn a check for $3,500 from McArdle. The skinflint had agreed to pay her 20 percent of any amount Bullwinkle shaved off from his original $50,000 figure. Severn needs more money to make boat repairs. Annie hatches a scheme to hire independent boatmen for a specified day. She leases a large lumber barge. The last day of Bullwinkle's work, with one last span to go, there's a steady flow of Deep-Sea and other tugs going back and forth in his way, and there's nothing he can do about it.

He finally agrees to transfer his tow contract to Annie, even though he will forfeit a penalty and late fee. As high tide approaches, Annie sets the barge beneath the discontinued cantilever bridge. The barge rises with the tide and lifts the span from its moorings. She then takes it to Watchikan, where she sells it to the town council, which needs a new bridge. With the towing fee plus half the penalty Bullwinkle faced, Annie tells Severn there's enough to spruce up the tugs and to put further money into his assistance fund.

• Bellingham in Whatcom County, [154] near the Canadian border, 52 miles from Vancouver, B.C., and 90 miles from Seattle, has a ferry terminal and is a departure point for visits to the San Juan Islands. It was previously known as Whatom and Sehome (for Samish Chief Sehome) and Fairhaven (from an aboriginal name for "quiet place"[155]).

27. Tugboat Annie Quotes the Law
(22 March 1947)

A storm rages at Cape Flattery as Tugboat Annie heads home from Portland, grateful for the relative calm of the Juan de Fuca Strait. The *Narcissus* has a dented ventilator and smashed deadlights and a small boat has been wrenched from its divots by the weather. Stopping at Neah Bay, Annie telephones dispatcher Fred that Clem is trying to repair the tug's ship-to-shore radio so it can again receive messages.

She learns the steamer *Harrowgate*, out of Melbourne, is in trouble. Stocking up on fuel and supplies, the *Narcissus* sets off. Suspecting Bullwinkle is following, she has Clem send a false radio message. Bullwinkle is wise and shows up at the *Harrowgate*. The ship's master and owner, Higgins, despite a blown cylinder head in the engine, refuses a tow. The storm pushes the ship against island rocks. Crew members take to lifeboats to join the *Narcissus*. Higgins says he will charge them with mutiny.

Higgins insists the cargo can be shifted and the ship will refloat by itself. Annie negotiates the crew's return to the ship. Higgins insists Annie cannot collect salvage, which covers cargoes but not human lives. He throws a towline to Bullwinkle. Annie reveals to Higgins that he is no longer master of the ship; the salvors (the old crew), own it now, since he gave an "abandon ship" signal, per his own witnessed statement, automatically terminating the crew's contract. She promises to share the salvage with the crew.

• Scholar Fred Erisman studied two fictional *Post* "legal experts," Annie by experience, Ephraim Tutt by education. In his "Tugboat Annie, Ephraim Tutt, and Popular Views of the Law," he notes: "Emphasizing her professional expertise is her sense of herself as a woman, a quality that give Annie her first level of significance. Widow of the alcoholic tugboat captain, Terry Brennan, from whom she inherited the Narcissus, she remembers fondly their turbulent life together; however, she sees no conflict between her sex and her profession and asks only to be judged on her expertise."[156]

• This episode was adapted to radio in 1947 and stage in 1998, as is noted elsewhere.

28. Tugboat Annie Gets the Works
(22 March 1947)

Annie is in a snit after her first-time visit to a beauty parlor and an unfortunate experience with a facial mud bath. Stomping home on Water Street, she encounters Bullwinkle, who makes fun of her when she inadvertently falls into a construction ditch. Bullwinkle alerts Big Sam and Shiftless on the *Narcissus* and they rush to help. Bullwinkle takes advantage of the situation to remove a lever from the tugboat's air starter, to slow her departure to inspect an area at Sockeye Cove where the city wants to contract removal of a garbage dump to clear the way for new docks. Barely back onboard her boat, Annie witnesses a great harbor explosion.

A 3,000-ton tanker has caught fire. Bullwinkle takes off to secure a tow; Annie has to wait for Big Sam to borrow a lever from the *Pansy*. Annie arrives in time to see Bullwinkle throw a line to the tanker, but she rushes through smoke and flames with fire ax in hand to sever the mooring rope. She then throws a line to the tanker, agreeing without enthusiasm to serve as his employee, as he claims the savage.

In the aftermath, Bechtel the city engineer tells Annie the city plans to award a contract for the dump work to Bullwinkle, in gratitude for his saving the harbor from a great disaster. One stray comment he makes prompts Annie to investigate the scene further. Then she visits Bullwinkle and they wrangle about her fee. With some fast talking, she agrees to give up the fee and any half-claim to salvage if Bullwinkle in writing agrees she can keep any amount she can secure from the oil company.

She said she intends to file a claim of salvage on two tankers that sat next to the fire ship. Although the city has state-of-the-art equipment at the docks for fighting fires, it was inactive due to a pipe break and the water was shut off because of the Water Street ditch Annie had fallen into.

Oh, and Bullwinkle's claim isn't what he thinks it is, as the city's two fire tugs are also eligible to file for two-thirds of the credit.

• Reader Clifford T. Crudington of Bridgeport, Conn., in a letter to the editor in the next issue said he loved the story but nitpicked: "More in sorrow than in anger, can't we get Artist Von Schmidt to read Author Raine's description on Page 18: 'Mr. Horatio Bullwinkle, the large, bullet-headed and bandy-legged skipper of a rival tugboat'?

"What do we see on Page 19? A tall and magnificently slender and straight-legged Annapolis graduate in tailored raincoat, with a sharp nautical cap on a noggin far from bullet-shaped."

The editor responded: "Von Schmidt's Bullwinkle may not be bandy-legged but he looks appropriately tough to us."[157]

29. Tugboat Annie Plucks a Goose

(10 May 1947)

The *Narcissus* has two assignments: take the *H.W McCurdy* from the oil docks to Port Chaklit then tow a lumber schooner to Bremerton and Olympia. But a misleading signal at Chaklit sends the tug into the wrong mooring and it grounds until high tide. It's a Bullwinkle trick, his way of getting even with Annie for a past prank. Bullwinkle grabs a towing job: half of a broken-up tanker, *Basra*. Alec tells Annie he's about to take Bullwinkle as a partner so he can purchase steel barges in anticipation of construction contracts. There ensues a complicated sequence of back and forth with Bullwinkle.

Annie cons her rival into an unwanted job and takes over the *Basra* task. She takes it to Foss Bay and sells it for $200,000 to electric power interests. Workers immediately connect the surviving section of the ship with boilers and engines to electricity-generating equipment. Developer "Nickel-or-Million" Connor can now build a new quick-freeze plant. Annie brings a tidy profit home to Alec.

• In Kitsap County directly west of Seattle, Bremerton is home to the Puget Sound Naval Shipyard. It was occupied by the Suquamish when German immigrant William Bremer arrived in 1891. Known for its many restaurants and shops, it has ferry links to Seattle to its east.[158]

"The Framing of Tugboat Annie" in the *Post's*
20 September 1947 issue is publicized in an advertisement
in the *Chicago Daily Tribune* for 17 September 1947.

30. The Framing of Tugboat Annie

(20 September 1947) *Tugboat Annie: Great ...* (Curtis, 1977)

Captain Craig of the Red Triangle Line is establishing a new terminus in Secoma. Leery of women skippers, he nevertheless allows Deep-Sea Towing a chance: bring the 10,000-ton cargo ship *Corinthian* out of London from quarantine in Port Townsend.

Annie asks to board the *Corinthian*. Captain Bogle is reluctant to have a woman pilot. As she guides the ship through a haze of forest fire smoke, Bogle and one of the cargo owners, Bandigo, question her about her navigation skills, including where the closest point near shore is. At Bush Point, Bogle grabs the annunciator and calls for full ahead,[159] then takes the wheel from the quartermaster and steers toward shore. Annie calls for full astern and retakes the wheel but the ship beaches on sand.

Bandigo claims he didn't see Bogle's actions. Annie is disturbed, as Craig had not yet signed a legal agreement that would have absolved Deep-Sea from blame for the matter. It turns out Craig had ordered Bullwinkle to bring barges to the scene earlier than he should have known about the need. In a showdown, Annie says Craig and the ship's owners are not at fault: Bogle and the cargo owners, in a scheme to shave costs, had staged the beaching and will be charged with barratry.

• Port Townsend in Jefferson County, on the Quimper Peninsula, has a Marine Science Center and an active shipyard. Once called Point Leavett, Bush Point projects from the shoreline of Whidbey Island.[160]

31. Tugboat Annie Meets Mr. Gallup

(13 December 1947) *Post Stories of 1947*, Hibbs ed. (Random House, 1948)

Annie is piloting a 6,000-ton cargo tramp *Titan* out of Yokohama, the *Narcissus* following in case there's recurring engine trouble. The third mate introduces himself: "Belial Gallup, ma'am, o' Truro, Nova Scotia.: He explains he's on this ship and not his regular *Jaipur Prince* because he was sidetracked by a bout of malaria in Auckland and this was his best way to get home. He's looking forward to seeing his wife and five sprats and rejoining Captain Sloan's ship in Boston. He will need to make a vital rail connection, however, to get across the country in time. Annie orders full speed ahead when she spots Bullwinkle's tug racing to get through a channel right of way first. Captain Anderson of the *Titan* orders half speed, and he and Annie argue over who has command of the ship.

That's enough time for Bullwinkle to dart ahead. He encounters a small commercial fisherman. Its wake tips Bullwinkle's tow and it sideswipes a railroad trestle. The result: twisted rails.

Annie delivers the *Titan* to Secoma and returns to the accident scene, feeling guilty because that rail crossing will mean delay of the run of Gallup's train west. She comfortably allows Bullwinkle to take a commission to bring a pile driver. Meanwhile, she persuades "Hair-Trigger" Harry Fremont, railroad division superintendent, that running a pipe from a nearby refrigeration plant to freeze the rail will enable speedy repair. It does, and the train stops to give Gallup a courtesy ride.

• Raine had as early as 1938 said Annie and Belial would share a story. It took a while. "I really love the old girl," the writer told a reporter. "They used to tell me I should be ashamed to let an old woman keep me, but that's actually what she did for three years… The two of them should have a lot of fun chatting over old times across the mess table."[161]

Brennan of course plied the Sound and Juan de Fuca Strait. Gallup shipped out of Victoria and Vancouver as third mate aboard the *Canadian Pioneer* of the old Canadian Government Merchant Marine.

Letter writer M.A. Swanson of Chicago took issue with Gallup's depiction: "Having known and liked Tugboat Annie Brennan since she first made port, I may be allowed to ask where her 'Mr. Gallup' picked up his diction… Not in or around Truro or any part of Nova Scotia. My birthplace in the Cape Breton end of Nova Scotia —Garabus Village — is close enough to Truro to enable me to speak their language. Mr. Gallup's constant use of 'wery' and 'wi' ' sounds absurd and incorrect to a Nova Scotian.

"Furthermore, we have 'young ones' down there and 'sprats' never. I'll willingly agree with Mr. G that we consider Boston merely next door to us in Nova Scotia, but no one calls it 'Bosting.' It's generally pronounced as though spelled 'Bostn.'"

The editor responded that Raine had modeled the character on a real-life Nova Scotia native who sailed with him years ago. "His dialect is a unique blend of Nova Scotia, British ship life — and rugged individualism."[162]

32. Tugboat Annie Finds a Leaphole

(27 December 1947)

The Greasy Spoon is a popular waterfront restaurant, "a clubby place where everything was on a positive note, from the rattle and clanging bells of the freight trains that chuffed along Water Street to the gravel-voiced persiflage of the stevedores, tugboatmen and other nautical characters who formed its patrons."

Annie, typically wearing her faded red sweater and old woolen skirt, a man's battered felt hat on her head, has $300 saved for a trip to California. Bullwinkle can't resist hectoring her into a wager: a test of one-upmanship, best two out of three.

First up, Annie finagles a tow of Malcom Ardle's *Lilian Morse*, with a captain out of commission. Annie claims salvage on the basis of the ship had no capable navigator — unaware that Bullwinkle had hitched a ride on the tuna clipper *Mabel Jester*, thus negating the salvage.

Annie doubles the wager and cons Bullwinkle into rushing a barge of fuel oil for the *Marcia*, only to be turned away as the ship makes it to Port Angeles — burning mayonnaise (vegetable oil) in its steam engine. Breaking the tie, Bullwinkle buys a barge of fuel oil from Annie — but it contains only barrels of Puget Sound salt water.

33. Tugboat Annie Crashes Through
(24 April 1948)

Severn is in Portland on business, and despite cautions from Fred the dispatcher, Annie decides to find new business opportunities. Specifically, she visits Henry Wismer of Wismer Steam Lines, who considers Annie a brawler, given some past routs she has with Bullwinkle at the Waterfront Welfare Club. Wismer does admit to Annie that he wishes he had the gumption to poke one party, Murdoch McArdle, who owns a ship-building yard. Wismer contracted for two cargo carriers from McArdle, and the first, in service between Australia and Europe, suffered a leak and had to jettison a load of grain, at Wismer's expense. Wismer is afraid the soon-to-launch second vessel will also fail.

Annie enlists Bullwinkle to take part in a fake spat at the Greasy Spoon waterfront café and to ram an empty steel barge being towed by the *Narcissus* with his *Salamander*. Annie takes the barge to the McArdle drydock, where it is repaired and passes a water test. With Big Sam's help, Annie investigates a tank used in the water test.

Meanwhile, Severn returns to the office, blows up at Annie's signing an agreement with Bullwinkle not to sue for damages and fires her. She nevertheless attends the launch of Wismer's new ship and reveals how McArdle rigged the water test. She takes the "repaired" barge to Puget Sound Shipyards for a true test. It leaks.

A pleased Wismer promises towing contracts to Annie and Bullwinkle.

34. Tugboat Annie to the Rescue

(14 August 1948)

Annie is at Fisherman's Jetty buying mackerel for Pinto to cook. She jaws with Ole and "Herring-gut" Barker and enters the halibut pool — whichever boat, as the season opens, is the first to return to port with a full load wins.

Annie heads out 70 miles west of Flattery to rescue the *Antha* loaded with 100,000 pounds of fish. On the trip, the crew enjoys a mess of flaky golden crisp mackerel, scalloped potatoes, Yakima tomatoes, curly lettuce with French dressing and buttermilk biscuits, with date pudding for dessert. To Annie's dismay they meet Bullwinkle, the *Antha* in tow — he'd told skipper Andy Ross that Annie had taken another call.

Per usual, Annie ruminates while staring at a picture of the late Terry Brennan — and hatches an idea. She stages a call from a French cargo vessel ashore on Duncan Rock off the Cape, and takes over the *Antha* from Bullwinkle, who has left it anchored east of Pillow Rock to dash after the new, non-existent salvage. La-de-da, with some further wrangling, Annie nets $6,450 for Deep Sea Towing.

• Real-life Andy Ross's wife was Thea Ross — tip of the hat.

Duncan Rock, called Rock Duncan by Captain George Vancouver, is a mile northwest of Tatoosh Island in northwest Clallam County.[163]

35. Tugboat Annie Races the Tide

(18 September 1948) as *Tugboat Annie Returns* (Peter Huston, 1949, Australia, hardcover with dustwrap)

Severn hints it may be time for Annie to think about retirement. She in expected manner disagrees. Losing her grip? Never. Severn goes out of town in Palm Springs, leaving Annie in temporary charge, under strict orders not to provoke Bullwinkle.

The Australian publisher Peter Huston retitles the story "Tugboat Annie Races the Tide" as *Tugboat Annie Returns* for book publication in 1949.

The *Salamander* skipper snags a contract to tow Bull Mountain Logging logs through Swift Current Inlet on the Panther River, despite not knowing the challenges. He loses his first log boom and asks Annie for help, especially since she intruded in Bullwinkle's bargaining with the Bull Mountain rep and he put up his towboat as insurance against loss.

Annie takes up the task, figuring she can move the rest of the 10 million board feet in eight trips. After the first, the mountainside cascades into the river at Devil's Slide not far from Juan de Fuca Strait. With Sven Anderson of Bull Mountain Annie schemes a way to slow the movement of the log booms, thanks to an unusual lunar pull on tides, and saves the day. Feeling a bit of remorse, she persuades Alec to cut in half the amount charged Bullwinkle — letting him save face.

• University of Rochester Professor Virginia Moscrip recognized in the story a paragraph reminiscent of Tiresias speaking to Odysseus (Od. 11.121-132): "Not me, brother! I'm gonna finish up the business o' Bullwinkle an' that loggin' company; then I'll take me savin's, such as they is, an' stick a oar over me shoulder an' start walkin' inland, an' when somebody axes me what the oar is, there I'll settle!"[164]

Bull Mountain may have been inspired by Sitting Bull Mountain in the Cascade Mountains in Snohomish and Chelan Counties, named for the Sioux chief.

Our Annie

Milton Palmer Holman of Inglewood, Calif., in a letter to the *Post*[165] questioned what Ann [sic] and her boss, Alex Stevens [sic], did with their windfall profits from wartime towing. Through intermediary Raine, the *Post* editors asked Annie herself, somewhat censoring her reply:

"You would come round askin' silly questions just when I ain't feelin' so good wid my gumbago and all. … The bos's name ain't Alex Stevens; it's Alec Severn — though there's another name or two I've called the little fat widget in times of past …

"Now I'll let you in on a secret what's knowed on'y to the readers of The Sattidy Evenin' Post. They was a long-winded tarradiddle about me in that once, on July thirteen, 1946, I think 'twas — called Tugboat Annie and the Prodigal Calf, about me an' Bullwinkle, the big — Well, never mind! Anyways, it told there all about the trust fund what Severn, havin' no kiss nor kin of his own had set up wid the company's profits, to take care of the widders an' youngsters o' men of our tugboat fleet what lost their lives in the war. Seven of 'em, all told. …

"That's where the profits o' the company's goin' an where they'll continue to go, long after that fat, sentimental little boss o' mine's gone to j'ine his flounderin' fathers.

"Anythin; wrong wid that?"

(Mrs.) Tugboat Annie Brennan
Secoma, Wash.

36. Tugboat Annie Smells a Mouse
(18 December 1948)

Bullwinkle barges onto the *Narcissus* just as Pinto is serving the crew roast pork with cinnamon-dusted apples. He's desperate that Annie take on an apprentice: Doc MacQuarrie, who has been obnoxious in the brief time he's been with the *Salamander* crew. Bullwinkle had responded to a request of his father, the Rainier Barge Terminal owner, hoping he would funnel information about likely tow work.

Doc needs experience as he pursues his post-graduate studies in law. He shows up in the tugboat's mess, lean, bespectacled, baby-faced and arrogant. Annie agrees he can join the crew. After Bullwinkle leaves, Doc shares word, gleaned through his "pipe line," of a three-mast schooner, the *Rauma*, carrying soybean oil, damaged in heavy weather and requesting a tow through the Underwriters office. Doc wants a 10 percent commission.

Annie takes to the water. Catching up with the *Rauma* west of Cape Flattery, she quotes her standard $800-a-day fee. The schooner's master counters with $500. McQuarrie urges Annie to lower her bid. Annie balks. She carefully scans the *Rauma*, which is pumping water. Bullwinkle shows up and enters the bidding, leaving Annie's last $300 figure to stand. After securing a line to the ship, Doc admits he and Bullwinkle own the schooner, having purchased it the day before.

Annie has to stick to her towing quote. But Annie expects to charge $30,000 salvage, citing maritime law regarding willfully concealing damage voids a contract. She points out irregularities in the pump flow. McQuarrie, chastened to realize Annie's job could have been jeopardized by the ultra-low bid, says he will buy out Bullwinkle's share in the boat. Sympathetic Annie keeps Doc on until he has to return to school.

37. Tugboat Annie and the Pirates

(14 May 1949)

Annie refuels the *Narcissus* in Port Hoogah. She has a barge in tow. The village has just learned of a theft, the fourth, from salmon Trap 12. She listens to the fishermen voice concern at McNab's cannery office. A Coast Guard cutter has been redirected to an emergency, a Canadian destroyer is nearby but can't cross the international boundary. What's to be done?

The pirates kidnap two men who are running a fuel launch, keeping one as hostage and sending the second back for more fuel. When the pirates strike Trap 4 after dark, Annie and Hank, undercover nearby, attach an aviation yellow die container to the vessel. They track the ship to Chinook Inlet. Bullwinkle had a similar idea, having punctured an oil drum on the pirate boat. There's a problem reaching the pirate ship from one section of the inlet — Bullwinkle tried fruitlessly to yank out old dock posts blocking the way.

Annie sends him to the other access, then removes the poles (winding cord around and around and pulling until they spin out. She has a false radio message broadcast about a shipwreck; under international law, a boundary can be breached in an emergency. Thus the Canadian destroyer confronts the pirates

• Chinook is in Discovery Bay.[166]

38. Tugboat Annie's Secret

(13 August 1949) *Contraband: Stories of Smuggling the World Over*, Phyllis R. Fenner & Charles Geer, eds. (Morrow, 1967)

The steamer *Starlight Victory* has turbine trouble at Anacortes and needs a tow. Annie goes after it, leaving two barges at Port Townsend. Along the way she hopes to snag the steam tug *Louise F. Danforth*, which has gone ashore at Ghost Inlet. But the *Salamander*, fresh from installation of new war-surplus radar equipment at the Bremerton Navy Yard, races through the fog and beats her to the steamer.

Bullwinkle has a problem with the *Danforth's* bilge pump not working, however. Annie takes it over and jerry-rigs an old compound marine engine to the propeller shaft, thus the turning propeller as the boat is drawn through the water is sufficient to operate the pump.

• In Skagit County, Anacortes, first occupied by the Samish, took its name from Anne Curtis Bowman, an early white settler. It is home to a state ferry dock that serves several islands as well as Victoria, B.C.

The *Anacortes American* was quick to note Raine's joining the University of Washington faculty, observing in its 11 June 1931 issue, when his story "Salvage" appeared in *The Saturday Evening Post,* he "was a visitor in Anacortes about two months ago."

As we will learn later, there's speculation Annie was born in Anacortes.

39. Tugboat Annie Opens Fire
(11 February 1950)

Again in Alaskan waters, Annie has a rush job picking up a war-surplus derrick barge at Wolf Creek village. She beats Bullwinkle to the tow, then docks overnight at the edge of mud flats. She'll be able to take the *Narcissus* further at high tide.

Meanwhile, she escorts the crew to a tavern, leaving Shiftless on watch. During the night, Bullwinkle, claiming the barge was abandoned, attaches a hawser and pulls it over the sand bar and heads for Secoma. Soon he sends an alert — he's caught at Chinook Cove during a sou'wester. The sea is broiling.

Annie stops at the cove, in sight of a Navy oil tank. She has Hank set up the Lyle gun — used to fire life lines — and directs Big Sam to heat some projectiles and shape their heads into points. Hank, who had mortar experience during the war, on his second shot punctures the tank, spilling oil which quickly spreads, calming the waves sufficiently for Bullwinkle to chug out of trouble. (The EPA wouldn't approve!)

Annie claims the *Salamander* and barge as salvage, but after the usual palaver, settles for the barge and a large fee.

40. Tugboat Annie Loses Her Ship
(25 March 1950)

The *Helix*, a 1,000-ton steam barge built for the Prudhomme[167] Company in 1902, breaks down. Being used for fuel storage for mills and canneries at Gray's Harbor, it's been purchase by Neils and Sunder Oleson of Neah Bay. The *Salamander*, towing it near Destruction Island, runs low on fuel and, when Tugboat Annie is slow to show up to help, cuts the *Helix* loose. Bullwinkle asks Annie to take over the tow so he can go arrange a four-month gig in Guam.

When the *Narcissus* shows up, however, the *Salamander* is again wired to the *Helix*. Jake tells Annie the anchor can't be raised as the steam pump isn't working. Annie sends for the *Pansy*, the last steam tug in the Deep-Sea fleet — the other vessels having been converted to diesel. As Annie takes over the tow, Jake tells her the barge's plates were skewed after it hung up on rocks. Annie has Tom, her assistant engineer, check the plates. They turn out to be worse than thought. She takes the barge to LaPush. Bullwinkle shows up; there's the usual confab. Bullwinkle agrees to return the barge to the Olesons; his ruse has thoroughly annoyed the community at Neah Bay.

During a late-night party on the barge, courtesy Bullwinkle, Jake reports the *Narcissus* has cut loose and drifted away. Bullwinkle retrieves it, then claims salvage. He heads for Neah Bay with the barge. Annie informs him there's no dockage available; every spot has been taken by gravel barges, oil tows, launches and rowboats. The people are angry. (Annie had alerted them to what's going on.) The Coast Guard is busy at Freshwater Bay, where the *Iris* has conveniently run onto a sand bar. The barge won't stay afloat long enough to reach Clallam Bay. An approaching sou'wester discourages Bullwinkle from going to Port San Juan on the Canadian side. If he sinks the barge, he'll be charged with barratry. Bullwinkle gives in and returns the barge, no charge, to the Olesons.

• The author's second wife would be Elizabeth "Betty" Prud-homme.

Juan de Fuca Strait between Washington and British Columbia — the international border runs down the center — was named by maritime fur trader Charles William Barkley for the Greek navigator. At the west end are the Salish Sea and Pacific Ocean.

Destruction Island is offshore of Jefferson County, near the mouth of the Hoh River.[168] Freshwater Bay is on the Juan de Fuca Strait between Angeles Point and Observatory Point.[169] Clallam Bay is on the Juan de Fuca Strait, in Clallam County.[170] Gray's Harbor may be Grays Marsh, near Dungeness.

41. The Wrath of Tugboat Annie
(12 August 1950)

Unhappy with the food served on the ocean liner she traveled on into Secoma — "It was so fancy pants I didn't know whether to eat it or rub it on me skin" — Annie can't wait to eat in the *Narcissus* messroom again — "I'll take a plate o' Pinto's slum anytime." On the way she stops at the Greasy Spoon for steak and fried onions, where Bullwinkle introduces her to Dandridge Merrypenny, who shows unbounding admiration for Annie. He's about to contract with Bullwinkle to run construction equipment to Juneau.

Falling for Merrypenny's attentions, Annie offers a bid 10 percent below whatever figure Bullwinkle offered, and hastily signs a contract. Later she learns no other tugboater would go anywhere near the contract, and when she reads it, she sees its onerous conditions as to timelines and penalties. Among other things, she has to get a drydock and landing barge from Portland within a certain time.

When Bullwinkle and Merrypenny visit her onboard, she learns she's been taken advantage of. Bullwinkle gets half of whatever he saves Merrypenny on the towing contract and she throws them into the bay, watching one crawl over the other to get out. That gives her an idea. She telegrams the two to come to Portland for "some good news." There she demonstrates sinking a drydock, sliding a dredge inside, then raising the whole to the surface and floating it. She'll take the drydock to Vancouver and reverse the maneuver, and collect on the contract, plus bonus.

• Annie says Deep-Sea at this time has 13 tugboats plus various scows and barges in its fleet.

Tugboat Annie, Colin Glencannon Join Forces as Authors Collaborate Here

To the followers of the adventures of Tugboat Annie, meeting Norman Reilly Raine, author of the stories, would be a surprising experience. Though he has served for four years as a seaman on a Canadian tramp steamer, short, dapper Raine has little in common with the rough, rugged and lovable lady sailor he created and made famous in Saturday Evening Post stories.

Raine, who sports a small mustache and speaks in a low, nervously rapid voice, has been in Santa Barbara for three weeks collaborating with Guy Gilpatrick, 1806 El Encanto Rd., on a new story. Hero of the story will be Gilpatrick's scotch-and-shilling-loving character, Colin Glencannon, while Annie will have more than a thing or two to growl.

"Oh, I love it," Raine said of Santa Barbara. "It's a friendly sort of a place. I've had three shops tell me I could get what I was looking for at a rival store. I live in Hollywood, you know—I do a lot of work with pictures—and this is one of my favorite weekend spots."

Academy Award

"A lot to do with pictures" is Raine's modest way of mentioning a screen writing career which

ries so much that it works out pretty well," Raine said. "Gilpatrick wrote a bit of Annie dialogue, and it was excellent—he's

HIGH SEAS adventures are the stock in trade of Norman Reilly Raine (left) and Guy Gilpatrick. Raine is the author of the Tugboat Annie stories which appear in the Saturday Evening Post, while Gilpatrick writes the adventures of Mr. Glencannon which appear frequently in that magazine. The two are conferring in front of Gilpatrick's 1806 El Encanto Rd. home on a story combining their favorite characters.

—News-Press photo.

Library to Offer Varied Program

A program of three interesting

By popular demand, Raine and fellow *Post* series writer Guy Gilpatrick collaborate on a novel featuring their two nautical characters. (*Santa Barbara News Press*, 12 February 1950)

42. The Glencannon-Tugboat Annie Affair with Guy Gilpatric (27 August, & 2, 9, 16, 23, 30 September 1950); as *Glencannon Meets Tugboat Annie* (Harper, 1950) (Glencannon Press/Maritime Books, 2002) serialized as "The Glencannon-Tugboat Annie Affair," *Sunday Sun Supplement* (October-November 1950, Australia) and *Sunday Mail* (March 1951, Australia)

The book pairs two veteran maritime writers and their respective popular characters. A thumbnail of the plot — besides Colin Glencannon wishing he could find some Duggan's Dew (to tipple in Seattle") and Annie Brennan wishing she could further one-up Bullwinkle and McArdle — is summarized on the book's dustjacket as the necessity "to purloin the *Inchcliffe Castle*. The theft of an entire freighter is no small operation, and in this case it involved a large cast of wholesome and unwholesome characters, the Coast Guard, an improbable salvage crew, a masked wrestler, and a deceptive Japanese mine guaranteed not to go off."

• *The Saturday Evening Post* introduced the co-written effort with a sad note: "Two of the most fascinating characters who have sparkled their way through Post fiction in modern times are Norman Reilly Raine's Tugboat Annie and Guy Gilpatric's Colin Glencannon. For years there has been a persisting reader demand to bring together — not in matrimony, just bring together for better or, more likely, for worse — the lusty female tugboat skipper and the freighter engineer with the high talent for quaffing Duggan's Dew of Kirkintilloch.

"For the first time, beginning on Page 17, and unfolding effervescently through our next five issues, the incomparable experiences of Annie and Glencannon are hilariously interwoven. This rare event is also happening for the last time. There will never be another Glencannon story. Guy Gilpatric and his devoted wife Louise died tragically on July sixth in their home in Santa Barbara, California.

"It is not easy to reconcile this tragedy with the chuckling pleasure that Gilpatric wanted everyone to derive from his pleasant collaboration with Raine. Perhaps it will give freedom to the readers; enjoyment to have in mind that Gilpatric wanted, possibly more than he did with any of his other novels or stories, to have his friends enjoy this climatic imbroglio of his beloved Muster Glencannon. Editor Erd Brandt, who labored so intimately and stimulatively with the authors to help inspire their deft blending of humor, joins with us in the sure belief that Gilpatric would want all of us to have a grand good time with this story, to laugh as freely as we will."[171]

Guy Gilpatric, Collaborator

John Guy Gilpatric (1896-1950) launched his series character Colin Glencannon with "Scotch and Water" in *Red Book's* February 1929 issue. He joined the *Saturday Evening Post* stable with "The Missing Link" in the 5 July 1930 issue and went on to sell 64 more Glencannon stories to the *Post*.

Gilpatric was born in New York, the son of a Scottish immigrant. After an initial career as a stunt pilot and flight instructor (training Canadian military pilots) he became a U.S. Army Air Service flyer during World War I. He began his writing career while living in Antibes, eventually relocating to Santa Barbara, Calif., with his wife, Maude Louise Pauline Lesser, in 1942. His early fiction writing was in the aviation genre.[172]

Thirty-nine episodes of a *Glencannon* television series were produced at Associated British Elstree Studios in Great Britain, starring Thomas Mitchell as Glencannon, Patrick Allen as Bos'n Hughes and Charles Carson as Captain Ball. The shows aired in 1957-1958 and were syndicated in the United States in 1959.[173] When Louise was diagnosed with breast cancer, they determined to die together.

(They had made a similar pact during the second World War, when living in France but fearing German occupancy.[174])

•

Raine's Mr. Gallup was not unlike Glencannon, so there was a natural fit for the two writers. How did they work together? Gilpatric wrote Colin's scenes. Raine, taking an apartment in Santa Barbara, did Annie's. Pages were traded, each writer able to polish his character as it appeared in the other's prose. Louise Gilpatric read the chapters out loud for further mild smoothing, then retyped them. Then they would work on the next sequence.

Raine commented: "Never have I known two people so closely attuned as Guy and Louise. Evening after evening, as we worked together in their big living room, Louise would sit nearby, reading or knitting, occasionally sparking our discussions with a word, a suggestion, a smile; and unfailingly Guy's eyes would light as he smiled his thanks in return. From the first it was impossible to imagine one without the other. It still is."

•

Post reader Pieter C. Hooft of Willemstad, Curaçao, N.W.I., was thrilled with the novel, writing: "I have in mind to wait until I have all six parts ... but I doubt whether I've the will power. Oh well, I'll just have a peek at the first ... Yes, just finished it. There goes the good intention."[175]

Roy Kervin, in a review in the *Montreal Gazette*, commented: "Mister Colin Glencannon, Chief Engineer of S.S. Inchliffe Castle, grew to manhood in Kirkintilloch, a suburb of Glasgow famed for its distillation of Duggan's Dew, a potent Scottish gargle. The salubrious fumes of the distillery gave him the bushiest moustache, the reddest nose and the greatest thirst in the British Merchant Marine;

the gutters and grog-shops of Glasgow contributed a mind both devious and original and a vocabulary lusty and loud...

"Meanwhile, in the less exotic area around Puget Sound, on the American Pacific Coast, another legend was being created by Mrs. Annie Brennan, relict of the late Terry Brennan, master of the deep-sea tug Narcissus ... Annie's seagoing adventures kept as many issues of the S.E.P. afloat as Colin's did. It seemed fated that the two should meet. The seven seas and the five oceans weren't big enough for Annie and Colin to live in without collision...

"In order to have the two meet at all, the tale had to be set in Annie's home waters. So Annie takes over direction of things from the beginning and overshadows Glencannon almost entirely until the end. Only in a couple of scenes is Gilpatric's rollicking farce allowed to run at full gallop. Most of the story follows the slower, heavy-footed Annie Brennan pace, with the accent on tricks of seamanship, rather than quirks of character.

"I am, it is obvious, a Glencannon fan. As such, I found this collaborative effort disappointing. Tugboat Annie enthusiasts may be happier with it."[176]

Al Chase in a review in the *Chicago Daily Tribune*, though, thought the "uproarious adventures" would "keep the devotees of Colin and the irrepressible Annie sailing in a full gale of laughter."[177]

Edmonton Reader, reviewer for the *Edmonton Journal*, observed: "Connoisseurs will probably not consider this the best chapter in the Glencannon and Tugboat sagas; both Mr. Gilpatric and Mr. Raine have reached greater heights of ingenuity in some of their short stories. Nevertheless, the book provides a good evening of excitement and rowdy fun."[178]

And a reviewer in *All Hands* opined: "Some there may be who'll find it heavy going, traveling Glencannon's Scottish brogue with the voluble Annie setting up a cross-chop of waterfront Irish. But if it's characterization you want, it's here, mixed with slow-going humor."[179]

Another reviewer, George Serviss, liked it: "Two of the whackiest scamps of the waterfront, Colin Glencannon and Tugboat Annie, collaborate in what is without doubt the greatest conglomeration of confusion afloat that ever swept the Puget Sound with gales of laughter."[180]

When the *Post* serialized the story, reader Lillian M. Smith of New York pointed out a boner missed by Raine and the Gilpatrics: Bullwinkle at one point was misidentified as master of the *Narcissus*, not the *Salamander*.[181]

43. Tugboat Annie and the Red Threat

(14 April 1951) (Sydney, Australia, *Sun Supplement*, 2, 9 & 16 March 1952)

Witnessing an American aircraft carrier and two Canadian destroyers west of Juan de Fuca Strait, heading into the Pacific for Korea, Annie rues her modest towing assignment, taking a couple of dumb barges to Bellingham. She passes Mooers Island, a World War II army base now being reactivated with new airstrips.

At a sawmill office, she spots a news item in a Canadian newspaper and hatches an idea. Without consulting Severn, she sends the *Narcissus* home with Peter and takes a bus to Vancouver, B.C.

Returning to Deep-Sea's office in Secoma, she explains to her boss that old rival McArdle has cornered the market on cement. But, a shipment of Japanese cement is due to arrive in Vancouver, and she bought it. Her plan is for Severn with "Nickel-or-Million" Connor to form a new construction company, Connor and Severn, and submit a runway bid in competition with McArdle.

Bullwinkle, who has a new pet ferret named Felix, remains connected with McArdle and after initially balking at what may be sabotage, agrees to help the conniving businessman destroy the Connor and Severn cement shipment. Just business rivalry, McArdle says.

The small leased freighter *George B. Hanson*, under Captain Ostrander, is carrying the cement to Mooers Island. On the second trip, a bogus quartermaster at the wheel disregards pilot Annie's command and steers the ship onto rocks. He then leaps overboard. Annie musters what barges she can and continues to take cement to the job site.

McArdle orders Bullwinkle to sabotage the barges, but Bullwinkle's plan goes awry when the *Salamander* breaks its screw on rocks. Annie drops the barge tow to help Bullwinkle save the *Salamander*. Then she figures a way to raise two half-sunken barges using portable irrigation windmills and a highway tow truck on loan from a garage.

When construction is nearly done, saboteurs dig up a telephone conduit that runs beneath Runway One, destroying it and necessitating reconstruction of 2,000 feet of pavement — which can't be accomplished within the contracted timeline — and the work will go to McArdle.

Bullwinkle, feeling a patriotic pang and sorry about the Annie rescue, comes through, offering Felix to run strings through the pipes. Like shooting a line, then a wire, then a hawser to tows, four ferret trips later, the wires are replaced.

Annie and Bullwinkle celebrate and get sloshed, but stop short of becoming bosom buddies.

Annie Explains

Two writers of letters to the *Post* editor took exception to Raine's saying two Canadian destroyers traveled at 45 knots. One reader said they had top speed of 35 knots, the other said 38.5.[182]

As noted earlier, Raine in 1927 wrote *War Stories* to correct a factual error he spotted in a pulpster's tale of World War I air warfare. That writer, Ralph Oppenheim, fessed up.

Raine, though, consulted the master of the *Narcissus*. She fronted for her biographer in a reply to two Royal Canadian Navy lieutenants, J.A. Davidson and John B. Boase: "Them Canadians is so far out in front wid so many things, as well as bein' swelligant shipmates, that I don't blame ye for not wantin' to be caught wid yer patent log down through underratin' them. An' asides, how was they to know what a congenial liar ye allus are?"[183]

The month previous, the *Post* related the retirement of the Foss tug *Sabine*, veteran of the Dressler/Beery motion picture, after being heavily damaged in a storm. "The report that she almost sank is credible as Annie wasn't aboard to bring her through."[184]

44. Tugboat Annie Tries a Bluff
(16 June 1951)

The *Narcissus* is towing a barge loaded with supplies to a U.S. Army garrison in Alaska near Glacier City. It's raining hard. She gets a call that a Red Funnel Line steamer, the *Buena Vista*, loaded high high-grade lumber, is beached at Porcupine Inlet on Quantako Peninsula, near a shut-down fishing cannery. The Port Muklatch gang of seal poachers, fish pirates and timber thieves hides out somewhere near there.

In town, Annie watches an Army training film with fellow towman "Dogface" Jackson and his friend Frenchy but finds it too loud for her taste.

She returns to her tug and learns Bullwinkle has snagged the tow. Severn is upset and cans her. She ignores him and gives pursuit. The *Salamander* is fired on by the pirates, two crewmen wounded. Bullwinkle returns the next night with a boatload of armed are men. Annie, meanwhile, treks by land along an old logging road and beats Bullwinkle to the grounded steamer. She and Frenchy play the training film as loudly as they can, touch off flares and otherwise create the experience of a military bombardment, frightening off the brigands. She claims the lumber steamer in the name of the owners.

"You're the captain's wife here, or the cook, perhaps?"—"Unh-uh, I'm
her skipper," replied Annie.

Annie abides a misogynistic businessman in "Tugboat Annie
Defies the Law," serialized in three parts in an Australian
newspaper. (*Sydney Sun*, 17 May 1953)

45. Tugboat Annie Defies the Law

(8 December 1951) (*Sun & Guardian Sunday Magazine*, 17, 24 & 31
May 1953, Australia)

Torpington Harris, representing Seaboard Towing of Boston, is
looking for a West Coast tie-up with either Severn or Bullwinkle.
Annie makes a rude botch of it at a meal at the Mount Rainier Hotel

with Severn, Harris and Bullwinkle, but Severn leaves her in charge as he goes to Vancouver, B.C., on business.

After she refuses to give Harris a rebate, he commends her integrity and says he will give the contract to Deep Sea and uses the company's office to finish some paperwork. He overhears Perry the night dispatcher send Annie to snag the oil barge *Sappho*, about to be cut adrift by the Portland tug *Acosta*, which ran into trouble in high winds near Cannery Cove. It will be a straight tow on behalf of the owners. When Annie arrives, Bullwinkle is already towing the barge, thanks to a tipoff from Harris.

But the *Salamander* had yet to replace a faulty bilge pump, and itself needs assistance. Annie takes over the barge and maneuvers it to protect the *Salamander* from strong waves as it limps to port. The oil station at Cannery Cove is anxious for the oil, but Bullwinkle, Harris and a federal marshal show up making claim. There is an agreed-upon lull. Bullwinkle paints draft marks on the barge so the oil can't be pumped off; he and Harris have already sold it to Murdoch McArdle. Annie talks with the barge owner, and offers an arrangement: the owner keeps the barge, Bullwinkle pays $5,000 to settle any claim for salvage of his tug and the contents of the barge.

Meanwhile, she gets a (fake) telegram from Severn saying she's fired. That's the clincher and Bullwinkle agrees to the settlement, only to learn later that Lars Larson, the Cannery Cove oil dock superintendent, and Annie have pumped out the oil and replaced it with water. Bullwinkle will be doubly burned when he fills McArdle's tanks with seawater.

• Portland, Multnomah County, Ore., in the shadow of Mount Hood, is at the confluence of the Willamette and Columbia Rivers. First occupied by Chinook and Multnomah and visited by the Lewis and Clark expedition in 1805, it took its present name from Portland, Maine, hometown of one of the white founders, Francis W. Pettygrove.

Cannery Point is on a southern shore of Hammersley inlet.[185]

The Seafair Cook Book, published in 1951, includes
Captain Brennan's instructions for Mutton Stew.

Mutton Stew

Tugboat Annie has a prodigious appetite and is appreciative of *Narcissus* hash-slinger Pinto's abilities in the galley. Witness her breakfast in "Captain Terry Comes Through": broiled ham, three eggs, a pile of wheat cakes drowned in melted butter and golden sirup, a stack of toast and a few mugs of coffee. She roundaboutly offered one of her favorite recipes for inclusion in *Seafair Cook Book; Favorite Recipes Gleaned From 100 Years of Cookery in the Pacific Northwest* in 1951.[186]

Here's the entry, under Outdoors Favorites:

By some mysterious means (probably waterfront scuttlebutt) Tugboat Annie Brennan heard that Norman Reilly Raine, that arch-prevaricator and chronicler of her misdeeds, had been invited to send a recipe to this *Seafair Cook Book*, in high dudgeon she laboriously dashed off the following:

Secoma, Wash

Deer Rain –

I heerd ye wuz goin to send a recete to that Seafare cook book, all I got to ay is you got youre nerv boy, what do ya no bout cookin or even eatin when the minute the Narcissus gits fifteen feet from the dock ye start givin like a overworked bilge pump. Well just don't try to fool them pore land folks an make them think ye git such to eat on board my tug, cuz here we go for real combustibles like this here stew and enyhow I don't want no one suing me fer rigor-mortises. Ye try this here sumtime.

Yores truly,
Tugboat Annie

MUTTON STEW
2 pounds neck, plate or shoulder of mutton
2 pounds spuds
6 onions
Salt and pepper
3 to 4 cups hot water
Cut meat in little pieces and put in stew pan, add salt and pepper and hot water. Put on lid and cook slow for an hour. Add the spuds and onions, peeled and cut up, cook another hour or so. Serve hot and it's better with dumplings.
Tugboat Annie

•

Courtesy Tugboat Annie's restaurant in Olympia, The Recipe Circus has posted online directions for making "Tugboat Annie's Almond-Crusted Halibut."

Cooks.com carries a recipe for "Tugboat Annie Bars."

And Rick Browne's *The Ultimate Guide to Grilling* (2011) includes how-to for "Tug Boat Annie's Sweet Potato Salad with Marjoram Honey Vinaigrette."

Her appetite is legendary.

46. Tugboat Annie Burns a Bridge

(24 May 1952) *Tugboat Annie: Great Stories …* (Curtis, 1977)

At Port Olympic delivering diesel oil to the small cannery and sawmill town, Annie feels off her feed and visits Doc Adams, who she knew when he was a boy. He finds her fit.

She's all ears when George Swimming Seal, a logger on the Koahkuddit River, tells her his boss needs delivery of 25 sections of logs before a storm strikes. Phone lines are out. By the time she passes an old logging railroad bridge with a hand-operated draw span, Bullwinkle is coming out with the tow. Scotsman McCann, the "bull of the woods" for the logging operation, has held him to a no cure, no pay contract plus half of any financial loss if the logs don't reach the mill before prices drop down.

Annie hastily instructs her crew to start a fire at the hinge-end of the lift bridge. When Bullwinkle shows up, his men can't get to mechanism to work. He finally turns over the contract and Annie has him release the tow. It floats under the locked bridge. Bullwinkle himself can't get out until Annie sends him a how-to: heat makes iron expand, cold allows it to shrink.

47. Tugboat Annie and the Sea of Flames

(15 November 1952)

At Jack-Pine Inlet, Annie watches a Lohrman Logging-hired helicopter flying over, making maps and training for fighting fires. At Port Whitley, a mill and canning village,, she meets Ole "One

Ear" Jensen, an old friend of the Brennans. He escorts her to a square dance at Scandia Hall to benefit the wife of a logger just killed by a "widow maker," a falling tree. Bullwinkle is at the dance. She teases him about buying a used hawser from his friend McArdle.

Bullwinkle plants a firecracker in Annie's bowl of Danish soup. It blows up and so does Annie, even more so Ole, who whops Bullwinkle, sending him off in an ambulance. Alec radios that the lumber ship *Lake Sappho* is on fire. The crew needs rescue. The ship is owned by McArdle and she's to work with Bullwinkle. She wrangles the role of boss on the retrieval, Bullwinkle to work for her. "Although inwardly acknowledging her rival to be a brave, skilled and resourceful towboatman, in danger or emergency Annie trusted no one but herself; and it was upon this hard-rock foundation that she had based her protest."

Annie's victory is short-lived. While she begins pumping water onto the flames, Bullwinkle successfully establishes a tow, and draws the ship away from dangerous shoals. Then the line breaks. The ship's crew members jump into small boats and flee. The ship beaches. McArdle and his marine lawyer appear in a water taxi. Full blame is fixed on Annie (and by contract, Deep-Sea) as she was the contractee. Bullwinkle — even though the loss of the towline was his fault — was not liable. Annie works out a deal. She'll admit liability if McArdle will turn the ship over to her.

Watching three buzzards take flight, and she has an inspiration. With "One-Ear's" assistance, the Lohrman "burlybird" drops CO_2 gas (dry ice) and puts out the blaze. The chopper then carries a shot line across and the ship becomes a quick tow to Secoma. The fire was confined to the engine room. Deep-Sea now owns the ship, free and clear.

• This story has some quotable quotes.

Bullwinkle calls Annie "cow-puss."

Annie calls Bullwinkle "a bat-eared, parrot-beaked, beetle-brained cross atween a blow-belly an' a faddom o'herrin' gut's...."

Annie's eloquence wins, hands down.

48. Tugboat Annie Loses a Tow
(21 February 1953)

"Alec Severn, pudgy, amiable little owner of the Deep-Sea Towing and Salvage Company of Secoma, stood for a few moments at his office window, staring abstractly at the rain-shrouded harbor and the misty reaches of Puget Sound, beyond," this adventure begins.

"Then, rubbing his bald, pink scalp, he turned back to his secretary, 'Where was I, Olive'"

Noah Svenson, once a successful maritime lawyer, after his wife died quit his career and opened Noah's Ark, a café on an old schooner. City engineers are blasting King's Bluff to make way for new docks at Jokisch Landing, and the construction is getting near Svenson's mooring.

Annie heeds a suggestion from deck hand Hank and offers to tow *Noah's Ark* to Wyant Island, where there will be a ready audience of hungry men because of construction work there. Svenson is in no hurry, until blasting does begin to rock his ship. He falls and is injured. The *Narcissus* begins the tow, but someone cuts the hawser and the *Ark* goes adrift in the dark. Bullwinkle picks it up, believing Svenson keeps a lot of cash in his safe. Bullwinkle learns Svenson is broke, and has a change of heart and takes the *Ark* to its new docking. Bullwinkle invites Annie to a bash at the Mount Rainier Hotel, with Svenson's family there. They didn't know his financial circumstance, and he has a moment to shine. Bullwinkle helps Svenson fix up the *Ark*, but has the hospital bill sent to Annie.

• Jeffersonville, Ind., was at one time home to a floating restaurant called Tugboat Annie's.

49. Tugboat Annie and the Amazon Star Mystery
(31 October 1953)

Alec Severn thinks of his head tugboat captain: "Rugged. Home-spun. Short of temper and raspy of tongue, but solid and dependable as a chunk of teakwood."

That was before he received a telegram: "Am in Mikmuk hoose-gow. Help. Annie Brennan." The place is a coastal resort town, the charge is burglary.

She was supposed to cinch a deal with Jack Shipley of Trident Lines while Severn was away in Palm Springs. Shipley said he was brining in the *Amazon Star* and would radio to arrange for a pilot through the Juan de Fuca Strait. Whoever got there first would get a contract. Bullwinkle of course wants the contract and shadows the *Narcissus* until Annie and Fred institute a new code for open communications. Bullwinkle can no longer get ahead of her.

But he has other means. He triangulates her call from Port Townsend and almost beats her — but the piloting has become a rescue, as a transport ship has rammed the *Amazon Star* and it has run aground on Galleon Shoal. A lifeboat with crew members is still missing and Annie goes to help.

Anticipating Bullwinkle's maneuvers, acting on a comment by Peter. Annie makes a quick stop at Mikmuk and she, two deck hands and the cook race into the village and return carrying certain items. A Canadian destroyer picks up the floaters.

By the time Annie reaches the lumber-hauling *Star,* Bullwinkle is ready to claim it. But Annie points out four shadowy figures on the deck — it hasn't been abandoned after all. She climbs to the deck and manages to get a line and secure the ship. The figures are clothing store dummies. The sheriff turns up. Yes, the dummies were "borrowed." The ship is a straight salvage job for Deep-Sea, the Trident contract assured. The only outlay: a $100 fine.

50. The Bashing of Bullwinkle
(9 January 1954) (June 2010)

Bullwinkle is laid up in Harbor Hospital with a broken leg. Annie visits. "Ye shouldn't ha' tried to trip me," she tell him. Bullwinkle figures he can still submit a bid for a Cascade Foundry job — hauling two steel barges to Bremerton Navy Yard. Annie and Sam drive along the river and see a narrow point, where there's a rotted old logging bridge and a "For Sale" sign.

At the shipyard, she observes how narrow the channel is. Returning to the office, she stops to see Bullwinkle again. He has a guest, Captain Paddy Gavin of Oakland, a huge man with plenty of experience who will pilot the *Salamander,* Bullwinkle says no cure no pay. They got the contract already. Annie tells Severn it's just as well, as the bid they were about to submit wouldn't have covered expenses. Instead, she will wait to step in when Gavin runs into trouble. And he does. Annie negotiates a takeover of the contract and $5,000 fee, still no cure no pay.

When Annie again surveys the Mennagonish River, she's surprised to see a floating pile driver anchored at the rotting bridge. It's Gavin's doing; he and Bullwinkle want to start a farm and have bought the property. As it's not an official navigable channel, there's nothing Annie can do. A comment from Severn gives Annie an idea, though. She hires house movers to take the barges to a different loading site, then dynamites new pilings so the two smaller Deep-Sea tugs and scows can get back to the Sound.

51. Tugboat Annie's Crazy Command
(6 February 1954)

At Port Zander, a sawmill and fish cannery village, Annie is on a tear. The roast beef is a disaster — it's too hard. Someone, it appears, put a plaster cast on it before it was cooked — that someone being Bullwinkle, getting even with Annie for one of her pranks.

An emergency job comes in. The steamer *C.C. Donslaugh* with a cargo of machinery has lost its generator power and been abandoned. The owner will pay Annie a per diem plus bonus to retrieve it. Bullwinkle is already there, with a dilemma as a fire on the ship makes it impossible to secure a line. The two captains consult and Annie has an idea — which Bullwinkle puts into action, burning a hole through the hull at water line and securing it that way.

When the *Salamander* approaches Port Zander's mud flats, where Bullwinkle intends to park the hulk, he encounters an individual riding on a log directly in the middle of the channel — Annie says she's fishing. She will hold up Bullwinkle into high tide, until they come to an agreement to her advantage.

52. Tugboat Annie Gets the Ax
(12 June 1954)

This story begins: "Alec Severn, the rotund little owner of the Deep-Sea Towing and Salvage Company of Secoma, brought his gaze down from thoughtful contemplation of his office ceiling, wiped his glasses vigorously and looked across at his secretary. 'And — er — furthermore – uh-uh —'Where was I, Miss Walker?'

"She read from her notes: 'And I hereby delegate to said employee, Mrs. Annie Brennan, the same power and authority to make disbursements and decisions affecting this company's business as if I had —' "

Ernie Judd of Judd Marine Salvage in Long Beach, Calif., and Captain Chuck Sloan, chief surveyor for Ajax Marine, ask for emergency help in removing the sunken *Starfish*, a cargo (bananas) carrier that sank at Tres Santos, 550 miles south, before a large reefer ship is due to arrive. Bullwinkle has already rented all necessary equipment for his own work. He tosses a ping-pong ball into Annie's libation at the barroom in rebuff. But this gives Annie an idea. She's temporarily in charge of Deep-Sea Towing in Alec Severn's absence.

She ignores a directive to make no large expenditures — and orders three million ping-pong balls. Alec threatens to fire Annie over the large purchase, but she impresses him and her clients when the boat is raised and removed in time to avoid damaging the reefer ship. She pumped the ping-pong balls into the hold to create buoyancy.

• Five years earlier, Dell comic book artist/writer Carl Barks used the ping-pong trick for Donald Duck and nephews to retrieve Uncle Scrooge's boat in "The Sunken Yacht" in *Walt Disney's Comics & Stories* for May 1949. They injected balls through a tube into the craft's flooded cargo area.

Would you be surprised if Tugboat Annie read comic books?

Raine repeated themes on occasion — clever and untried ideas, knowledge of seamanship and maritime laws, understanding of terrain, comeuppance, proving her capabilities, besting Bullwinkle, etc. He also recycled openings. Compare how this tale begins with that of "Tugboat Annie Races the Tide" from 1948.

53. Tugboat Annie's Long Shot

(30 October 1954)

Transporting oil barges from Port Townsend to Port Hoskins, Annie is greeted at the dock as "cook" by a dandy named Widdiken S. Triptoe, who turns out to be vice president of White Water Logging. He intends to observe Annie in action before deciding on a lucrative new towing contract with Deep-Sea. She's sent to Siwash Cove Mill to pick up a 20-section log raft but Bullwinkle has overheard Severn's impatient radio message and beaten her to it. The *Salamander* has gone through Suicide Narrows, and Annie follows.

Bullwinkle offers to share the tow with Annie, so he can go off on a more important job. Annie guesses what Bullwinkle is up to, flares up briefly with Triptoe, and takes Bullwinkle in tow when he admits he has run out of fuel. With no time to spare, they race through the increasingly angry waters. Annie tells Bullwinkle his boat was knowingly unseaworthy, but she will let him get away with it for $2,000 in lieu of a salvage claim. Triptoe, impressed, gives Deep-Sea the job. He admits to Annie that he, too, is hooked on trite joke books and they go enjoy a beer in Secoma.

• Siwash Creek is in northeastern Okanogan County. Siwash Slough is in northwest Skagit County.

54. Tugboat Annie Tames a Tempest
(6 April 1955)

Suffering a toothache, Annie is in no mood to take on, at Severn's request, monitoring Freddy Dunphy, a recently mustered-out infantry officer. This is a favor to John Dumphry, his father, owner of Inter-Ocean Steamships, who is planning a West Coast expansion and waves a major contract. Of large stature, Dunphy is at odds, a growing alcoholic leaning toward brawling. Of course he and Bullwinkle hit it off and he leaves with the *Salamander* taking a schooner load of pipe to a construction site on Wedell Island. Annie has snuck Freddy a bottle, a mix of alcohol and cold medicine, that knocks him for a loop.

Meanwhile, Bullwinkle's tug encounters very rough waters. Suspecting he'd have problems, Annie is nearby and tells Bullwinkle how to retrieve his broken towline. She makes a quick return to the Army dock to acquire an over-sized section of pipe, then picks up the *Salamander* after the line has broken a second time. She spots Freddy on the scow, where he'd fallen asleep after drinking Annie's concoction. She and the crew rescue him, then pick up the towline and, with their pipe dead weight, bring it safely to port. Straight salvage.

Freddy expresses remorse, swears off liquor and praises Annie and her crew for their skill and bravery. They remind him of the heroes on Heartbreak Ridge in Korea, he says. She scolds him aplenty but is pleased to be assured a new towing contract.

55. Tugboat Annie Loses a Race
(24 September 1955)

With heavy storm warnings, coasters, cannery tenders and purse seiners head to the protection of Port Glacier. The *Narcissus* has just delivered a derrick barge to an Army base at Cordova when its propeller wraps a seiner net. Hank, a Navy "toadman," as Annie calls him, frees the prop.

An emergency call comes in from underwriters for a vessel ashore off Skag Island. It's the *Fort Yukon*, a 1,000-ton freighter. Bullwinkle catches the same radio message, his eyes on salvage. To make her way through a narrow channel in dense fog, Annie has Shiftless toss scrap nuts and bolts into the water, to detect hazards.

Once past an old Native American burial ground, she spots a flame — a distress signal. Annie picks up Captain Sorensen and crewmen. Bullwinkle has already tied onto the ship. Sorensen demands he leave the vessel until examiners have assessed damages. But it makes sense to Annie that Bullwinkle tow it to a safer inlet nearby. The ship is heavily damaged, however, and sinks. Bullwinkle is in a spot. Under maritime law, a master leaving his ship to find help has technically not abandoned it. But she has something in mind, and for $1,000 she'll tell her rival. Sorensen had tried to drag a large tarp under the hull to stem the break, but it didn't work. Crewmen tell Annie they were well fed before leaving the ship.

Putting the pieces together, Annie asserts Sorenson, given a timeline, purposely ran the ship aground. He had blown a hole in the bilge. He wanted to collect insurance. After a Coast Guard hearing, Deep-Sea earns 20 percent of the insurance payoff. Annie volunteers to give Bullwinkle back his check. But Bullwinkle says no worry, it was written in invisible ink.

• Glacier Bay port and Glacier Bay National Park & Preserve are on the Alaska coast as is Skag Island, one time a winter camp for a Norse Greenlander named Thorvald.

56. The Treasure of Tugboat Annie

(5 May 1956) (last illustrated by Von Schmidt)

A man named Steed from Kansas City is looking for Bullwinkle, who is supposed to locate certain salvage items for him. Consulting Captain Henry Foss, an old friend at Navy HQ, Annie figures out from an inventory of junked military surplus that he's after anchors. She visits Sven Larsen's scrapyard on Ghost Island, and buys some 700 old anchors from him for $1 each. Bullwinkle chaffs and sputters and pays her $3,700 for them, only to brag Steed is willing to pay $10 each for them, and they go for $20 each on the current market.

But Steed has gone home, having given Annie $1,000 for good information — these are not fish-hook-style anchors, but sea anchors, 50-foot hoops wrapped around a canvas-covered core. The metal is nearly all rotted away. They're worthless. But now they are Bullwinkle's.

• Real-life Henry Foss was speaker at featured speaker at the *Tugboat Annie Sails Again* premier at the Roxy Theater in Tacoma in 1940. He served as Port of Tacoma commissioner from 1951-1952.

The *Saturday Evening* Post collects Secoma
yarns in a hardcover book in 1977.

57. Tugboat Annie Loses Command

(13 October 1956) (first illustrated by James R. Bingham) *Tugboat Annie: Great Stories ...* (Curtis, 1977)

Captain Price of the Navy Procurement Office has called a meeting of Severn, Annie and Bullwinkle — the latter two on 90-days probation if they fight again — to talk about moving heavy equipment to Alaska. Severn posts $15,000 bonds for each of them and assigns Captain "Truthful" Tomkins of the *Daisy* (which is in drydock) to travel with the *Narcissus*, towing a barge to Port Ragluff, in case he is needed to take over as master. Annie is of course miffed, and itching to razz Bullwinkle as usual. It's a stormy ride.

On a layover to wait out the bad weather, Annie visits Olaf Torgeson on the *Cascade*, an ancient steam tug now without its boiler. The gale batters the coastal cargo ship *Chilcoot* of Nome (Captain Bardett). Annie can't take the salvage job, as she is committed to her towing chore.

But with some quick thinking, she lets word leak to Bullwinkle, who predictably completes his companion tow then races back for the *Chilcoot*. But Annie, who turned over her *Narcissus* command to Tomkins, already has secured that ship, having used Torgeson's *Cascade*, equipping it with an unwanted logging train locomotive power plant.

Darned Shame

The month "Loses Command" appeared in *The Saturday Evening Post*, Annie wrote to the media reporter for the *Province* newspaper in Vancouver, B.C., Les Wedman, to talk about the television show then filming: "It's a darned shame you ain't more handy to Toronto, Else we could uv sent you an invite to come visit with us. You're missin something because Pinto, he's my cook, makes a special Tugboat Annie caseroll with lobster sauce and I'll bet you never tasted nothin like its so good.

"But there you are in Vancouver, stuck far away from it all. So Shif'less, he's my deck hand, he woke up enough a couple days ago to say Annie why don't you and Bullwinkle fone that Mr. Wedman who rites that kolum in the Vancouver Province.

"So what this is all about is would you let our publicity people have a couple of times you'll be in your offis soon. And that old goat Bullwinkle or me will give you a ring and chew the fat."[187]

58. The Firing of Tugboat Annie
(1 December 1956)

Severn hopes for a lucrative contract with Angus Campbell, commissary contractor for defense bases and hydroelectric projects in the Aleutian Islands. Campbell is impatiently waiting, in Port Ugachak, for a barge loaded with ice-cooled fruits and vegetables. Severn takes him to meet Annie, who tumbles out of the Pribiloff Café, mid-brawl with Bullwinkle. Campbell tromps off. Severn says Annie's done when she returns from delivering construction material to Amatka Island.

On the water, Clem hears an emergency call. Red Halloran's *Firefly* is in trouble. It's hauling the fruit barge. Clem also says Bullwinkle's radio is on the fritz. So she fakes a breakdown and transfers her tow to Bullwinkle, then takes off for the *Firefly*. She finds the crew on shore, whooping it up. The *Firefly* has beached. She gathers the men and then locates the fruit barge. But Bullwinkle had fixed his radio, secured Annie's tow and hooked onto the salvage.

Annie informs him he ignored an SOS signal and is subject to a heavy fine. He concedes and hands over the fruit barge. Suspicious, Annie checks the barge; the cooling equipment has conked out. Halloran tells her not to worry, and gives her a plan. Thirty hours later, she delivers the fruit barge. Severn can claim salvage, but he asks for a contract instead. Annie reveals the barge had a carbon-di-oxide fire-suppression system, which she and Halloran redirected to harmlessly cool the veggies.

• This is the fifth time Severn has (or strongly threatened to) let Annie go. Previous times were in "Tugboat Annie," "Tugboat Annie Crashes Through," "Tugboat Annie Tries a Bluff" and "Tugboat Annie Gets the Ax."

59. Tugboat Annie's Reunion at Sea
(12 January 1957)

Annie, in yellow oilskin, pilots the British tramp steamer *Inchcliffe Castle*, Colin Glencannon's old ship, into Secoma. A stowaway jumps overboard. When she eventually retrieves him, he's Robert Rankin, who says he's looking for a cannery or logging camp job. Annie takes him on for the task of towing the *Gen. B.G. Appleby*, an old attack transport now condemned, to Unalaska to become a caisson at a new Army base harbor. Rankin meets Bullwinkle at the Greasy Spoon, but gets into a fight. The crew is unhappy. Rankin has a chip on his shoulder. The tug has a rugged time of getting the *Appleby* through a gale.

When the towline snaps, Rankin hastily volunteers to swim a new line across. But he doesn't tie it on. He stands at vigil as the ship sinks, only its funnel showing. Rankin, it turns out, had Post Stress Disorder Syndrome before it was called that. Considered a deserter, he had served on the *Appleby* and missed getting back in time when it left Pearl Harbor. Many of his shipmates were lost during the fighting. Masters and crews of the *Narcissus* and *Salamander* subscribe for a simple granite monument for Rankin.

• The story is a nod to fellow writer Guy Gilpatric.[188]

60. Tugboat Annie and the Hoard of Heroin
(30 March 1957)

In stormy weather, Annie is headed for a log boom at Sail River when she is re-directed to a steamer, the *Sonora Star*, which is having engine trouble. It had departed Mazatlán south of the Columbia River. Alert to the situation, she waits out the tempest at Clallam Bay. Bullwinkle is there too.

Bullwinkle gets Pinto drunk, weasels out Annie's plans and takes off for the *Sonora Star*, as the master will sign on with the first tugboat to arrive, for a $900-a-day tow. Bullwinkle persuades Annie to take the *Star's* fireman, who has a broken leg, to the Marine Hospital at Port Angeles. Customs agents meet the *Narcissus* and ask a lot of questions.

When Bullwinkle pulls in, Customs agents search his tugboat and find a waterproof package holding a kilo of pure heroin, when cut worth $150,000. Bullwinkle is under heavy suspicion despite Annie's testimonial to his (general) honesty. A Customs agent drops a torn section of newspaper, which Annie scoops up, wondering if it's a clue. She hatches a plan, wrestles a fee from Bullwinkle then recruits her rival and selected of their respective crewmen to cruise through Port Angeles.

At the Chinook Bar & Grill they find the *Star* crew, and through a ruse cooked up by Annie and Bullwinkle, get the *Star's* bosun, Hawkins, to provide evidence he's the smuggler.

61. Tugboat Annie and the Dangerous Cheapskate
(24 August 1957) as Tugboat Annie and the Cheapskate (May 1981) (May/June 2001) *Chicken Soup for the Gardener's Soul* (Health Communications, 2000) Government contacts have dried up and the fleet needs overhaul. Alec brings in a financial expert named Bolzer then heads to New York City for the Sea Freight Carriers Convention. Bolzer to cut costs takes existing gear out of service

and replaces it with substitute equipment, including a hawser that Annie deems rotten. She goes on a salvage tow of the steamer *Chesil Bank*, which is sitting at Seal Reef near Nanaimo, B.C. The ship has been filled with timber by a new owner. Bolzer, who has charge, replaces Annie with Captain Peewee Jorgensen and sends him off with the *Narcissus*.

Annie commiserates with Bullwinkle then hires him to follow the *Narcissus* while she goes into town to do some research. The *Salamander* shadows the *Narcissus*, during a strong sou'wester, and is ready when the hawser snaps. Using all their skills, Bullwinkle and Annie attach a new line to the steamer and take it to Secoma. An angry Severn and Bolzer meet them at the dock.

Finally given a chance to explain, Annie says Bolzer as an employee (something she'd insisted on) is liable if he knowingly places faulty equipment on a ship. Too, Bolzer struck out a disclaimer-of-damage-liability clause in the contract and gave the new owner of the steamer a 20 percent discount. To top it off, Bolzer through a dummy company owns the steamer and had been unable to secure his own insurance because underwriters were suspicious.

Thus, Annie says, the ship and cargo are worth $300,000. She pays Bullwinkle $25,000 and gives crew members a bonus. The rest goes to Severn, as she had taken on Bullwinkle's hire in the name of Deep-Sea Towing. The money can go toward re-equipping the fleet. Severn doesn't know what to say.

• Annie was on her way to television screens, as the *Post* noted in Keeping Posted.[189]

When the magazine reprinted the story in 1981, reader Nellie King of Oradell, N.J., wrote: "It was wonderful to read one of those great yarns after so many years. In fact, I read it twice. Won't you print some more of them in future issues — please?"[190]

62. Tugboat Annie's Secret Stratagem
(25 October 1958)

The *Narcissus* is directed to the Tidewater Bay logging terminus to pick up a 60-section boom for McArdle. Annie is suspicious, and calls in the *Daffodil* to handle the logs while she investigates the *Salamander*, which has gone beyond Cape Flattery to pick up a cargo steamer that's blown off course south of Port Delta. The crew sent out an SOS and abandoned ship. It's the *George Havard* of the Trident Line — for which McArdle is Secoma agent. Bullwinkle has already claimed the ship, but is waiting out a storm at the docks near an old cannery.

Bullwinkle has set up a set of brilliant lights so he spot Annie, should she try to poach the ship. Annie refuels and backs out to watch. Shiftless discovers a stowaway, a hep cat named Benny Wilson, who is on leave from the nearby Air Force base. Annie knew his father, a decorated pilot. She learns from Wilson, a radar and electronics specialist, is skilled at using a bow and arrow. She sends Wilson to the military base to secure some tinfoil; he ties one end of the foil to an arrow and shoots it over the power lines, causing a short, darkening Bullwinkle's lamps and all of the village. She then rushes in, secures a line and removes the *George Harvard*.

• There was a Tidewater station for the Northern Pacific Railway at Commencement Bay in Tacoma.[191] Delta is a small municipality near the Canadian boundary in Whatcom County.

Raine married actress Elizabeth "Betty" Prudhomme in 1958. He didn't reveal the wedding until six months later, among his excuses being busy writing a two-part Secoma story. The only two-parter published would be "Tugboat Annie's Sentimental Journey" in 1961, his next-to-last Puget Sound tale.

He disregarded a rude *Post* letter writer, John D. Mee of Hollywood, who apparently disliked any maritime stories, urging the periodical's editor: "Please introduce [C.S. Forester's Horatio]

Hornblower to Tugboat Annie. Put 'em on a slow boat to China and sink it!"[192]

63. Tugboat Annie and the Killer Ship
(17 October 1959)

Transporters are busy shuttling supplies to Operation Glacier, a chain of radar and air bases and installations under the control of Allied Detection & Interception Command, headquartered at Port Tundra. The 3,000-ton *Kalshan* and slightly larger *Cairngorm* collide in dense fog after their radar equipment goes askew. This is not the first such collision, Annie and Bullwinkle are told at a high-level military meeting. In each case, a mysterious craft is seen through the thick air. It has no name, no markings, a bare deck, a windowless and enclosed bridge.

The tugboat operators are recruited to help port Superintendent Bartlett, Coast Guard skipper Sorenson and Royal Canadian Navy Captain Hughes of the destroyer *Saguenay*. Locate the mystery ship, they are told, and earn a $25,000 reward. Bullwinkle through a ruse takes off before Annie, but limps back, his boat shot-up and the crewmen injured. He lies about where he went, but eventually reveals he'd found the Kaltog Inlet on Mishkan island where the craft simply disappeared. Annie comes up with a plan to block the inlet with two barges. Bullwinkle recklessly ends up bashing the unknown vessel onto the rocks, damaging it with a bargeful of dynamite. Annie meanwhile has cut off any means of escape.

It was a submersible ship owned by an unfriendly nation, we learn. It was equipped with sophisticated radar-blocking equipment. Annie tells Bullwinkle she expects to collect on full salvage as she tows the *Salamander* back to Port Tundra — but relents when she learns he intends that all the reward money go to the families of military personnel injured or killed in the contrived collisions.

• This story is a departure, as much an espionage as maritime tale.

64. Tugboat Annie's Hot Cargo
(2 January 1960) (April & May 1991)

Annie has a new assignment, the first tow from Williwaw Island Atomic Power Plant. She and the crew celebrate at a dance at the Port Chilkat Cannery Workers' Monthly Ball, leaving Shiftless on the *Narcissus*. Jealous, Bullwinkle, needing fuel and having to wait until morning, gets Shiftless drunk and pumps fuel from the *Narcissus* into the *Salamander*.

At Williwaw, Annie receives instructions from Commander Owen Beam and Professor Langley on towing the steel barge with decking over the hold and protective locked hatch covers. Over water 1,000 feet deep, she's to activate the compressed air pumping mechanism, which will swing open the hold's bottom doors, dropping 1-ton containers into the sea water. They contain radioactive waste from construction of atomic units for Navy nuclear-powered vessels and submarines. The containers' sodium contents will explode if mixed with water.

The *Narcissus* runs out of fuel. Annie figures out what happened. She uses some of Pinto's cooking oil to get her tug to Deep Cove, where she refills her tanks with government-owned fish oil stored there. The *Salamander* has its own problem — a jammed propeller. Annie takes the barge out to sea and returns, demanding a large fee from Bullwinkle. She later admits she enjoys the back-and-forth with her rival.

• Deep Cove has also been known as Fox Cove, on the western shore of Sucia Island, near Fossil Bay. Henry Wiggins once raised foxes on the island.[193]

Keeping Posted provided a Raine anecdote in this issue. The writer appeared at a testimonial dinner for a retiring homicide officer with the Los Angeles Police Department. "When Raine was introduced, a gentleman in the audience, noting our man's unpoliceman-like bearing, inquired, 'What does he do?' — meaning, was he a stoolie or a trusty or what? 'Do?' the master of ceremonies roared, 'Why Raine doesn't do a thing. He's being kept by an old woman!'"

A likeness of the lady in question appeared on Page 17.

Times changed, and so did the *Post*. Not all readers were pleased with a profile of architect Frank Lloyd Wright, among them George E. Blanchard, a Methodist pastor in Chattanooga, Tenn., who wrote: "Does being a genius in some line permit all disregard for common decency?... Why not more Tugboat Annie and less about illegal elopements and dirt?"[194]

65. Tugboat Annie: House Mover
(17 June 1961)

Peter the first mate is in a snit. Port Tidewater where he and his wife, Mary, have lived for 30 years, has taken his house, for less than he thinks it's worth, along with five other houses on his street, for a new freeway. Louis Hogan, head of the Freeway Commission, is sympathetic but can't help. Peter has filed all sorts of appeals and made other delaying moves.

Alec Severn has Annie deliver his bid to tow construction supplies to that town for a new defense research facility. George Manning of Industry Construction will entertain his and Bullwinkle's bids. Bullwinkle, under duress, tells Annie his bid is "2 percent below Severn's," no matter what.

Annie has an inspiration. She learns there's a severe housing shortage in Port Tidewater for the new defense workers. Peter agrees he will drop his appeals if he gets what it's worth for his house. She arranges a deal with Port Tidewater officials. The homes haven't been removed because the contracts are all pending. She offers to move the six houses from the property within 10 days. When Bullwinkle stymies her plan to hire Charles Jessup's Secoma House Moving Co. to transpose the buildings, she takes an even better course: using Deep-Sea barges.

• Annie has no apartment or house of her own. As is pointed out in the next story, she is "homeless" other than her quarters behind the *Narcissus* wheelhouse.

66. Tugboat Annie's Sentimental Journey
(26 August & 2 September 1961)

Returning from the far north, where the *Narcissus* has spent six months running shipments to the Dew Line Supply Base on Glacier Island, Annie is grumpy and tired and spouts off after Severn mischaracterizes her loss of a converted LST by an errant ship. Crew members have homes to go to, she only has her onboard cabin.

She ruminates about early days in Port Henry, on the ocean side of the Olympic Peninsula, where she met her late husband Terry, and they and Lars "Snoosebox" Larson ended up spending a night behind bars for a barroom brawl. She decides to look up her old friend to talk about the *Sura Star*, a schooner loaded with sawn cedar (worth $90,000) that was never salvaged after a dam gave out and wiped out most of the village. Severn sends her to buy 250 feet of wire to replace what was lost in the LST incident, and she ends up paying more than necessary, egged on by Bullwinkle's bidding.

The *Narcissus* goes into drydock for maintenance and Annie takes a bus to Port Henry to find Nilson, now proprietor of a ship model shop. She learns the dam is being rebuilt and will power an electric power plant. Tim O'Dowd, head contractor, will soon blow up the *Sura Star* and Annie hatches a scheme. She buys it, with the proviso she will refloat it into the new channel through Dogleg Spit within four days. In Secoma, she explains her plan to Severn, who accepts its legitimacy but, smarting from an Annie insult, insists he will skipper the *Narcissus*.

A visitor from London, Charlie Cove, accompanies the tugboat. Bullwinkle learns of the plan and shows up and picks up the schooner when the cable Severn insisted she purchase ends up wrapped around the *Narcissus* propeller after a gust of wind. Ben the diver is unable to cut it off with an Army "hot stick." Bullwinkle as usual wrangles a deal and ends up taking the *Sura Star* to Secoma, claiming salvage. Annie returns to Secoma overland, obliging Severn to use specific language in making a deal with Bullwinkle. One provision is he covers any money owed O'Dowd for excavating the old schooner.

Meeting with Severn and Bullwinkle and Cove watching, Annie challenges Bullwinkle's claim, noting the schooner was close to land, in Washington state waters, in fact, and covered by state, not international, laws. The cargo per state statute goes with the owner — Annie conveniently purchased it from the insurance underwriters, the original owners being out of the picture — and Bullwinkle himself was responsible for the *Narcissus'* inability to clear its propeller. Cove — who turns out to be Captain Sir Charles Covese, late of the Royal Navy Reserve, now in charge of British Commonwealth Steamers — says because of his wartime service, Bullwinkle knew the hot stick was of a Naval variety, as was the hawser, and thus worked differently than Army gear. Ends up, Cove gives a lucrative contract to Severn.

• The working title for this two-part story was "Tugboat Annie Takes It with Her," as described in a Between the Covers Rare Books online sale listing for a 38-typed-page ms. and 15-page unbound galleys typeset proofs, offered for $3,500.

Named for Midshipman Wilkes Henry, who died in Fiji in 1840, Henry Island is east of San Juan Island.[195]

67. Tugboat Annie & The Sunken Gold

(9 December 1961) *Tugboat Annie: Great Stories ...* (Curtis, 1977) (last story of 11 illustrated by Bingham, and last story published)

Returning through the Inside Passage of Alaska, Annie is alerted to an urgent call for help. Barney Hogan, woods boss for Frost King

Logging, and his men are trapped by a fast-moving forest fire. She goes to Cougar Landing camp to pick up the men and tow a log raft away from shore. Hogan is reluctant to leave, not knowing the fate of the Snowman, a white-haired hermit who probably set the fire.

She shifts the men and logs to Bullwinkle, who is on his way to pick up the job, and he takes them to a hospital at Kupreanof Island. Annie returns to Cougar Landing and locates the Snowman, injured and babbling about gold dust pokes. Bullwinkle returns, having learned of the hermit's ravings, determined to find the treasure. Annie goes to Kupreanof and seeks out Potlatch Murphy, who recalls two ships sinking in the vicinity of Lost Pass. One was the steamer *Quinault,* on its regular run from Secoma to Skagway northbound.

But Annie suspects it was the *Kenbarra,* southbound with some $460,000 in gold dust coming from the Yukon fields. Bullwinkle has already brought in a salvage barge and diver and brings up a mess of old leather straps and a safe. Annie identifies the straps as dogsled harness. Annie strikes a deal with Bullwinkle; he can keep anything he finds from the wreck if he pays Annie $5,000 and the remainder of the Hogan contract. He agrees, thinking of all the cash in the safe.

Annie explains the *Kenbarra* was years ago destroyed as a menace to navigation. This was the *Quinault,* and the Snowman was Herman Slager, a notorious wanted international crook who bought up gold in Africa and took off.

It's a time bomb.

In her last words to appear in print, she explains: "An' it won't explode till Bullwinkle axes the Gov'ment to change his $200,000 into clean new bills. Meantime, he'll have scallions o' fun spendin' it in his mind. But when he does — *Boom!* Because ye see, pal, Slager — that cheatin' old Snow Bum — used to pay off his suckers wherever he operated, wid counterfeit dough!"

• Kupreanof Island is part of the Alexander Archipelago and was critical to the early maritime fur trade.

Of the 67 Tugboat Annie adventures to appear in *The Post*, 40 were never reprinted in books.

68. Tugboat Annie and the Crying Dollars
(1962, unpublished)

Navigating home to Secoma, the *Narcissus* receives a wireless message from Fred at the home office that a small British cargo steamer, the *Aldgate*, Ken Lawes the skipper, has lost power off Astoria, Ore. Annie decides the next morning will be soon enough to depart for a tow; she and Peter have tickets to the fights that evening.

Meeting with Severn, she learns wharf neighbor Bullwinkle has become a 10-percent partner with Mike Halloran of Golden State Tug based in San Francisco. (He's no relation to long-time Secoma tugman Red Halloran.) It means stronger competition for Deep-Sea Salvage & Towing. Severn leaves for Mexico and puts Annie in charge, with the usual cautions.

Annie confronts her rivals, nevertheless, and sets a trap. Bullwinkle, as expected, swipes the boxing arena tickets from the brim of her hat, purposely left behind when she was aboard the *Salamander*. That evening, with an usher and constable at her side, Annie fully expects to confront Bullwinkle and see him carted off to the pokey. But Bullwinkle has fooled her; he traded the tickets with someone else. Annie raises a stink, and she and Peter are shown the door.

Annie sets off for the *Aldgate*, which has wired it was obliged to take a tow from the *Condor*, a Halloran vessel, and has been taken to Neah Bay, instead of to Nanaimo, B.C., where it needs to make a delivery Alleging the Condor was never informed of the *Aldgate's* broken propeller, Halloran makes a salvage claim and acquires at bargain discount several outstanding liens against the *Aldgate* with the intention of foreclosing on it himself then selling it for profit.

Annie figures a way to circumvent Halloran. She tows the *Aldgate* to Canada. Based on a written payment refusal by Lawes she files her own claim and seeks a rapid sale at the Canadian Admiralty office. She gradually reveals her plans to Lawes. At auction she buys the ship for $10,000,. With repairs made, the steamer soon docks in Secoma to deliver the rest of its cargo. Halloran and Bullwinkle show up, planning to take possession of the ship. But Annie has hired a sharp young lawyer, Knud Sunneson, to handle legalities. He advises the men that Annie has bought the ship and her claim has precedence over all others. Mission accomplished. Lawes keeps his steamer, and will repay the debt to Deep-Sea thanks to a lucrative new contract in California.

Halloran and Bullwinkle are out big bucks.

Annie has the last words.

• A cover sheet and 18 typed manuscript pages for this story (printed on Manilla paper using severely diminished carbon paper) plus a one-page outline and four pages of notes, are in Boston University's Howard Gottlieb Research Center's Norman Reilly Raine Collection.

The top page of the ms. carries this penciled notation: "Mailed at airport, 11.00 p.m. Sunday, Mar. 25, 1962."

And "No sale. <u>Series cancelled.</u>"

It was the magazine's decision to end the series, not Raine's. After the glorious 1940s and 1950s, the reading public's interests changed. *Life* and *Look* were the fresh upstarts.

The conservative *Saturday Evening Post* lost readership. It began to stress current events and de-emphasize popular fiction. *The Country Gentleman, The American Magazine* and *Colliers Weekly* were already gone, in 1955, 1956 and 1957 respectively.

After 323 covers, artist Norman Rockwell, smarting at Lorimer's dictate to only show Blacks in subservient roles and the magazine's growing use of photo covers, departed for greener pastures the next year. The *Post* went through several publishers and editors. Heavily in debt, Curtis Publishing ended publication with the February 1969 issue. New owner Beurt SerVaas resurrected the venerable periodical in 1971. It has had other owners since. And it has reprinted four Tugboat Annie stories for nostalgia's sake.

Rigorous Story Preparation

Raine worked out all the plot angles before starting the actual 5,400-word story. The characters flowed comfortably from his fingers.

The archive as mentioned holds a detailed a 14-point story outline for "Tugboat Annie and the Crying Dollars," starting with "Narcissus returning to port. Annie looks forward to fights" and concluding with a tag line: "Yer net loss on this deal is $50,000. (grins) So what was that ye said, about 'dollars don't cry'...?" (A variation appears in the final typescript.) The reference is to a snide remark Halloran made to Annie earlier in the story.

Other surviving pages include one with notes on Admiralty law, radio malfunctions and the potential for far north locales. He used a far north background for "Tugboat Annie and the Killer Ship".

Another sheet has a handful of plot ideas, several X'd out, having been used. A telephone conduit beneath a runway shows up in "Tugboat Annie and the Red Threat." Another story idea is used in the same story: a shipment of cement from Japan. A defective hawser is used in "Tugboat Annie and the Dangerous Cheapskate." The idea of either Annie or Bullwinkle becoming suspicious of a radio message works nicely in "Tugboat Annie Wins Her Medal."

Raine marked as "used" an idea of Bullwinkle taking advantage of Annie's habit of feeling the mooring lines "to judge the dampness and thus the weather" to pull one over on Annie and sneak off. An idea involving false damage claims was earmarked for a Gallup tale.

He employed another tidbit that if a tug is towing a barge and, because of a broken hawser, has to anchor it, the tug master is not liable for any resulting damage and may recover the towing fee, but not the cost of a new hawser.

One paragraph about solving a problem of fog at the mouth of a port (a ship-shore phone; or a mail boat with a whistle buoy; or cars on a pier honking their horns) came from conversations with Henry Foss.

One sheet of technical notes includes the observations that the drums of pawl bitts are called "gypsy-heads" and an important whistle signal between tugs is: "Nearing to heave line: is ---! -! ---! -! -!" (long, short, long, short, short).

A last sheet, headed "Ship's Business (Legal Duties of Ship-masters)," collects Board of Trade and other maritime regulations, including the liability of a skipper if he exceeds his authority in making contracts.

Annie of course never exceeded her authority.

"Sometimes he [Raine] permitted his love of the water to seep into his early writing in too large quantities and one of his tales contained 10,000 words of atmosphere and 2,000 of actual fiction."

— "Buffalonians in Hollywood,"
Buffalo Evening News, 24 July 1935

Chapter 8

Creating Her Own Literary Berth

Raine worked in a literary maritime tradition that began with Homer's *Odyssey* was nurtured by such writers as Daniel DeFoe, James Fenimore Cooper, Herman Melville, Jack London and Frederick Marryat. Raine's contemporaries Guy Gilpatric's Colin Glencannon and C.S. Forester's Horatio Hornblower had strong followings, as did in recent years Patrick O'Brien's Jack Aubrey and Stephen Maturin.

Tugboat Annie broke sea waves as one of, if not the, first of popular literature's female series character of physical stature — let's just say, she was of sturdy build and had a healthy appetite, for which she was neither ashamed nor apologetic. Her equivalent on the male side was Rex Stout's crime-solving Nero Wolfe.

Annie came to accept her relationship with abrasive husband Terry as normal. As a widow she was on her own. Big Sam and Peter and Hank and Shiftless and Pinto were her family. So was Alec. And while she wouldn't admit it, so was Bullwinkle.

Insults from rival Bullwinkle roll off her oilskin like raindrops. Bullwinkle satisfies a need for Annie: a rough-and-tumble adversary. He is her equal in maritime skill and in playing tricks, though his are often dirtier than hers and often motivated by financial gain. She misses him when he is away. He is her comfortable foil.

Richard J. Lane and Jay Wurts in their 1998 study *Women Warriors in Popular Culture*[196] posit Tugboat Annie was a Hiordis-type character[197] — tough and strong as any man who excelled at a man's profession: driving tugboats in the Pacific Northwest. "Her adventures included all the derring-do one might expect from a nautical setting: battling smugglers and pirates and braving squalls on the high seas… However, the idea of a waterfront Brunhilde[198] never caught on with the post-war public, particularly when they had other, more culturally acceptable icons to adopt."

Women hither and yon were likened to Brennan.

Women of Stature in Popular Literature

Large women appeared in prose with modest regularity in the 1930s, two in pulp fiction magazines — so-named for the inexpensive paper they were printed on — others in slicks and books.

One of the first fictional female private eyes, D.B. McCandless's hefty Sarah Watson headed her own detective agency in 11 stories that appeared in *Detective Fiction Weekly* (1935-1938).

Cleve F. Adams' equally robust Violet McDade solved cases in 14 stories in *Clues Detective Stories* (1935-1936).[199]

Erle Stanley Gardner, whose writing career began for the pulps, under his A.A. Fair alias turned out 30 novels featuring ample Bertha Cool. Her associate Donald Lam did the legwork. The first book appeared in 1939, the 30th and the last in 2016.

In recent years, mystery readers have enjoyed "traditionally built" Precious Ramotswe, Botswana's adept lady private detective, in Alexander McCall Smith's book series that began in 1998. Another private eye — in Sacramento — is Misa Ramirez's Lola Cruz. Meg Cabot's Heather Wells, an assistant dorm director, and Joanne Fluke's bakery owner Hannah Swenson are also plus-size amateur crime solvers.

Tugboat Annie was not a detective in the traditional sense, but she had the investigative skills — and gumption — to have made a good one.

She's not a woman of girth, but she's in the Tugboat Annie bailiwick: Vancouver, B.C., author Owen Laukkanen's McKenna Rhodes is a salvage tug captain in his thriller *Gale Force* (2018). The heroine encounters unexpected obstacles as she attempts to aid the freighter *Pacific Lion* out of Yokahama, floundering 200 miles off the Alaska coast.

"The Lord will perwide …"
— Colin Glencannon's general philosophy

Chapter 9

Belial Gallup & Dandy Man 1929-1960

Belial Gallup is third mate (most of the time) of the tramp steamer *Jaipur Prince.* Played by J. Carroll Naish, he was featured in the "Mysterious Cargo" episode of the CBS television series *Playhouse of the Stars,*. Raine wrote the script.

These are the Mr. Gallup short stories:

1. Mr. Gallup
(*Saturday Evening Post*, 19 October 1929)

A long-winded storyteller, Belial Gallup, who believes firmly that "The Lord will perwide," is third mate on the *Baluchistan*, about to debark from Tahiti when the first mate suffers an injury while operating a windlass by hand and the captain breaks a leg when taking a fall. Gallup, with 30 years' experience, puts up a strong argument for taking command when the owners want the second mate to assume the responsibility. Gallup has a master's license, Cameron doesn't.

On board is Mr. Wilkeson, who is impatient to return home so he can take over management of the company. He takes an instant dislike to Gallup, who often quotes Board of Trade regulations. The dislike intensifies when the ship periodically slows to make engine repairs; when it reverses course to pick up Sir Charles Brentwood and others on the steamer yacht *Sirius*, which piled up on Frigate Bird Atoll; and when it returns to Tahiti to take on more stores to feed the 30 folks brought on board.

"You, sir," Gallup roars at young Wilkeson, "are nothing but ballast aboard this wessel." Wilkeson takes a mail boat home, and when the *Baluchistan* steams into port, fires Gallup. Gallup isn't upset;

he's received an offer from Brentwood to become master of his new yacht, the *Orient*.

2. The Lord Will Perwide (*Maclean's* 1 July 1932)

3. Mr. Gallup Goes to Chiny (*Saturday Evening Post*, 23 March 1935)
    The Argosy (UK) January 1939

4. Mr. Gallup Loses His Hat (20 July 1935)

5. Mr. Gallup Gets Command (21 September 1935)
Who's Who and Why (11 January 1936)

6. Mr. Gallup Minds His Ps and Qs (28 March 1936)

7. Mr. Gallup Is a Terror to Snakes (*Maclean's*, 1 June 1936)

8. Mr. Gallup Tends to His Knitting (9 May 1936)

9. Mr. Gallup Has Conniptions (4 February 1939)

10. Mr. Gallup Gathers No Moths (25 October 1941) (*Australian Women's Weekly*, 10 March 1942)

11. Mr. Gallup Backs a Cockroach (7 March 1942)

12. Mr. Gallup Delivers the Goods (11 January 1947)

13. Tugboat Annie Meets Mr. Gallup (13 December 1947) *Post Stories of 1947*, Hibbs ed. (Random House, 1948)

14. Mr. Gallup Has His Day (26 June 1948)

15. Mr. Gallup and the Mysterious Cargo (5 February 1949)

16. The Shanghai Stowaway (20 May 1950)

17. Red Flag on the High Seas (4 November 1950)

18. Treacherous Cargo (26 January 1952)

19. Dangerous Derelict (26 September 1953)

20. Mysterious Cargo (3 December 1955) (11)

21. The Mutiny of Mr. Gallup (9 June 1956)

22. The Inquisitive Mr. Gallup (26 April 1958)

23. Mr. Gallup and the Cargo Snatchers (21 November 1959)

24. Mr. Gallup and the Claim Jumpers (26 November 1960)

25. Mr. Gallup Lets Freedom Ring (1950, unpublished)

●

Peter Trumpet, aka Dandy Man, is a veteran master of cargo steam ships with the Maori Line.

1. Dandy Man
(*Saturday Evening Post*, 15 March 1930) (*The Story-teller*, October 1930)

The Old Man, Captain Peter Trumpet, 75, is sharp-tongued and conceited and good at his job. Arriving in Sydney with less than a full hold of fruits from Ratahiva island, he is dismayed to be retired by Maori Line Steamships executive John Constable, who wants to appoint a younger man to a new vessel, the *Phoenix*. A rival company, Inter-Ocean Steamship, is cutthroat in undercutting Maori Line's contracts.

Weeks later, Constable summons Trumpet to brainstorm ways to save the company. To go any lower in its bid is to sail at a loss. Trumpet speaks with business contacts who have amalgamated as Island & Antipodes Produce. He speaks with Max Abelman, managing director of Inter-Ocean. The fruit growers sign a two-year contract with Inter-Ocean, after which the owners expect to set their own price.

After two years pass, Trumpet announces to Abelman there will be no renewal, as the fruit growers are going to ship their own product from then on. Maori Line had to sell off its cargo ships, one by one, all but the *Phoenix*. But with the proceeds, it purchased Island & Antipodes Produce stock. The two companies are now one. So there, Mr. Abelman.

2. Able Wackets (18 October 1930)
3. Salvage (13 June 1931)
4. Heads I Win (17 August 1935)

Illustrator Harold von Schmidt visited the *Tow Line* office in January 1951 to discuss with staff pilot-house details on the tug *Edmond J. Moran*. Doing his homework.

Chapter 10

Artists Define Annie's Image

"TUGBOAT ANNIE," now at the Palace, stars Marie Dressler and Wallace Beery in a comedy of life on the waterfront. Robert Young and Maureen O'Sullivan also have featured roles in the picture.

Newspaper cartoonists had a field day depicting Marie Dressler and Wallace Beery in the 1933 motion picture *Tugboat Annie*. Ralph Faulkner was responsible for this drawing that ran in the *Washington Times* for 12 March 1933.

Tugboat Annie was earmarked but never depicted on a *Saturday Evening Post* cover, nor were any of her fellow fictional series characters delineated on the cover. But the interior art made up for it.

• Anton Otto Fischer (1882-1962) had the first fling of the paint brush, illustrating with bold images the first Tugboat Annie story 11 July 1931 and continuing the assignments through 13 May 1939, 23 stories in all — excepting a Daniel C. Sweeney fill-in for the 22 September 1934 number.

Warner Brothers commissioned Fischer to produce illustrations for a *Tugboat Annie Sails Again* pressbook in 1940.[200] His art for the first Annie story was reconfigured for a *Post* reprint in Summer 1971.

Born in Munich, Germany, Fischer was orphaned at an early age, was a deck hand on Norwegian, Swedish and British galleasses, barques, steamers and trawlers — his depictions bore the sea breezes of experience — before lingering in the United States to study art in New York City. He then studied in Paris at the Academie Julian, before again crossing the Atlantic and establishing a studio in Wilmington, Del. He was influenced by Howard Pyle's illustrative style. His first sales were to *Harper's Weekly, Everybody's Magazine* and *The Saturday Evening Post* beginning in 1910. He also did book illustrations.

Fischer had a passing acquaintance with the Puget Sound, as he related to Raine: "I was there in a British sailing ship called the 'Gwydyr Castle' and we took wheat to Callao, Peru. Tacoma was in those days (1901) a wild and woolly place, practically a frontier town, and I can still see myself at a seamen's place, conducted by an attractive Norwegian lady called Miss Funnymark, playing the parlor organ, accompanied in the singing of hymns by a crowd of about 75 sailors of all races and denominations. I had some funny experiences in Tacoma."[201]

Anton Otto Fischer, Marine Artist: His Life and Work assesses his craft.[202]

• Sweeney (1880-1958), born in Sacramento, Calif., by 1914 was well known as a book illustrator. He provided images for *Collier's, Overboard Monthly* and other periodicals. He had an eye for exotic subjects and came to specialize in large posters for hotels in Asia and elsewhere. He illustrated a single Deep-Sea story.

• Harold Von Schmidt (1893-1982) carried on the Fischer style from 15 June 1946 — author Raine had taken a break during World War II and screenwriting obligations — to 5 May 1956.

This artwork by John Gulbransen appeared in the
Seattle Star in 1933, when the Dressler-Beery film opened.

Another Californian — he was born in Alameda — and another orphan, he worked on a ranch and on construction projects before attending Grand Central School of Art in New York City, where he was exposed to leading illustrators of the day including the Leyendecker brothers, J.C. and Frank, and Norman Rockwell. He settled in Westport, Conn., to work on assignments for *Collier's*, *Liberty* and *Cosmopolitan* as well as the *Post*.

Ashley Halsey Jr. in *Illustrating for Magazines* said Von Schmidt's Annie had "crustier features and more delineation of lies than in the previous artist's drawings."[203]

Raine called on Von Schmidt in Connecticut in 1957. It was their first meeting. "Fortunately, they liked each other very much," observed the *Post*.[204]

The Western Art of Harold Von Schmidt collects the artist's frontier works.[205]

• A Pittsburgh native, James R. Bingham (1917-1971) finished the *Post's* run of 11 Annie stories, 13 October 1956 to 9 December

1961. During World War II, he illustrated propaganda for the U.S. Navy. His Annie style for a dozen issues was lighter than his predecessors', Annie's garb more modern.

• Phil Smith illustrated the *Post*'s reprint of "Tugboat Annie and the Cheapskate" in 1981. He also provided artwork for the magazine's reprints of Jeeves and other stories.

Unsolicited Endorsements

Raine, a subscriber to *Tow Line*, a magazine issued by the East Coast maritime company Moran Towing, wrote to praise the 1949 calendar: "It is by far the most arresting I have seen; and of course its subject matter, to one who has presumed to write about towboating — a field wherein so few angels treat — is particularly appealing...."

Attached was: "P.S. — Me too gents, and knobs on it! TUGBOAT ANNIE."[206]

Brennan herself wrote Commander R.M. Munroe of Moran Towing & Transportation's magazine in February 1955 to exult over a cover artist: "Again I experience the intense pleasure of receiving the Moran calendar. What a fine artist Charles [sic, Carl] Evers is! Does he, I wonder, know Anton Otto Fischer? He is, I think, fully 'bows abreast' with that old master of marine art.

"As for Tow Line, it is always my most welcome ... arrival. You do a fine job with it, not alone in the illustrations, but also in the infallibly interesting articles and fillers. And incidentally, I would like to have a copy of the Christmas number cover for framing, if I am not applying too late.

"And may I extend to you and to all the Moran fleet and personnel, ashore and afloat, the best of all good wishes for 1955, from yours admiringly, Tugboat Annie Brennan (writ wid me ball-bearin' pen) ...

"and all hands of the tug Narcissus, and even from that old horse's tail, Horatio Bullwinkle, "and all hands of the tug Salamander, and from their faithful chronicler and friend of all towboatmen and seafarers around our coasts, Norman Reilly Raine."[207]

Evers (1907-2000), a native of Germany, emigrated to the United States in 1947. A collection of his paintings was published in 1975: *Maritime Paintings of Carl G. Evers.*[208]

Taken with another piece of art, Annie sent a Western Union night letter from Hollywood to Commander R.M. Munroe, Moran Towing, in January 1959: "Dear Bob If a art print is a copy o yer Christmas cover ID sure like to have one. It's the best pitcher I seen since I was in twaddlin clothes... Yours respeckfully Tugboat Annie (Per Norman Reilly Raine). Spelling passed per copy."[209]

Annie wired Monroe again from Hollywood in December 1960: "ME AND ME BOYS ON THE OLD NARCISSUS WISHES A WET AND MERRY XMAS TO ALL HANDS ASHORE AND AFLOAT AND HALF SEAS OVER OF THE HULL MORAN SHIPS COMPANY. GUESS BILGE CREEPER BULLWINKLE WOULD WISH HE THE SAME BUT WID NO TIME OFF FOR GOOD BEHAVIER HE DON'T GET OUT TILL MARCH. THAT SHOULD LARN HIM NOT TO TAKE ON MORE THAN SIX COPS AT ONCE. GOD BLESS YE ALL. TUGBOAT ANNIE BRENNAN. (Per Norman Reilly Raine)"[210]

It's ironic the issue carried a query from "The Boys on the Fireboat" wondering if Munroe knew of any tugboat captains in New York harbor of Irish heritage. There was one in Secoma harbor — mentioned on another page.

Raine was good friends with another magazine and children's book illustrator and newspaper cartoonist, Robert Brinkerhoff (1880-1958), according to *Los Angeles Times* columnist Lee Shippey: "Norman and Bob Brinkerhoff are old friends. When Norman was a struggling writer he was almost on the point of giving up, for the time, at least, when a magazine which had taken one of his stories decided to play it up with art. Brinkerhoff was the artist selected to make the illustrations and he did such a striking job that the story attracted immediate attention, and thousands of readers realized for the first time how good Norman was."[211]

Al Hirschfeld's distinctive style is evident in a cartoon in the *San Jose News* for 3 April 1934.

Women Re-define Stereotype

"No other blue-collar heroine has endured as long in popular culture as this bosomy mariner of the Puget Sound," according to in a story in *The Dispatch* in 2004.[212]

Raine admitted Dressler and Foss were big influences on how he shaped her character, "but, as I later discovered, there were other women engaged in seafaring besides the lady in the east, and three of them were in or close to the Puget Sound waters that I had chosen for a background for the series."[213]

Captain Myrtle "Molly" Kool (1916-2009) of St. John, New Brunswick, daughter of a Dutch four-mast seaman, was the first woman in Canada — in fact, North America — to obtain a master's ticket. She was regularly at the helm of the barge *Jean K* in the 1930s, taking loads of lumber and other goods across the Bay of Fundy. Unlike Annie, she wore a blue jacket with brass buttons, sailor's trousers and cap. Her most exciting misadventure, she related, was squabbling over dock space with a Norwegian steamer. But she knew her sea law.[214] A Canadian Coast Guard icebreaker was christened the *Captain Molly Kool* in 2019.

Captain Dorothy Blackmore of Port Alberni on Vancouver Island's west coast, a qualified tugboat skipper, marine engineer and tugboat and ferry service operator, was certified in 1940 when she was 25. She took over her father's operation a year later.[215]

Dr. Eve Forrest Gulliford, the daughter of a tugboat captain in Port Coquitlam, earned her own master's papers in British Columbia. Sexist remarks? "Just don't act like a man, that's all," she said. "There's no secret; just be yourself."[216] She eventually earned her medical degree.

Some resented being compared with the Secoma boatwoman. In 1969, during a hearing on President Richard Nixon's nomination of Helen Delich Bentley to be head of the Federal Maritime Commission, Rep. Edward A. Garmatz of Maryland cited a *Sunday Star* story by Miriam Ottenberg headlined "Tugboat Annie or Knowledgeable Lady Our Highest Ranking Woman Appointee."

Asked about that comparison, Bentley testified, "I don't really think I'm a Tugboat Annie. I'm a very plain-spoken, hard-working and I think fair-minded person … a twentieth century woman with a certain amount of conservatism, which undoubtedly fits in with Republican Party thinking.

"I have always felt that each person should stand on his own two feet. I've worked since I was 12, never dodged anything, nor asked for any favors. I try to meet everyone on his or her level. I don't like phonies, don't like pseudo socialites and I particularly don't like lazy people."[217]

And she wasn't a Tugboat Annie?

"The preconception of tugboat workers is we're all big and we waddle," Captain Jean Pinto said. "The public expects to see people with thick arms, fat and tattooed."

According to writer Maria Brooks, "Pinto, a tugboat operator on San Francisco Bay for 18 years, looks trim and shapely."

In one regard, little has changed for towboat women. [218] "Annie works twice as hard as the guys," Brooks quoted Marina Secchitano, San Francisco Bay Regional Director of the Inland boatmen's Union. "She's a super achiever, but even so, she's constantly suspect for being a woman…

"She may beat men at their own game, but the price she pays is her womanliness."

"Some companies say they'd rather have guys of any age than hire a woman," Maine Maritime Academy graduate and operator/owner of the World War II-era *Nokomis* on San Francisco Bay Melissa Parker said. " 'You're too young. You don't have the experience.' "

She added, "I love tinkering around the engine room, taking them apart, repairing them, trouble shooting…."

"Tugboat Jennie" — the implication obvious — was Mrs. Lee B. Jensen of Portland, the first Oregon woman to hold a pilot's license, was usually found in the wheelhouse of the *Jensen* escorted logs in the Sound.[219]

Freda Hough of Tacoma heard the nickname frequently after she took over her late brother's tugboat in the early 1930s. It didn't deter her from learning all she could about engine mechanics.[220]

" 'I think her image, even for my generation, is a good one. Being female in a man's world isn't easy. Tugboat Annie wasn't willing to lie down and die … Now, when I'm called Tugboat Annie I feel it's complimentary. Annie drove boats because she loved it. I'm here for the same reason. There's nothing I love better than to captain a tugboat.'"

Captain Maura Hackett expressed the same pleasure as she navigated Tugboat Roundup guests on a brief Hudson River run from Lockport, N.Y., during Tugboat Roundup in 2019. She was at the helm of the wooden-hulled, steam-driven *Russell I*, launched in 1930, the last boat built by Long Island Machine and Marine Co. The *Russell I* now berths at South Street Seaport under its new name, *W.O. Decker*.[221]

"Both [Wallace] Beery and Miss [Marie] Dressler had to learn to handle the help, trim the boat and steer a course…," according to one report.

> — "Tugboat Lore," *Evening Star*, 11 June 1933.

Raine "acted as instructor, being an experienced tugboat hand… A complete ship was rented and set up on a sound stage, its stock including even a patent London taffrail-log."[222]

> — *My Own Story*, Marie Dressler,
> as told to Mildred Harrington (1934)

Chapter 11

Marie Dressler's *Tugboat Annie*

Author Raine and actress Dressler look over the script for *Tugboat Annie*. (*New Movie Magazine*, August 1933)

"M-G-M Buys Dressler Vehicle," *Film Daily* reported 19 July 1931, the studio having acquired rights from "Major Norman Reilly Raine, Canadian [sic] short story writer."

Raine received $10,000 for rights to three stories, the *Province Sun* said, his first sale of film license.[223]

The Toronto *Star Weekly* misidentified the character as "Gun-Boat Annie."[224]

Raine's short story "Tugboat Annie" was timely, as Metro-Goldwyn-Mayer was in search of another star vehicle to pair Marie Dressler (1868-1934)[225] and Wallace Beery (1885-1949).[226]

Dressler was paid a reputed $100,000 to play Annie.[227] Beery by his arrangement with MGM was paid $1 more a year than any other contract player, probably in the neighborhood of $50,000, to take the part of Terry Brennan. Mervyn LeRoy (1900-1987)[228] directed; his salary was $70,000.

It didn't matter to the studio that the screenplay would vary significantly from the *Post* story. In fact, it had to in order to work Wallace Beery into the action, according to veteran cinema scribes (*The Thin Man, It's a Wonderful Life*) Frances Goodman and Albert Hackett, who were considered for the assignment.[229]

A call went out for ideas. Some 50 synopses were submitted,[230] including one from playwright Bayard Veiller.[231] The scenario accepted was by actress Zelda Sears and script clerk Eve Greene with additional dialogue by Raine, whose contract came with an invitation to Hollywood to write new scripts.[232]

The changes to the storyline wouldn't go unnoticed. The *Boston Globe* observed after the picture was released, "The rakish, rowdyish heroine of the published stories has been made softer and more tender-hearted. And in only one scene does that impudent lone feather flaunt its defiance from Tugboat Annie's 'best hat.' One suspects that the authors of the scenario took Annie right out of the stories and wrote a completely new series of experiences for her, emphasizing maternal affection and wifely loyalty. Certainly the adventures of Annie and her shiftless, drunken, but lovable husband, played by Wallace Beery, center around a pleasant domesticity that was lacking in the original tale."[233]

Also appearing in the film were Tammany Young as deck hand Shiftless, Paul Hurst as engineer Big Sam, Jack Pennick as First Mate Pete, Willie Fung as Chow the cook, Willard Robinson as Severn and Robert Young and Maureen O'Sullivan as the love interest.

The script created a son for the Brennans. Young recalled, "Marie said the thought of her and Wally having such a handsome son was shocking. She was very ill with cancer by then and could only shoot a few scenes every morning and then she'd retire exhausted. She acted in the silent fashion, full steam ahead, and for her it worked. Wally loathed being part of a team with her because she was twenty five years older than he was."[234]

Dressler was 63 at the time of the filming, Beery 47.

Mervyn LeRoy, director of Metro-Goldwyn-Mayer's *Tugboat Annie*, is flanked by the stars Marie Dressler and Wallace Beery. (Publicity still)

Tugboat Annie's stars share an intimate moment. (Publicity still)

The actress acknowledged an interesting challenge to her role: "Here was a story written more or less with myself in mind. That is flattering, of course. The author wrote of me as he saw me on the screen in a certain role. Then, as the stories began to gain more and more success in the Saturday Evening Post, he amplified the character he was writing about. Annie became a real entity.

Willie Fung as Chow the *Narcissus* cook shared a dubious recipe with Marie Dressler as Tugboat Annie. (Publicity still)

Tugboat Annie surveys the horizon from the *Narcissus's* lower deck. (Publicity still)

"The stories were good — more widely read than any sea stories in years. That means that the public conceived a very definite idea of exactly what kind of a woman Tugboat Annie was. Then, in the picture, you see, it was up to me to try to fit that idea. In other words, I was given the task of living up the public's conception of the character.

"The author had no idea when he wrote the stories that they'd ever be made into a picture. But the minute I read the first of them here was an ideal character. It wasn't until Mr. Raine came to the studio to help adapt them that I learned that he'd gotten the first idea for them from a role of mine."[235]

"I love any role which shows that if you aren't afraid of life, life can't hurt you," Dressler said in a *Washington Evening Star* article. "That's what Tugboat Annie does. She licks fate because she can look it in the eye and not be afraid. I always love a role in which I can get that idea over to the audience, because I think that's the kind of stimulant that we need in American life right now."[236]

The actress actually cooked the meal of spare ribs and sauerkraut she served to Wallace Beery, Young and O'Sullivan in the movie — to celebrate the first time she and Beery appeared together, in *Min and Bill*.[237]

Beery revealed how he unintentionally achieved a realistic effect in *Min and Bill*: "In the couple's row in the sailor boarding house it seems that Wally unknowingly stepped on Marie's toe, with the weight of all his 204 pounds, and after that when Marie punched, kicked and cuffed him she did it with a fury that included no pretense.

"Beery did not know about stepping on Marie's toe until afterward," according to George Shaffer. "That was after Marie busted the picture over his head. Marie's toe was infected for months.[238]

There are two allusions to Terry stepping on Annie's toes in the nine-reeler.

Beery said he abandoned his old ways while making the film. "When a fellow gets a character such as he's never played before, he's better off if he forgets all his old tricks, lest he resort to some of them in the new character.

Norman Reilly Raine, seated right, joined the cast and crew of *Tugboat Annie* on the set. (Richards Studio)

The *Sea King* performed as Horatio Bullwinkle's *Salamander* in the 1933 film. (University of Washington collection)

"I had to coil hawser, work in an engine room, steer a tug, all at sea," the actor related. "So I got in with the regular tugboat workers, learned their trade and absolutely forgot I was an actor and tried to be a real tugboat man. In other words, I tried to use their bag of tricks, rather than mine."[239]

Sound Locations

Some California sets and locations were used in filming *Tugboat Annie*, but "Most of the picture was shot in Puget Sound in the actual locales of the Norman Reilly Raine stories, which gives the picture an extraordinary sense of authenticity," the *Seattle Daily Times* said.[240]

Director Leroy was impressed, when scouting potential film sites with Raine, to find so many relics of Jack London's days in Seattle harbor.[241]

"The famous 'Inside Passage' from Puget Sound into Alaskan waters, terror to all but the most skillful navigators, and traditional among men who follow the sea, figures in the thrilling details of 'Tugboat Annie' ..." the *Corvallis Gazette-Times* elaborated.[242]

"The 'inside passage' is a channel formed by the mainland on one side and thousands of small islands, with channels between that deceive and mislead the mariner into reefs and other perils.

"Because the islands protect the 'inside passage' from heavy storms, it is a favorite course northward. Countless legends have arisen about the islands, many of them still unexplored...

"Puget Sound tugboats built to withstand the terrific storms of winter in the northern port, cameras slung from cables, or from their booms, to film them in churning seas, a great liner, chartered for a picture and placed in the center of a raging storm at sea — these are among the amazing technical feats accomplished in the filming of 'Tugboat Annie'...," one newspaper reported.[243]

"In 'Tugboat Annie,' Miss Dressler runs a tug into this playground of perils to rescue a liner, caught on a reef. Many thrills are interspersed among the poignant heart-interest episodes and the smashing dramatic climax, in which Beery enters the firebox of a seagoing tug to plug its boilers and thus make possible the rescue of a stranded liner. Much of the picture was actually filmed in Puget Sound and Seattle Harbor, original locale of the Raine stories."

Dressler said in her autobiography: "The most grueling piece of physical labor I ever put in was during the filming of the gale scenes in 'Tugboat Annie.' One coastwise sailor in the cast told me that in twenty years' experience aboard tramp steamers he had never encountered rougher seas than those manufactured in our studios. They should have been good. Mr. Mayer spent $30,000 on the dock alone! Able-bodied men were slapped down by waves the script described as mild. There was more than one arm in a sling, and at least one leg in a plaster cast before we got through." [244]

Confirmed the *Seattle Daily Times,* "An entire ship chandlery was reproduced for one scene. Robert Young [as the Brennans' son Alec] is seen on an actual steamer bridge, as a captain operating navigable instruments. A complete engine room was used as a floating set for another of the vivid scenes and a Puget Sound tug was moved in toto from Seattle to San Pedro harbor for 'close-ups.'"[245]

"The technicians knocked down a tugboat and transported it by trucks 40 miles from the ocean to the studio where it was reassembled on a sound stage," according to Captain Roscoe Fawcett. "A ship-chandler's shop, complete with propellers, taffrail logs, lamps, buoys, hawsers and other sea-going supplies, and a section of pier also were transported in the same way."[246]

The *Wallowa* (later renamed *Arthur Foss)* of the Foss Launch & Tug Company was used in scenes filmed on Lake Union and Elliott Bay. Captain Clarence Howden did the piloting duties.

Studio technicians made an unexpected discovery when readying the ships old triple-expansion engine and boiler, according to columnist Fawcett. "Built in Scotland forty years ago, the machinery has had only two repairs in that time although it has been in constant heavy service. On these occasions broken petcocks were replaced. The boilers have been cleaned but have never needed repair. Government inspectors believe the machinery will be good for still another period of the same length."[247]

So the tug was slandered in the motion picture's plotline centered on a malfunctioning boiler.

Some of the cast traveled to Bellingham and Port Angeles for scenes. The *Wallowa/Narcissus* was briefly renamed the *Municipal Garbage Tug*. J. Razore's City Sanitary Service's real garbage scows ferried cameramen around for view of Bellingham Bay and the San Juan Islands.[248]

A broad casting call went out for upwards of 5,000 people, regardless of clothing or appearance, for a Bell Street Dock scene filmed 21 April, to welcome Annie's son upon his return from his first experience as an ocean liner commander.[249] Mayor John F. Dore was an extra.[250] The city official also rubbed elbows at dockside with Director LeRoy and author Raine.[251]

R.H. Herzog of Lake Union Drydocks painted new names on the tugboats and steamer.[252] But George D. Hubbard, U.S. Collector of Customs, took notice of Foss's *Wallowa*, Puget Sound Tug & Barge's *Sea King* and Libby, McNeil & Libby's *General Gorgas*, and sent investigators. "It is against customs regulations to alter the name of a vessel without first obtaining the Treasury Department's permission, a procedure that requires about a month and runs into money."[253]

"As far as I can determine," Hubbard said, "not one of the owners of the three ships applied to this office. — in violation of regulations, but it was let slide as Customs Collector George Hubbard felt it was not an attempt at fraud.[254]

Getting the right images from the *Sea King* and *Wallawo*, rechristened the *Firefly* and the *Narcissus*, was another matter. "What was wanted," according to Dorothy Brant, "was a good coal smoke, the nice black kind the neat housewife dreads on washdays And when the *Narcissus* smoked up, the *Firefly* 'went out' and when the *Firefly* did get up a black smoke, the *Narcissus* was lost to view.

" 'She's smoked before,' shouted Mervyn LeRoy, the director, from his position on the top of what was a cross between a high diving tower and a tennis referee's platform. 'Why can't she now?'

"And faintly, from the stern of the tug — 'We just put a tire in.'"[255]

Real-Life Crewmen

Walter House, later with the Delta V. Smyth tugboat line in Olympia, worked/acted as mate on the faux *Narcissus*. He recalled with amusement a "misunderstanding in orders that resulted in the actual collision of the tugboat and ferry. Although the wreck was planned, it was to be faked, but no faking occurred when the nose of the tugboat plowed into the ferry. The squall portrayed in the picture was filmed in the Strait of Juan de Fuca, off Clallam Bay. Twenty days were used in the actual filming on board the tug."[256]

Wedell Foss assisted with maneuvering vessels from his fleet, while O.O. Dull, an MGM production coordinator, handled human performers.

Some scenes were of course fabricated; MGM's model shop's wooden and metal 34-in-long tugboat replica made for the film 85 years later went up for sale, but had no takers, according to Heritage Auctions.[257]

Puget Sound newspapers had a grand time following the production. " 'Tug Boat Annie, Ahoy!'" *The Seattle Daily Times* titled one photograph of Seattle Mayor Dore with LeRoy and Raine,[258] to accompany a story, "Movie Director Finds Local Tugs Temperamental."

Raine's Seattle secretary June Pat Wetherell tested at Elliot Bay and Lake Union as an extra, was accepted and ended up doing further scenes on a lot in California. She reported for the *Seattle Post-Intelligencer*: "Each time they finished a scene she [Dressler] meekly asked Director LeRoy: 'Was that all right?'

Each time he shot back: 'Fine, darling!' "[259]

Wetherell was awe-struck: "There I saw the *Glacier Queen*, the same liner that all Seattle turned out as extras to welcome when scenes were shot in that city — confetti, gangplank and all, but it was a movie set now, made in Hollywood. Mervyn LeRoy, the director, was pacing back and forth, cigar in mouth …

"Nils Asther, big and brown and handsome; Maureen O'Sullivan, Walter Huston and Stuart Erwin brushed past me as I went up the stairs. The studio policeman examined my ticket. The place was jammed with actor, stars, extra, directors and writers."

She said one way to distinguish shots filmed in Los Angeles and from those in Bellingham is the garbage scows in the latter contain oranges.[260]

Extras named Tammany Young and One-Eye Connelly gate-crashed and played two tugboat firemen in a spitting duel.[261] The scene was never used.

Housewife Maria Fisk, "spotted on the rear of her houseboat throwing out coffee grounds," was cajoled into spending several hours one day doubling for Dressler, who needed to conserve her energies. "Director Mervyn LeRoy said Mrs. Fisk made a fine double," according to a United Press story.[262]

"A fleet of Foss tugs, chartered for the picture, steamed fussily in and out of the moorings, smoke pouring from salt-caked funnels. Batteries of cameras perched on new timber towers, upper decks and along the doc itself. "LeRoy was there directing," reported the *Seattle Post-Intelligencer*.[263] "So was Raine, standing around the way authors do. W.O. Foss, president of the Foss Company, leaned out of a pilot house window, shouting directions to his tugs through an enormous megaphone. O.O. Dull, production manager, sat on a string-piece at the end of the dock, watching the tugs steam by under their drifting clouds of smoke, think about how much it was costing per minute...

" 'There aren't any seagulls!' someone shouted.

"A conference convened hastily. A messenger was sent posthaste for a loaf of bread. He returned panting, clutching a large loaf. A man was appointed to go throw the bread on the water. He departed at a gallop for the end of the wharf.

"Everyone stood around waiting. The man threw bread with passionate anxiety. Dull, as production manager, is responsible for business details like costs, groaned as he scanned the sky for a gull.

"After awhile a gull hopped off the yardarm of a big square rigger across the way and circled down to see what was going on. A couple of others followed. Soon there were lots of gulls.

"Foss hauled the whistle rope of the 'Narcissus'— in real life the tug *Wallawa*. In response to the signal the tugs standing by offshore came charging by with their smoke, which drifted off across the background of ships. Cameras began to grind."

When the cameras were turned off, "The gulls ate all the bread and flew around waiting for more."

The next day, someone placed a classified in the *Post-Intelligencer*: "NORMAN REILLY RAINE Please quit fooling around with the motion picture industry and get back to your job of writing some more 'Tugboat Annie' stories. It's been quite awhile, now —!"

Captain James A. Hersey, former owner of the barkentine *Conqueror*, went to California "to take charge of the floating equipment of Metro-Goldwyn-Mayer," the *Seattle Daily Times* reported.[264] Besides the *Wallowa*, as the *Narcissus*, the *Sea King* belonging to Gilkey Brothers Towing of Anacortes was brought in, also the *Sabine*.[265]

That last vessel, sunken during the filming, was revived and sold to the Royal British Navy and saw actual service during World War II. It successfully retrieved a number of British naval vessels from the North Sea.[266] It was rundown when it visited the Tyne in 2012, on her way to the J.J. King & Co. of Gateshead breakers yard in U.K.[267]

"Norman Reilly Raine will consider this melancholy news, for it was aboard the *Sabine* that Marie Dressler and Wallace Beery once lived Tugboat Annie adventures while the movie cameras whirred. The Sabine's last run was outlandish enough to seem fitting to Raine, though it probably didn't to the crew. Built in Baltimore way back in 1917, long in the service of the Foss Tug and Launch Company, of Tacoma, Washington, before going into war-salvage work, the Sabine was getting fed up with it all. She ran into awful weather beating up the English coast, her hull began to unfold like a window blind opening, and she finally made port with 750 tons of sea insider her, which is not good. The report that she almost sank is credible, as Annie wasn't aboard to bring her through," said a writer in *The Saturday Evening Post*.[268] It was salvaged in 1950 at Gateshead's J.J. King & Co.[269]

Non-tugs included the *Lilly* aka *Bounty* and the *Nanuk* aka *Pandora*, square-riggers, also Gloucester fishing schooners *Oretha F.* and *Spinney*, which were brought in from the Great Banks. (Tugboats imported to the M-G-M lot were also adapted for another film, *Louisiana*, set in a bayou.)[270]

•

Theaters on the Puget Sound pulled out all the stops in
promoting the premiere of *Tugboat Annie* in 1933.
This is the Liberty Theater in Walla Walla.

World Premiere

The film's producers were Harry Rapf and Irving Thalberg. Music was by Paul Marquardt, cinematography by Gregg Tolland, art direction by Merrill Pye, costume design by Lucia Coulter, editing by Blanche Sewell.

Ontario-born Dressler appeared as Tugboat Annie on the cover of the 7 August 1933 issue of *Time: The Weekly Newsmagazine*. She and Beery were also on the cover of the 3 February 1934 issue of *Picture Show*.

The world premiere was at Seattle's 5th Street Theater.[271] Gov. Clarence D. Martin and Lt. Gov. Victor A. Meyers were in the audience."[272] Tacoma hosted its own premiere three weeks later.[273]

"The crowds saw a picture that more than measured up to expectations — a picture glorifying the doughty spirit of a woman mariner...," said Everhardt Armstrong in the *Seattle Post-Intelligencer*. "Scenic backgrounds, including many a familiar flash of the Seattle waterfront are superbly woven into the texture of the film... it was a master stroke on Frank L. Newman's part to arrange its world premiere for the Fifth Avenue."[274]

New York Times reviewer Mordaunt Hall opined, "Miss Dressler is admirable, giving a genuinely human touch to her role. As for Mr. Beery's performance, he is very amusing when showing Terry's penchant for strong drink, particularly in the scene where his brain becomes so muddied that the task of dressing is almost impossible. Tammany Young makes himself noticed as a deckhand on the Narcissus."[275]

A Washington, D.C., *Evening Star* critic carped about the humor: "Soap in sauerkraut. Wallace Beery wearing a stiff collar and derby and ambling along without his trousers. Marie Dressler drinking every glass of punch Terry attempts to guzzle and getting drunk for it may have been the irresistible comedy climaxes of some more naïve age. It is doubtful if they are today. And yet, when it departs from this time-worn path of amusement, 'Tugboat Annie' is a very funny picture."[276]

Troy, N.Y., Theatre manager Leo Rosen in cooperation with distributor zone advertising chief Charley Smakwitz, came up with eye-catching tie-ins for the debut. He displayed giant letters, two each day, asking passersby to guess what they would spell out. The day of the first show, a row of automobiles lined the street, each displaying a huge letter:

TUGBOAT ANNIE.[277]

In St. Louis, Mo., a motor vehicle altered to resemble a tugboat parked in front of Loewe's State the week the Dressler/-Beery picture opened.[278]

A German moviehouse gave out small bottles of schnapps with a card reading: Why should you be worse off than Wallace Beery?"[279]

Inspired by the movie, J.C. Jenkins in His Colyum doggereled:

When 'Tugboat Annie' comes to town
She'll turn the whole town upside down.
She'll make you laugh, she'll make you sigh,
And then again she'll make you cry,
She'll make you glad that you're alive,
She'll make your front look like a hive
Of bees, in a balmy summer clime
When they come out at swarming time.
You'll hear the quarters plunk until
You'll say, 'By gosh! They'll bust the till,'
And you'll not see a single frown
When 'Tugboat Annie' comes to town.[280]

Theaters in Beemer, Neb., Lathrop, Mo., Dayton, Ohio, Collinsville, Okla., and Rochester, N.Y., misspelled the name in advertising the movie: "Tugboat Anna." A few theaters billed it "Towboat Annie."

That didn't deter audiences. The picture tied for fourth place with *She Done Him Wrong* in the box office earnings listing for 1933 pictures, according to *Motion Picture Herald*.[281] It brought the studio some $1.917 million in North American ticket sales, $655,000 overseas, $2.572 million overall. With a budget of $614,000, it showed a profit of $1.1 million. According to Ultimate Movie Rankings, its adjusted domestic box office take as of 2024 is $250.8 million, worldwide $336.4 million.

Publicizing the 1933 motion picture's release, Arthur Catlin, manager of Cleveland's Loew's State Theater, arranged for a quarter-hour radio show over WHK the Saturday evening after the picture's Friday opening.

"Life Savers were placed in special envelopes with the copy: 'A Life Saver — if you laugh too hard at Marie Dressler and Wallace Beery at Loew's State,' etc. These were passed out on the streets by two young ladies attired in white sailor suits with ribbons reading 'Tugboat Annie' across their shoulders," *Motion Picture Herald* reported.[282]

Dressler's image appeared on a 1940 European collector card packaged with Max Cigarettes, No. 28 in a series issued under the umbrella Cinema Cavalcade.

"For a generation of women, many heading households alone and struggling with the nearly non-existent employment opportunities for women in the 1930's, Tugboat Annie was a hero and role model. She could outsmart her nemesis, Captain Bullwinkle, at every turn and if necessary she could roll up her sleeve and sock a brutish chin that deserved it."

— *Immigrant's Path,* Tacomahistorylive, 16 February 2017

Chapter 12

Raine's Career in Hollywood

Raine settled into the flow of the cinematic community in California.

Canadian journalist Gordon Sinclair visited Raine at the MGM studio: "I stalk down a corridor past two Russian dukes and a camel. Three wax dummies in dress suits are being loaded on a truck; Helen Hayes, prim and neat, goes by in nun's costume, fingering a rosary. A Barrymore in need of a shave lounges against a wall reading mail. I'm directed to a low crowded building by a cop. 'Authors in there,' he says. 'You an author?' 'Yes.' 'Thought so — go right in.

"Norman Raine, creator of Tugboat Annie, is getting Annie ready for the screen. He has to chart her every move. Marie Dressler, the grand old gal of the flickers, is going to play Annie, only Miss Dressler is pretty sick right now; flat on her back with the miseries."

The reporter notes 22 writers at work on a story about beer; napping in a corner, Gary Cooper is dressed like a British soldier. Wallace Beery walks by holding a fistful of letters and orders a lettuce sandwich. Helen Hayes, "with a pair of 'teen' age lads in tow, eats a vast meal of beans and molasse, sausage and friend potatoes. Jimmy Durante in heavy makeup flirts with Joan Crawford.[283]

And a screenwriter was expected to get work done?

In a feature article for *Maclean's*, Raine told what he learned of the inner workings of the movie-making capitol. Stories go through several steps before an idea is run up various rungs of a ladder to the head of the studio, he said. Writers are asked to do a treatment.

"A treatment is an extended synopsis, written in scene and extending to thirty or fifty typewritten pages. It contains the full feature story, with high lights of business and dialogue fully written out, so that the studio head, as he reads it, may have a running picture in his head of what the finished product is to be like . He says 'Lousy' or beams and grunts 'Great! Swell! Okay!' and the delighted and incredulous writer hops off before the head changes his mind to write a full continuity-dialogue script. This is the document, generally running to about 130 typed pages, from which the picture actually will be shot.

"The finished script, the writing of which may take from four weeks to three months, again must have approval of the studio head; and this secured, the script — a number of copies having been made — is turned over to the director. He breaks it down into scenes, and it is from this list of scenes that the shooting time is estimated and the shooting schedule made."[284]

The writer, once actors have been engaged and shooting begun, must remain on standby through editing and preview screenings in case major changes are necessary.

"Often, after a preview, extensive retakes are necessary in the studio — which is why, after a picture has been shot, the cast stands by, and the set are not torn down, until the picture is in the can and on its way to the distribution centres."

Major studios, he said, keep from 50 to 80 writers on staff.

Brother Malcolm Visits

The screenwriter's older brother Malcolm, taking leave of his association with the *London News Chronicle*, spent several months with Norman in Hollywood in 1938 before settling with his two daughters and son in Buffalo.

"While I was visiting him, he worked 32 hours without stopping even for sleep," Malcolm told columnist H. Katherine Smith. "His working day usually starts at 7 a.m. and ends at midnight; and he accepts a week-end invitation only on condition that he may go off by himself and write for hours at a stretch."[285]

That's a far cry from a decade earlier, when he set aside only from 2 to 4:30 each afternoon for literary endeavors.[286]

Malcolm's sister-in-law Joyce more than holds her own with Hollywood starlets, he said. While on a four-day cruise on a yacht that appeared in the picture *Waikiki Wedding*, Malcolm swam with Marie Wilson (then appearing in *Boy Meets Girl*), attended a reception for Spanish pianist Amparo Iturbi and hobnobbed with Stan Laurel and Oliver Hardy.

Among his impressions: Everyone in Tinseltown dressed informally; actresses ate lunch, had their hair done and took in a fashion parades simultaneously. And everyone had a dog. (Norman's was a wirehaired terrier, a four-year-old runt of the pack "Mickey" or Miss Mickey Twink per the American Kennel Club.[287])

Malcolm was in awe of Hollywood movie sets: "A New York tenement rising in the midst of an Italian village, with a Bowery saloon and an Egyptian pyramid for their neighbors. It looked like a bad dream. All those buildings were shoved together on one section of a movie lot and deserted until there's use for them in another picture."[288]

Peter B. Kyne, Fellow Word Wrangler

Raine was on the MGM studio lot one day, half listening to conversation as he scanned proofs, edited copy and glanced at a desk clock, when, as opportunity provided, a bespectacled stranger took a seat.

" 'Working on "Tugboat Annie" film, I understand!'

" 'Yes, yes; quite so.'

" 'These surroundings and "Tugboat Annie" rather remind me of the days when we filmed "Cappy Ricks." '

" 'Oh, did you work on the "Cappy Ricks" series?'

" 'Yes, I wrote them.'

"And then Captain Raine apologized for not catching the name in the first place and he and Capt. Peter B. Kyne did a little honest-to-goodness back slapping, went out to lunch together where kindred spirits talked and talked about ships and field guns, soldiers and sailors and the romance of the wide-wide world," the *Seattle Daily Tribune* reported.[289]

Works by Kyne (1880-1957),[290] beginning with *The Three Godfathers* (1913), were adapted into more than 100 motion pictures. His best-known character, Cappy Ricks, operated a West Coast shipping and lumbering trade.[291] Ricks drew on real-life experiences for many of his plots.[292]

Thus a kinship with Raine.

Advice to Writers

"My writing is a business with me, an extremely commercial proposition," Raine told the *Buffalo Evening News* in 1935, suggesting to budding writers: "There is no need for the walls of a successful writer to be papered with rejection slips. Know your product. Study the magazines. Saturate yourself with the material that the popular reader wants. Be imitative, if necessary."[293]

He admitted, "I prefer magazine writing, as there is more opportunity to be your own boss. In the movie world one can become a story doctor too easily. But it is good fun once in a while."

Does apparel matter? Raine "always works with a knitted cap on his head," according to one columnist. "When he mislaid it recently, he astonished a casual visitor by appearing at the door with a substitute: a knitted stocking belonging to his wife."[294]

•

Raine was convinced writers were born, not made.

"You have to have the ability to tell a story — to have a sense of dramatic values. A little bit of talent will go a long way," he told a *Daily Toronto Star* journalist in 1936.[295] "I have seen men with loads of genius that couldn't turn out a thing."

He continued, "Sit down and decide just what type of stories you want to write. If you want to write about travel get out and travel. If you want to write about adventure you must go where it lies. You can't sit down in the library and write adventure or travel stories. You have to get the authentic background, the atmosphere."

Does freelancing pay?

"Free-lancing is a bit tough at the start, but if you have a typewriter, lots of paper and lots of time, you can, with a little ability and lots of hard work, make a living at it…

"It is a matter of self-discipline and training. There are a lot of smart people going hungry on the street today because they won't write for the large 'commercial' magazines. They think it is beneath them. They have talent but won't discipline themselves."

•

Raine spun off his fictional characters based on traits of individuals around him. Sometimes that got him into hot water, he told the *Toronto Star Weekly* in 1932. "An amusing instance of this occurred while he was a member of the editorial staff of a well-known magazine. Mr. Raine happened to get into an argument with a certain Miss Winnie S——, also an editorial staff member. Neither was willing to cede a fraction of an inch to the other, and as the day progressed the argument grew warmer…"

Raine went home, still steaming.

"To work this off, he turned his attention to a certain story which, up until that time, had proved a little stubborn in the working out. Next morning, he handed the finished story to the editor.

" 'I like your story, Mr. Raine,' said the editor. 'But don't you think you could have made the character, Winnie the barmaid, a little more attractive personality?'

"The author shook his head. He happened to catch the eye of the argumentative Miss S——. 'No,' he said. 'That is, unless I change her name again. You see, I didn't want her a charming character, but I couldn't seem to make her live as I wanted until last night, when I re-christened her 'Winnie' after Miss S—— here. And after that the story just unfolded itself time without any further difficulty whatsoever.'"[296]

Audiences Change

Raine witnessed change in Hollywood. He remarked to a newspaper in 1939, "Producers once thought their audience had a mental age of 10 or 12. That idea was killed by the box-office success of recent serious biographical films. Since the depression people have demanded some solid content to their entertainment. As a result, studio efforts toward realism and accuracy have become almost unbelievably detailed."[297]

An inveterate investigator, Raine in 1939 tracked down a hunting group organized by Major-General Robert E. Wood, head of Sears, Roebuck, and Major Wendell Endicott, president of Endicott Shoe Co., who were going on a hunting trip in the Yukon — so he could interview the party's third member, Col. William "Wild Bill" Donovan, famed commander of the Fighting 69th Regiment, as Raine was writing a scenario for a Warner Brothers film about the war heroes.[298] Raine and Donovan became seatmates on a train traveling from Chicago to Seattle.[299]

Raine located Captain John T. Prout in New York. Prout had been commander of G Company, 69th Regiment, during the war and was serving as technical director on the picture.

"I'm Norman Reilly Raine," the author introduced himself. "Just flew in from Hollywood. Been working on the script of 'The Fighting 69th.' Want you to read it and see if there is anything we have to do here before we fly back to Hollywood. Must leave tomorrow night. They've already made reservations on the plane."[300]

Raine's old friends the Moores visited him in Hollywood in 1939 and he gave them a tour of the Warner Brothers lot.[301]

Raine registered with the U.S. government in 1941. Living at 2730 Outpost Dr., Hollywood, he indicated Walter Wanger Pictures Inc., Universal Studios, Burbank, was his employer.[302]

Joyce Raine in 1943 sang as part of a St. Patrick's Day musicale put on by the Opera Reading Club Juniors of Hollywood and in another musical show put on for USO centers in Los Angeles she played the role of a Red Cross nurse.[303]

•

Raine, in response to a request from columnist Robbin Coons for a guest essay, launched into a diatribe against columnists — "How long we screenplay writers have endured from those self-anointed pundits…" — and directors who get more credit than they deserve, "since a director works from the script, where all of the dialogue and most of the business is written in for the guidance of himself and the cast …."

But his beef was mostly with the columnists who "without having read the screenplay, thus blithely can bestow his critical but spurious largess.

"How does he know that the 'masterly use of pantomime' which so aroused his admiration, was not written into the script by the scenarist, with the director's sole contribution the meticulous application thereof? What magic insight causes him to label 'inept' a screenplay he has never seen? …

"Recently I wrote the screen version of a rather important historical play which we called 'The Private Lives of Elizabeth and Essex' intended for two of our more prominent stars. In adaptation for the screen, the producer stressed the fact that I should adhere as much as possible to the story in the play. That was no trick. The main problem lay in transcribing into vigorous, contemporary language the blank verse of the play with its many archaic phrases, and in shortening and livening up its long and ponderous speeches so as to give it fast action and amusing lightness.

"This was done, to the enthusiastically expressed satisfaction of all concerned. But the director, who has an imperfect knowledge of English, took a copy of the play on the set with him and in an idle moment read it. Those sonorous, rolling speeches seemed pooty good to him; so, disregarding the screenplay, he threw back in huge indigestible chunks of the medieval blank verse I so rigorously and painstakingly had streamlined. Result: When the picture was released those tinkered portions never did climb out of their morass of words.

"But ah, the columnist-critics! Those omnipotent, all-seeing fellows. How unerringly they castigated the wrong culprit, one saying: 'The brilliant direction of So-and-So did its utmost to give charm and lightness to a heavy script,' and another, in proud demonstration of his historical knowledge, deploring the ignorance of the screenplay writer in distorting historic fact — when, actually, I had only followed the plot and detail of the original play."[304]

The Warner Brothers film, starring Bette Davis and Errol Flynn, was based on *Elizabeth the Queen* by Maxwell Anderson. Raine co-wrote the script with Aenaes Mackenzie. It was a money-maker and earned five Academy Award nominations.

Raine in 1941 visited Ottawa for a project he wouldn't mention for the Dominion government.[305]

He was given a rousing welcome to College Station, Texas, in 1942, the Texas A&M band and entire cadet corps greeting his arrival at the Southern Pacific depot. He was in town to gather material for a scenario he was writing for the motion picture *We've Never Been Licked*, about the Aggie Twelfth Man (E. King Gill) and how the *Aggie War Hymn* was written by Pinky Wilson. The picture was being produced by Walter Wanger at Universal Studios.

In 1942, Raine worked on the script for *Captains of the Clouds*, one of the first Hollywood pictures to be filmed on location in Canada. A joint production of Warner Brothers, the Royal Canadian Air Force and the Canadian National Film Board, the film spotlighted Canadian pilots during World War I. It was directed by Michael Curtiz, whose next project was *Casablanca*.[306]

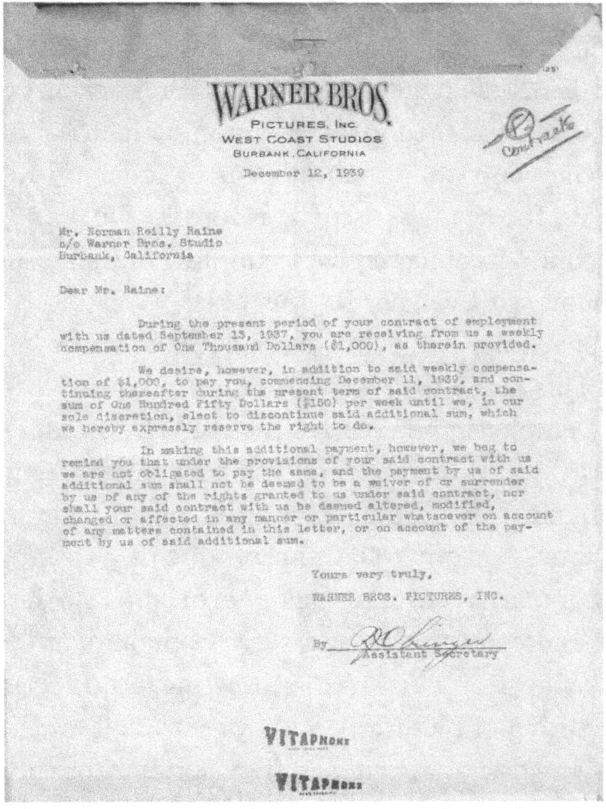

WARNER BROS.
PICTURES, INC.
WEST COAST STUDIOS
BURBANK, CALIFORNIA

December 12, 1939

Mr. Norman Reilly Raine
c/o Warner Bros. Studio
Burbank, California

Dear Mr. Raine:

During the present period of your contract of employment with us dated September 13, 1937, you are receiving from us a weekly compensation of One Thousand Dollars ($1,000), as therein provided.

We desire, however, in addition to said weekly compensation of $1,000, to pay you, commencing December 11, 1939, and continuing thereafter during the present term of said contract, the sum of One Hundred Fifty Dollars ($150) per week until we, in our sole discretion, elect to discontinue said additional sum, which we hereby expressly reserve the right to do.

In making this additional payment, however, we beg to remind you that under the provisions of your said contract with us we are not obligated to pay the same, and the payment by us of said additional sum shall not be deemed to be a waiver of or surrender by us of any of the rights granted to us under said contract, nor shall your said contract with us be deemed altered, modified, changed or affected in any manner or particular whatsoever on account of any matters contained in this letter, or on account of the payment by us of said additional sum.

Yours very truly,

WARNER BROS. PICTURES, INC.

By _________________________
Assistant Secretary

This 1939 letter outlining a contract extension is attached to a typical contract Norman Reilly Raine had with Warner Brothers Pictures in Burbank, Calif. (Drew collection)

Warner Brothers Contracts

Raine created a scrapbook of news articles about *Tugboat Annie*, clipped mostly from Seattle and Hollywood newspapers.[307]

After his dialog assignment on *Tugboat Annie*, Raine had found a more permanent employer: Warner Brothers.

He was initially represented by the New York literary agency Brandt & Brandt[308] — the same firm that promoted Booth Tarkington, Rafael Sabatini and Stephen Vincent Benet.

After an initial contract with Warner Brothers, Raine signed with a new agent, Harold Nordling Swanson, whose office was at 9018 Sunset Blvd., West Hollywood. Swanson (1899-1991) also represented F. Scott Fitzgerald, William Faulkner, Ernest Haycox, Frank Gruber, Ross Macdonald, Raymond Chandler, Steve Fisher and Cornwell Woolrich, among dozens of others.[309] Raine mostly consulted with the agency's associate Dorothy Duncan.[310]

Several contracts at hand give a sampling of Raine's negotiations and agreements with Warner Brothers.[311]

• A 17-page pact dated 14 March 1936 contains 26 numbered provisions. This is the first: "The Producer [Warner Bros. Pictures Inc.] hereby employs and engages the Author to render his exclusive services for and during the period of this agreement in and about its business of producing motion pictures and/or without talking sequences or other sound reproducing accompaniment or synchronization, as a writer of dialogue, original stories, scenarios, adaptations and continuities, as a supervisor, and, at the option of Producer, to direct or assist in the directing, co-directing, cutting, titling and editing of pictures, and to perform all other duties pertaining to the work of a writer, supervisor, and/or director, upon the express condition that all the duties, obligations and agreements assumed or entered into by the Author shall be fully performed and kept by him."

His compensation is to be $700 a week for 52 weeks.

Following sections are largely boilerplate. Warner Brothers spells out its right to lend out the Author to other studios. There is a built-in option to extend the contract for another 52 weeks at the rate of $800 per week. A second extension would be for $900 per week. The Author may write for publication, but the Producer has the right of first refusal to produce a motion picture based on the material.

• A 12 December 1939 document bumps Raine's compensation to $1,000 a week plus an additional discretionary $150 a week. By letter 5 February 1940, Warner Brothers extended the contract another 52 weeks, at $1,150 per week. These papers and others are bound to an earlier 16-page, 13 September 1937 contract. There is also a one-page Office Memorandum dated 21 September 1937 from Alan J. Miller of Swanson suggesting changes to the proposed contract renewal that year.

• A 24-page 10 March 1940 document with riders is for 104 weeks at $1,500 per week compensation, the annual equivalent of $3,320,705 in 2022 dollars.[312]

Raine's work "off campus" is evident by the various film releases by other studios.

• A 7 January 1942 letter notes he is to complete his work for Walter Wanger Productions before taking his annual allowed 12-week leave.[313] This is in addition to a 22 August 1941 letter from Warner Brothers' executive offices.

• A 26 January 1944 agreement notes in legalese that only one other film, *Tugboat Annie Sails Again,* was made as allowed under a four-picture arrangement spelled out in the 1939 contract, now opted to select the following enumerated short stories, which said short stories are numerically equal to the number of motion pictures unproduced by us, to wit: 'Mr. Bullwinkle Earns His Pay,' 'Tugboat Annie Blows a Man Down,' 'Welcome Home.' "

• A 1972 letter from P.D. Knecht, chief counsel, West Coast, Warner Bros. Inc., to Elizabeth Raine, the writer's second wife, who was living 1652 South Curson, Los Angeles, noting that of her late husband's original assignment of 18 stories for film purposes, 14 of those stories were reconveyed to him. "The picture 'Tugboat Annie Sails Again' was sold in 1956 and is now owned by United Artists

Corporation, which also owns the rights to the underlying story entitled 'Tugboat Annie Sails Again.'

"The other 3 stories listed in the letter of January 26, 1944 to Mr. Raine were never produced by Warner Brothers and I believe are still owned by Warner Brothers.

"Thus it would appear from the files that Mr. Raine acquired full ownership of 14 of the 18 stories (I believe there are some other 'Tugboat Annie' stories owned by M-G-M which he may or may not have gotten back), so that he, or his successors, could license the production of motion pictures and television films based upon stories not owned by either United Artists or Warner Brothers."

• Attached to that letter are other communications between Warner Brothers and Raine/Swanson, specifying the original 18 stories conveyed were: "Old Mefoozelum," "A Man of Few Words," "When Greek Meets Greek," "The Last Laugh," "Iron John," "Mr. Bullwinkle Earns His Pay," "Welcome Home," "If the Cap Fits," "Tugboat Annie Saws Off a Log," "Tugboat Annie Blows a Man Down," "Tugboat Annie Borrows Six Bits," "The Other Cheek," "A Matter of Business," "Captain Terry Comes Through," "A Great Day for Mahoney," "Horse of a Different Color," "Tugboat Annie Sails Again" and "Tat for Tat."[314]

Besides these documents, of course, there were ones for Universal, Columbia, Republic and others.

The documents confirm Raine was a contract screenwriter; if a movie became a big hit, it was reflected in the next contract negotiations.

"I don't believe in waiting for inspiration. I go to the office at 10 o'clock in the morning and work until 4 o'clock whether I feel like it or not. Having once been a newspaper reporter, I have learned to write at any time."

— Norman Reilly Raine, "Back in Secoma,"
Seattle Sunday Times, 21 August 1932

Chapter 13

Screenplays 1933-1960

Norman Reilly Raine and co-writers took home Oscars in 1937 for *The Life of Emile Zola*. (Publicity poster)

As Raine and co-writers Heinz Herald and Geza Herczeg "approached the task of writing the screenplay [for *The Life of Emile Zola*] they were under the handicap of having too much story material," according to a reviewer in *Hollywood Speculator*. "To keep the busy life of Zola within the limits of a motion picture was no easy task. But they committed the fault of not balancing evenly their condensation and their elaboration. The result is a picture which is too long for those who view pictures for their story content and not with an eye to its technical merit. Another difficulty the writers faced was the fact of our knowing at the outset what was going to happen. The Dreyfus Affair is history, and there can be no surprises in its retelling … The elaborate and brilliantly presented court room sequence was for the purpose of showing the unfairness of the trial of Zola. Witness after witness was used to register a fact which was planted by the first one. If the story had been fiction, so many witnesses might have been permissible, but as we knew in advance how the trial had ended, hint of the unfairness would have been sufficient...."[315]

The critic praised actor Paul Muni's depiction but doubted the picture's success.

Raine may have had doubts himself.

But it became the highlight of Raine's Hollywood career when he received an Academy Award in 1938. He and Joyce were in the audience, their first time at an Academy of Motion Picture Arts and Sciences ceremony.

"He was discussing the next award when his name rang out and filmdom's assembled royalty broke into applause," according to journalist Harry "Hye" Bossin. "To Norman Reilly Raine for the best screen play of the year, 'The Life of Emile Zola,' announced the chairman. Then came the names of the other two who collaborated. There isn't one among Hollywood's toiling thousands who wouldn't pass up the Kohinoor Diamond for the miniature gold statue that symbolizes this hoor.

"The red-headed Canuck was so frozen to his chair that they had to pry him loose for the march to the head table and the coveted trophy."

Raine had no inkling that the Oscar would be his. Academy rules, in fairness to Hollywood's 400 newspaper correspondents, call for strict secrecy until the Academy dinner.

"Raine thought highly of 'Zola.' It won several awards besides the one Raine helped bring in. But he hadn't included himself in his surmises."[316]

The Life of Emile Zola, a Warner Brothers production, starred Muni and Gloria Holden and was directed by William Dieterle. The film also won the best picture award.

This poster promoted the French version of
Les Adventures de Robin des Bois. (Promotional)

Raine, according to Bossin, had "one of Hollywood's rarer contracts — a long-term one without option clauses. The option clause permits the studio to drop you at any sixth month."

Actor Muni's agent Herald and German expatriate writer Herczeg at producer Hal Wallis's request turned an 18-page treatment about journalist and novelist Émile Zola's defense of French officer Alfred Dreyfus, who was unjustly convicted of treason, into a 200-page script that would have run three hours. Raine took the draft and condensed and shaped it to prize-winning quality.

Raine, according to Matthew Bernstein, "specialized in 'conversion narratives' depicting solipsistic characters [such as Robin Hood] who suddenly discover a greater purpose in their lives; in his award-winning [Zola] script, Raine spent nearly half of the film portraying the title character as a complacent, successful writer, stirred from his smug existence by the injustice of the Dreyfus affair."[317]

A Self-Adopted Canadian

Two decades later, "On the Square" columnist Hy Bossin remarked to Raine that Canada took minimal notice to his winning the Oscar.

"Canada seems to have less appreciation for Hollywood than Hollywood has for Canada" came the reply. "It appears that there exists an indifference at home to the doings of the film capital. They won't take Hollywood seriously. Yet hundreds of Canadians work here in every branch of the industry and are thoroughly welcome. Dozens have distinguished themselves. The world honors them, but Canada pays little attention."[318]

Raine told Bossin, " 'Home' for me will always be spelled 'Toronto'; and I cannot tell you how pleased I was when I learned that the [Tugboat Annie television] series would be produced there."[319]

Welford Beaton, editor of *Hollywood Spectator*, had in 1938 taken note of an evolution in Hollywood.

"As motion picture production had become merely a matter of photographing stories or plays, it was logical for producers to employ authors and playwrights to provide them with story material," he wrote. "Many brilliant writers, therefore, came to Hollywood. Many of them have done brilliant work for the screen. The great improvement talkies have made in the last two or three years is a tribute to the excellent workmanship of those who wrote the scripts. Among the recruits from the field of literature is my friend, Norman Reilly Raine, an author with a national reputation in the world of fiction. Since coming to Hollywood he has mastered the technique of talkie writing, has developed enthusiasm for his work and has turned out some excellently constructed scripts."[320]

Another columnist, Frank Filman, in 1941 singled out Raine as a sterling example of talent coming from the north country.

"If you heard a group of people arguing about who should be raked as Canada's outstanding contribution to Hollywood, we'd bet a dime to a diamond that you'd never even hear Norman Reilly Raine mentioned. That's because nobody ever reads or remembers the screen credits. And exploitation departments don't publicize writers. What's glamourous about a typewriter pounder?" [321]

The newsman inquired how Raine ended up in Hollywood with a lucrative Warner Brothers contract.

"You know, I've only had three rejection slips in all my literary life," came the reply. "It's not as easy as it sounds. I had always wanted to write and I determined to do my best. So I set a harsh standard for myself. I wrote and rewrote endlessly, until I was convinced that the article or story represented the best that was in me. Then I sent it out."

Mechanics of Scriptwriting

"One cannot learn how to write scenarios in schools," Raine told Harry Westgate in 1939, "but what one can learn is how to avoid errors in writing. A knowledge of screen construction is an absolute necessity, and this, too, can be learned in school courses teaching the subject."

Westgate added: "Journalism experience is invaluable, as the majority of successful screen writers claim that background. Raine's three and a half years as an able seaman on a tramp ship has proven of considerable aid in writing original stories, particularly those with a sea background, such as 'Tugboat Annie.'

"When a writer is at a loss for story, he doesn't sit around and wait until a stroke of inspiration comes. Waiting for that 'happy day' is a waste of time. Raine imposes regular office hours upon himself regardless of how he feels. He invariably writes several thousand words a day. At least some of this day's effort is good enough to use in the story he is working on.

"Laughingly, Raine said, 'I have done some of my best work while suffering from a stomach ache or some such ailment. Of course, this probably was due to taking my work more seriously under these unusual conditions.'

"Concentration upon the story doesn't stop after office hours. Raine sometimes thinks of situations to put into his story at home, or even on the golf course. Often Raine will get ideas that cannot be used for the story he is writing at the time, so he files them way for future use.

"One can visit a waterfront, logging camp, or even sit an hour in a hotel lobby and absorb enough atmosphere to give rise to a story. Raine recalled a dense fog one time in Puget Sound, in which it was almost impossible to see his hand before his face. In a sea story, he could picture such a situation by remembering his experience in a fog.

"When Raine uses material with which he is unfamiliar, for instance a scene which takes place in the operating room of a hospital, he tries to visualize the atmosphere of the setting. He might recall an operation he was once subject to and in that way write from experience, or he might visit an operating room until he was thoroughly saturated with the atmosphere of blood."

In writing the screenplay for *The Adventures of Robin Hood*, he consulted reference and other books. He molded the character to fit the swashbuckling personality of the star, Errol Flynn.

It is critical the screenwriter understand the elements of tragedy, drama, comedy and so on "to know where and when to place these elements of story structure. To understand these elements is an essential fundamental of story writing. After all, to become a master of the trade, one must know his tools," Raine said. [322]

Hard-Working Screen Scribes

Considerable work went into historical subjects particularly. Heinz Herald and Geza Herczeg spent seven months in initial research. Raine picked up from there, he told Harry Coulter: "The creation of characters such as Zola and Dreyfus is a 50-50 proposition between the writers and the actors and director. There was such a wealth of material, however, that it was more a process of elimination than of creating. Therefore, we used only material that would further the dramatic action of the story."[323]

As an example, the writer gave Zola an eye for selecting good lobsters when going to market — as a human touch. Zola was often irritable — as would be anyone suffering a serious cold.

J.E. Smyth in *Reconstructing American Historical Cinema* includes Raine with a group of screenwriters who "had more autonomy and power over film production than directors did. At the time, the power of a writer was often connected to his or her status as a historical screenwriter."[324]

The screenwriter was usually on set, on call to make changes as needed.

As to Raine's power, sometimes yes, sometimes no.

The writer appealed to producer Hal Wallis about changes director Michael Curtiz had made in his *Zola* script: "It is hard to understand why the studio assigns a professional writer in whom the studio presumes to have confidence, then lets his judgment be over-ridden by a director with an imperfect knowledge of English."[325]

In a letter to Wallis dated 7 September 1937, Raine on another matter voiced concern about filming scenes in Chico, 350 miles from Los Angeles, due to likely autumn rain there slowing progress and increasing costs. "Do you think that the locations there are so vastly superior to the ones we can secure down here in [Lake] Sherwood?"[326] he asked.

Curtiz prevailed.

On location at Bidwell Park in Chico, making last-minute script revisions for *The Adventures of Robin Hood*, Raine complained 23 September 1937 about director William "Keighley's sincere but misguided attempts, further to bugger up Robin Hood...."

Raine pleaded to producer Hal Wallis to remove a jousting tournament inserted by William Keighley, who was co-director with Curtiz.[327]

Raine prevailed. Lances were dropped.

Advantages of the park setting allowed numerous changes to the script, and Raine on this rare occasion was at the set. [328]

Wallis heard from Raine again 4 January 1939, regarding the making of *Each Dawn I Die,* being directed by Curtiz, later replaced by Keighley. Raine didn't want to dilute the character of hard-boiled crime reporter Frank Ross played by James Cagney. But the star wanted to soften his screen image. "What audiences love about the guy is that they get instant blistering, crackling action from him the moment his toes are stepped on."[329]

Modest compromise. Cagney, who was first cast to play the part of imprisoned gangster Stacey, switched roles with fellow actor George Raft.

On another occasion, "Norman Reilly Raine, writer on 'Captain Kidd,' is practically in jail," Hedda Hopper reported in 1945. "You can't reach him by phone, and you have to go through three offices to get at him. One of the last hurdles is the room of Producer Benedict Bogeaus himself. They want to start next Monday, and with a finished script."[330]

Raines' humor showed in a guest editorial for 20th Century Fox's *Action* publication for September 1943. It begins: "THIS, brothers and sisters, was to be a very profound piece. Something, I decided last night when about to hit the hay, about the importance, if any, of writers to the Motion Picture Industry. It would contain such erudite and pungent and even witty ideas, I thought, as I pulled back the counterpane, that producers and even directors would realize instantly the uselessness of claiming credit for the, Something — and that is as far as I got, because, resting neatly between pillow and folded-over sheet, was a gift. A neatly molded and dried-out little ball of Gaines's dog food...."

The rest is about his wire-haired terrier, Mickey, and other dogs he has known.

Now Showing

This list of Raine's Hollywood work was assembled from print and online sources:

Tugboat Annie (MGM, 1933) theme and characters, additional dialogue. Screenplay was by Zelda Sears and Eve Greene.

White Woman (Paramount, 1933) screenplay by Samuel Hoffenstein and Gladys Lehman, based on the play *Hangman's Whip* by Raine and Frank Butler. A woman joins her new husband on a jungle rubber plantation in the Congo, "Where men are profane and women calloused."

China Clipper (Warner Brothers/First National, 1936) screenplay by Frank Wead, Raine uncredited additional dialogue. Entrepreneurs struggle to establish an airline to China.

The Gentlemen from Kimbe Whiperley (unproduced, 1936).

Sapphire (1936), an original story by Raine was considered, according to Louella O. Parsons,[331] but apparently not produce by Paramount.

God's Country and the Woman (Warner Brothers, 1937) script with William Jacobs (uncredited), based on the novel by James Oliver Curwood and story by Peter Milne and Charles Belden. Families feud over timber harvesting in the Northwest.

Mountain Justice (Warner Brothers, 1937) script with Luci Ward, featuring George Brent, Josephine Hutchinson and Guy Kibbee. An Appalachian woman finds romance.

The Life of Emile Zola (Warner Brothers, 1937) script with Geza Herczeg and Heinz Herald, based on their story. Biograph of the French author.

The Perfect Specimen (Warner Brothers, 1937) script with Lawrence Riley, Brewster Morse and Fritz Falkenstein, based on a story by Samuel Hopkins Adams. A man raised in luxurious isolation ventures into the real world.

The Adventures of Robin Hood (Warner Brothers, 1938) script with Seton L. Miller. Numerous scenes were shot on Warners' Sound Stage 25 (as were *Casablanca* and *Batman Returns*) and for a dozen years it served as the set for television's *The Big Bang Theory.* The hero of Sherwood Forest battles the Sheriff of Nottingham.

Men Are Such Fools (Warner Brothers, 1938) script with Horace Jackson and Stanley Logan (uncredited), based on a *Saturday Evening Post* story by Faith Baldwin. Raine, to get the psychology of his script correct regarding "how the business girl of today actually behaves on the job," polled 2,200 women employees of Warner Brothers asking nine questions such as Do you dress to please your boss? Does he know it? Do you use men's brains to help you in creative work? Do you 'lean on' men who have equal rank in your organization? Do you ask men to cover up your mistakes? Do you date your boss? Raine told a journalist the "idea was suggested by his secretary — who is the first girl on the lot who refused to answer."[332] The romantic comedy is set at an advertising agency.

The Career of Sarah Bernhardt (1938) According to columnist Louella O. Parsons, "Jack Warner has ordered Norman Reilly Raine to write the film biography of the great tragedienne." Bette Davis was to be featured[333] as the French actress.

He was considered to write a script for Sigmund Romberg's 1926 operetta Desert Song,[334] but nothing came of it. Warner Brothers produced *Desert Song* in 1943, with other writers.

The Oklahoma Kid (Warner Brothers, 1939) script with Jerome Odlum (uncredited), Warren Duff, Robert Buckner and Edward E. Paramore Jr., based on story by Paramore and Wally Kline. The Land Rush oater featured Humphrey Bogart and James Cagney.

Each Dawn I Die (Warner Brothers, 1939) script with Warren Duff and Charles Perry (uncredited), based on Jerome Odlum's novel of the same title. Raine visited San Quentin as part of his research.[335] A corrupt district attorney frames an ambitious big-city journalist.

Island of Lost Men (Paramount, 1939) Horace McCoy and William R. Lipman, based on *Hangman's Whip* by Raine and Butler. A woman singer searches for her Chinese father in the Malaysian jungles.

The Private Lives of Elizabeth and Essex (Warner Brothers, 1939) script with Aeneas MacKenzie, based on Maxwell Anderson's stage play *Elizabeth the Queen*. One working title was *The Knight and the Lady*, announced as featuring Errol Flynn and Bette Davis.[336]

He reportedly was to work in 1939 on a *The Life of Beethoven* script (to feature Paul Muni), but it did not materialize.[337]

Indianapolis Speedway (Warner Brothers, 1939) script by Sig Herzig and Wally Klein, revisions by Raine. Working title was *The Roaring Road*. The action centers on the famed race track.

Tugboat Annie Sails Again (Warner Brothers, 1940) story and characters. Screenplay by Walter DeLeon. An advertising copywriter had a sense of humor: "The S.S. Fun (Tugboat Annie, skipper; Horatio Bullwinkle, first hate), decks tomorrow at this theatre. Don't miss what Annie would call 'the celegration!'"[338]

The Fighting 69th (Warner Brothers, 1940) script with Fred Niblo Jr. and Dean Franklin (working title *Father Duffy of the Fighting Sixty-Ninth*). A heroic World war I Infantry unit is featured.

The Gentlemen from Kimberley (1936) apparently unproduced, or at least not under this name, 147-page draft in Norman Reilly Raine Collection, Boston University.

Santa Fe (Warner Brothers, 1940) One iteration, *Diary of the Santa Fe Trail*, was scripted by Raine based on a diary by Captain Stanley.[339] The Warner Brothers release, scripted by Robert Buckner, starred Errol Flynn as J.E.B. "Jeb" Stuart and Olivia de Havilland as his romantic interest Kit Carson Holliday. The storyline is critical of abolitionist John Brown (Raymond Massey).

Captain Horatio Hornblower (Warner Brothers, 1939) uncredited; newspapers reported Raine's involvement with Aeneas MacKenzie.[340] The action takes place during the Napoleonic wars.

Benjamin Franklin (1939) Raine and Aeneas MacKenzie were assigned to write a script for a bio-pic for Earners, to feature Edward G. Robinson. But MGM had something in mind at the same time with Spencer Tracy.[341] So no-go.

Virginia City (Warner Brothers, 1940) assist on script by Robert Bruckner and Howard Koch. Screenwriter Buckner complained to Producer Hal Wallis about, among other things, revisions made by Raine with Director Michael Curtiz' instructions, using Libby Prison in the opening scene, rather than riders on a stagecoach, as Buckner had written. The prison intro remained. A Union soldier escapes a Confederate lockup and heads west.

The Sea Wolf (Warner Brothers, 1941) script with Abem Finkel based on Jack London novel about a brutal ship captain played by Edward G. Robinson.

Footsteps in the Dark (1941) Raine worked on one version of the script,[342] based on two plays, *Footsteps in the Dark* (1935) by Ladislas Fodor and *Blondie White* (1937) by Bernard Merivale and Jeffrey Dell. The final script is credited to Lester Cole and John Wexley. A banker writes lurid detective novels on the side.

Captains of the Clouds (Warner Brothers, 1942) script with Arthur T. Horman and Richard Macaulay, based on their story, working title *Bush Pilots*. It looks at brash Canadian fliers who enlist in the Royal Canadian Air Force.

Eagle Squadron (Universal, 1942) based on a C.S. Forester story. Raine accompanied Walter Wanger to England to "view scenes already made by a Wanger photographic unit attached to the Eagle squadron of the RAF and Raine will finish his script in London," according to a news report.[343] It features American pilots and the Battle of Britain.

Yankee Cavalcade aka *Goodbye Nellie Gray* aka *Goodbye Dollie Gray* (1942), unproduced treatments based on the life of Edith Wilson.

Sons and Soldiers (MGM, 1943) Raine returned to this studio after five years to script an Everett Riskin production based on Irvin Shaw's *Labor for the Wind*, which had run on Broadway. It was to feature Geraldine Fitzgerald, but apparent was not made.

We've Never Been Licked (Universal, 1943) script with Nick Grinde, based on Raine's "The Fighting Sons of Texas A.&M.," released as *Texas to Tokyo* in the United Kingdom, also known as *Texas Aggies* and *Fighting Command*. Raine lectured on writing at Texas A&M Press Club the year before as part of his visit "gathering material on which to base forthcoming screen story, *American Youth Has Never Been Licked*."[344] War picture.

Ladies Courageous (Walter Wanger Productions, 1944) script with Doris Gilbert, from a Virginia Spencer Cowles novel; working title *When Ladies Fly*. World War II Women's Air Service pilots are featured.

Wing and a Prayer (20th Century Productions, 1944) Raine & Erskine Caldwell wrote a draft script *Torpedo Squadron 8*, a historically factual account of the Battle of Midway which was reconfigured into a fictionalized story by 20th Century Studios and director Henry Hathaway, Jeremy Cady writing the final script.

Nob Hill (20th Century Productions, 1945) script with Wanta Tuchock, adapting a Eleanore Griffin story. George Raft is a Barbary Coast saloonkeeper.

Captain Tugboat Annie (Republic, 1945) theme and characters. George Callahan supplied the screenplay.

The Bells of St. Mary's (RKO, 1945) Raine lunched with director Leo McCarey to discuss the Bing Crosby/Ingrid Bergman pic, Hedda Hopper reported,[345] but Dudley Nichols ended up writing the script based on a story by director Leo McCarey. The musical comedy-drama reprises Crosby's priestly role from *Going My Way*.

Romantic Life of Charles Dickens (1945) Raine was reportedly preparing a Warner Brothers screenplay incorporating Charles Dickens' "Life of Christ," once he was done with *Captain Kidd*.[346] It would be a Benedict Bogeaus production featuring Charles Laughton.

A Bell for Adano (20th Century Productions, 1945) script with Lamar Trotti, based on a John Hersey novel. An Italian village is rebuilt after the war.

Captain Kidd (United Artists, 1945) script from a story by Robert N. Lee. Charles Laughton played the historic pirate in a picture that also featured Randolph Scott and Barbara Britton. "When Ben Bogeaus proposed that I play Captain kid for him, I said, 'Have you got a script?' Whereupon he placed in my hands a literary creation by Norman Reilly Raine which, in my opinion, is as fine a contribution to screen literature as you'll uncover in a month's search...," Laughton told Hedda Hopper.[347]

Day of the Conquerors, Niven Busch's novel about soldiers returning from World War II duty, got a Raine treatment in 1946 but apparently found no studio support.

Unconquered (Paramount, 1946) uncredited, adaptation of a novel by Neil Swanson, revising Fritz Lang's script for his 1931 version. Pauline Goddard and Gary Cooper starred in the frontier epic.[348]

A Miracle Can Happen (1946) Hedda Hopper announced Raine and John O'Hara would co-script the pic, to feature Jimmy Stewart and Henry Fonda.[349] It apparently was released in 1948 as *On Our Merry Way*, with other writers.

Personal Column (1947), a psychological mystery, was scripted by Raine, as Warner Brothers and producers James Nasser and Henry Kesler sought actress Joan Leslie to star.[350] Leo Rosten eventually did the screenplay and Lucille Ball was featured in the crime drama.

Case of Millie Pearson (MGM, 1948) original screenplay for a Skid Row bargirl film (not produced), to feature Angela Lansbury.

Streets of Laredo (Paramount, 1949) uncredited story about three outlaws.

M (Columbia, 1951) script with Leo Katcher, additional dialogue by Waldo Salt. Joseph Losey directed this child killer drama, a remake of Fritz Lang's 1931 original.

Custer's Last Stand (not produced) Raine told Bennett Cerf of a commission from a Hollywood mogul that went through seven iterations and still was turned down. " 'I really slaved over this last script. It's the best I can do. Just what is there about it that displeases you?' 'I'll tell you,' confided the magnate slowly. 'I … hate … Indians!'"[351]

Woman of the North Country (Republic Pictures, 1952) script adapting a story by Charles Marquis Warren and Prescott Chaplin. Gale Storm and Rod Cameron were among actors in this story, working title *Minnesota*, of a mining empire in the Misabi Mountains.

The World in His Arms (Universal, 1952) script with Frank Richardson Pierce, based on a Rex Beach novel, working title *Seal Poacher*. A Russian countess flees an arranged marriage in San Francisco in the 1850s.

Kangaroo (20th Century Productions, 1952) Raine in 1949 worked on a script variously known as *The Land Down Under* and *Sundowner*, later *The Bushranger*, drawing from an original story by Martin Berkley, but the material was largely scrapped and Harry Kleiner is credited as the writer upon release.

Sea of Lost Ships (Republic, 1953) story only, Steve Fisher screenplay. The story is about Coast Guard sailors.

Born in Freedom: The Story of Colonel Drake (American Petroleum Institute, 1954) short about the discovery of underground petroleum.

We Who Serve (1958), short directed by Wilhelm Thiele, set at an American Legion convention.

The American Doctor (National Osteopathic Museum/Ronald Reed Productions, 1960) about Dr. Andrew Taylor Still and the development of osteopathy.

Raine through the Swanson agency apparently discussed writing a screenplay for producer John McCadden for a Treasure Island feature, but there's no further information.[352]

The Story of Dr. Lister (Warner-Lambert Pharmaceutical, 1965), directed by Arthur Pierson.

The Norman Reilly Raine Collection at Boston University also includes outlines for *The Angel of Dien Bien Phu* and *Gangway.*

"All I do is go to the greasy spoons on the waterfront, take a seat and listen. I get ideas and plots and all. And if I've pulled some boner the guys give me hell."[353]

— "He gave us 'Tugboat Annie,'"
Seattle Daily Times, 30 July 1971

Chapter 14

Print Fiction 1924-1963

Raine returned from his 1920s overseas ventures and one day "burst into *Maclean's* with a series of short stories so vividly the editors of some of the largest publications in the United States sat up and took notice," the magazine's editors said.[354]

The awe shows in this blurb: "NORMAN REILLY RAINE, author of 'Mutiny,' in his wandering across the world, brought up, one day, in a tiny Arab town in the Anglo-Egyptian Sudan, where the Nubian Desert dips its parched hem in the waters of the Red Sea. As a result, in a month or two there will appear in *MacLean's* a novelette, a two-part serial, 'The Pariah Dog,' a fast-action story of mystery and intrigue, involving a charming English girl; the British officers of a Sudanese Camel Corp; Egyptians, dogged little fellaheen soldiers; the wild, raiding tribesmen of the desert; Baggara Arabs; Bedouins; and those fanatic fighting men made famous in Kipling's 'Fuzzy-Wuzzy,' the Hatendoas. *MacLean's* editor has no hesitation in recommending this tale to its readers as probably the best Mr. Raine has yet written."[355]

Raine's first magazine contribution had been a factual piece, "Pearl of the South Seas," for Canadian National Railways' *Canadian Magazine*, 1 August 1922, about sailing into Tahiti. His first work for *Maclean's* was another non-fiction article, "Sunlight Through Shadow" (1 March 1923), about mental healthcare in Canada.

Then he began writing fiction....

Bones of a Story

Raine explained to *The Editor* readers in 1924 how he crafted an idea into publishable prose.

"Captain Spring, master of the *Canadian Britisher* bound from Vancouver to Bombay, drawled a yarn about a small-time ship owner with a regular route carrying horses from Australia to India. A larger competitor began to constantly undercut him in pricing for the return trade in jute. But the businessman didn't wither, he prospered. How? He invested in jute manufacturing at both ends, in Calcutta and in Australia, and took advantage of his competitor's rates.

"Here was the skeleton for a short story, complete in itself, and needing only flesh and clothing to present to the public," Raine wrote. "When I tackled the writing of it some weeks after Captain Spring related it, the first problem was to localize it in juxtaposition with the markets for which I write. True, the yarn might have been left in its original setting without detracting from its story value, but why not, if possible, add interest. By bringing the scene more closely home to the bulk of my Canadian and American readers? This question was answered by placing the main action in Montreal, a city more or less familiar to most North Americans, which conveyed a more vivid mental picture, even to those who never had been there, than any Australian port could do.

"The keynote of the story was latent power, unsuspected, and brought to the surface through opposition. This thesis must be developed in the main character. It is my custom to write of people with whom I am acquainted, garbing and changing them to conform to requirements, but with a familiar basis which is of tremendous assistance in conveying reality and building dialogue. Thus, the central figure, Oliver Johns, was written around a former fellow-officer in my old regiment, stout, good natured and easy-going to the point of laxness, but with a most astou8nding recklessness and tenacity in battle.

"In contrast against Johns' outward lethargy, was created Old Man Winter, head of a gigantic Montreal shipping combine; a colossal figure, ruthless in business, merciless over opposition.

"Here were the two main figures, strongly drawn and detailed. The supplementary cast was sketched only sufficiently to balance each one's part in working out the plot, and the story was carried on as in the original anecdote; but in order to make convincing the idea of a great ship-owner (essentially a business man) being willing to go to any length, even against his most deeply rooted commercial instincts, to put Johns out of commission, it was necessary to create individual antagonism and vindictiveness as well. This was done in the beginning of the story, by Johns becoming engaged to Marion Winter against her father's will. Old Man Winter then had a keen personal interest in smashing the younger man."[356]

Raine used a variation on this ploy in his 1930 story "Dandy Man."

The writer offered a truism — "that burning inspiration and a Pegasus flight of fancy are not essential to the construction of a workmanlike story. Not that I am decrying the value of spontaneous thought; but I have written in all climates, at all hours of the twenty-four, in the nervous tension of a morning paper city-room, with the last edition shrieking to be put to bed, and during long leisurely days on a summer sea...."

Byron H. Christian in an essay, "Getting Through to Newspaper Readers," conveyed advice given him by Robert W. Jones, professor of journalism at the University of Washington: "Just tell what the folks said. Just tell what the folks did."

Christian, who taught journalism at the same school, said he looked for "that touch in a student's story that indicates a painstaking search for colorful statement ... Norman Reilly Raine of Tugboat Annie fame told me he spent an hour coming up with the phrase, 'the insect threnody of a jungle night.'"[357]

Raine kept in touch with compatriots old and new. He spoke on the subject of short stories at the California Writers Club's 6th Annual Writers' Conference in Oakland in 1960.[358]

He told attendees if they write for a living, they can't wait for inspiration. They must pursue it.[359]

On the Newsstands

Tugboat Annie and the author's two other series characters have been covered. Here's a list of Raine's other published short fiction and a handful of novels:

"Canada Expects," *The Sailor*, June 1922.

"Heritage" (*Maclean's*, 14 April 1924) (*Adventure*, 10 May 1924) (*20-Story Magazine*, June 1924) Johnnie Barker is a member of the "flea-bitten, hard-working, hard swearing fraternity, the marine fireman" and, having quit the Blue Funnel ship *Tyndareus* out of Liverpool, stows away on the *Paladin*, headed toward Suez. Discovered, he is assigned by the "Deucer," the second engineer, to the hottest, dirtiest job on the ship.

"And David Took Thence a Stone" (*Everybody's Magazine*, September 1924) (*Maclean's*, 1 September 1924)

"Mutiny" (*Sea Stories Magazine*, April 1925) (*Maclean's*, 1 November 1925)

"Seven Days" (*Maclean's*, 1 July 1925)

"The Captain's Holiday" (*Maclean's*, 15 July 1925) (*Sea Stories Magazine*, December 1925)

"The Lonely Passenger" (*Maclean's*, 15 January 1926)

"The Argonauts" (*Maclean's*, 15 April 1926) (*New Stories for Men*, Charles Grayson, ed. Doubleday, Doran, 1941)

"The Pariah Dog" (*Cassell's Magazine of Fiction*, April 1925) (*Maclean's*, 1 June & 15 June 1926)

"Silver Night" (*Maclean's*, 1 May 1926)

"The Wind-Ship Man" (*20-Story Magazine*, July 1926) (*Maclean's*, 1 October 1926) (*The Shrine Magazine*, October 1926)

"The Sing-Song Girl" (*Maclean's*, 15 December 1926) (*London*, August 1926)

"The Trimmer of the Ispahan" (*Maclean's*, 15 July 1927) (*Toronto Star Weekly*, 16 July 1927) (*Chicago Sunday Tribune*, 17 July 1927)

"The Little Things" (*Maclean's*, 1 August 1927) (*20-Story Magazine*, September 1927) "The Little Things; A Story of Heroism on a Hoodooed Ship" (*Adventure*, 1 May 1928)

"The Blood Feud" (*Saturday Evening Post*, 5 November 1927) (*The Goat*, Guild of the Royal Canadian Dragoons, December 1927 and November 1933)

"Funky Villiers" (*Maclean's*, 15 November 1927)

"Care to Lay a Little Wager?" (*Elks Magazine*, December 1927)

"What'll You Bet?" (*Maclean's*, 15 January 1928)

"Czar of Waitaea" (*Canadian Magazine*, February 1928)

"Stone House" (*Maclean's*, 1 April 1928)

"Deep Water Mate" (*Maclean's*, 1 October 1928) (*Sweetwater, Storms and Spirits: Stories of the Great Lakes* ed. Victoria Brehm, University of Michigan Press, 1991)

"A Simple Man" (*Liberty*, 28 July 1928)

"The Creed of the Desert" as by Captain N.R. Raine (*Boys' Life*, November & December 1928, January 1929)

"Master of His Ship" (*Short Stories*, 25 November 1928) (*Short Stories* UK early April 1929)

"A Fresh-Water Mate" (*20-Story Magazine*, December 1928)

"Home for Christmas" (*Canadian Home Journal*, December 1928)

"Seventy Below" (*Everybody's Magazine*, March 1929)

"The Chinese Ring" (*Maclean's*, 1 April 1929)

"A Valor-Ruined Man" (*Adventure*, 15 April 1929) "A Valour-Ruined Man" (*Windsor Magazine* No. 414, June 1929)

"Doctor Lamartaine's Wife" (*Everybody's Combined with Romance*, June 1929)

"Fresh-Water Ways" (*Sea Stories*, June 1929)

"The Hide-Out" (*Detective Fiction Weekly*, 8 June 1929)

"Old Dog" (*Maclean's*, 15 July 1929)

"Outward Bound" (*Maclean's*, 15 August 1929) (*Argosy* UK February 1936)

"The Wind" (*Everybody's Combined with Romance*, October 1929)

"The Supercargo" (*London Sunday Dispatch*, 7 October 1928)

"The Sixth Man," *Saturday Evening Post*, 7 November 1929)

"Pariah" (*Saturday Evening Post*, 16 November 1929) as "A Man to Tame the Termagant" (*Pearson's*, April 1930)

"A Stokehold David" (*Popular Magazine*, first December 1929)

"Home from the Sea" (*West Briton and Cornwall Advertiser*, 26 December 1929).

"Old Brimstone Sees It Through," (*Pearson's*, December 1929)

"Go to Toronto!" (*Canadian Magazine*, January 1930)

"The Chief of the Pegasus" (*Blue Book*, February 1930)

"A Man to Tame the Termagant" (*Pearson's Magazine*, April 1930)

"Death at Jack Pine" (*Canadian Magazine*, June through September 1930)

"Tramp Ship" (*MacLean's*, 1 June 1930)

"The Bride Blushes (*Hearst's International Cosmopolitan*, July 1930)

"The Glasgow Keelie" (*Saturday Evening Post*, 30 August 1930)

"The Sixth Man" (*Saturday Evening Post*, 13 September 1930)

"Able Wackets" (*Saturday Evening Post*, 18 October 1930)

"Iron Cross" (*Country Gentleman*, November 1930) (*Pearson's*, 1930)

"Thirty-Five Quid a Month (*Saturday Evening Post*, 31 January 1931)

"Goin' Home" (*Windsor*, February 1931) (*Maclean's*, 15 May 1931)

"Salvage" (*Saturday Evening Post*, 14 June 1931)

"Barratry" (*Saturday Evening Post*, 1 August 1931)

"Singapore Jack" (*Saturday Evening Post*, 19 August 1931) (*Pearson's*, April 1931)

"Windy Bill" (*Collier's*, 20 December 1931)

"Star of the Sea" (*Maclean's*, 1 February 1932)

"Going Home" (*Windsor*, February 1932)

"The Old Shellback" (*Saturday Evening Post*, 11 June 1932)

"Success" (*American Magazine*, December 1934)

"Heads I Win!" (*Saturday Evening Post*, 17 August 1935)

"White Trader" (*Argosy* UK, October 1935)

"The Bride Blushes" (*Cosmopolitan*, July 1936)

"Down to the Seas Again" (*Argosy* UK, November 1936)

Adventures of Robin Hood (Warner Brothers, 1937) novelization based on screenplay

Captain Kid (World, 1945) novelization of screenplay based on story by Robert N. Lee

"Shanghai Stowaway" (*Saturday Evening Post*, 20 March 1950)

"Red Flag on the High Seas" (*Saturday Evening Post*, 4 November 1950)

"Buckskin and Blanket Days" (*Saturday Evening Post*, 24 August 1957)

"Disaster Course" (*Saturday Evening Post*, 16 December 1961)

"Coffin Ship" (*Saturday Evening Post*, 9 & 16 June 1962)

"The Karimata Ghost" (*Argosy*, March 1963) This gritty last-published Raine story is about out-of-shape, out-of-job, alcoholic Welchman Rhys Morgan who stows away on the *Karimata* tramp steamer, hoping to wrangle work as a stoker. He learns the deucer (second mate) and others plan to steal its cargo and sink the ship. Morgan had previous experience on the vessel when it was the *Moenwyn* out of Glasgow, before he was disgraced for a navigational incident. He musters the courage and strength to overcome the deucer, save the young fourth engineer Leahy, close a safety door to shut off the ship's flooding, take it to port and save the insurers a bundle.

Mad Magazine parodied *The Saturday Evening Post* and *Tugboat Annie* in "Tugboat Annie Sinks" in its issue No. 39, distributed in 1938. The heroine is manhandling Captain Kangaroo.

Comics and Comic Books

It seems a missed opportunity for Tugboat Annie to never have been featured in a newspaper comic strip or comic book adaptation.

Here's what has appeared:

Tugboat Tessie is a takeoff on the Secoma heroine. The character is skipper of *Harbor Lady*. Running characters are daughter/First Mate Melody and Captain Bill Jetty. *Seven Seas Comics* ran for six issues published by Leader/Universal Phoenix, 1946-1947. Tugboat

Tessie was in all but No. 4. A seventh, unpublished story survives. The plots were by Manning Lee Stokes (as "Lee Stoken"), art by Alex Blum and Matt Baker.[360]

Mr. District Attorney himself goes undercover with his assistant Harrington to crack a diamond smuggling ring in "Operation Annie K." in the 33rd and final issue of DC's comic book *Mr. District Attorney* in May 1953. The tugboat's name, "Annie K," suggests a tip of the hat to Tugboat Annie. Howard Purcell did pencils, Charles Paris inks on the 6-page story.

"The Saturday Evening Pest" in *Mad Magazine* No. 39 (July 1958) includes a parody, "Tugboat Annie Sinks," written by "Dietrich Dunstan Drizzle" (Tom Koch writer, Bob Clarke artist).[361]

Rival *Cracked* No. 16 (October 1959) mirrored that with a two-page spread of "Magazine covers just a little bit different." A blurb on "The Saturday Evening Pest" touted: "Tugboat Annie Sinks to the Bottom." Jack Davis did the artwork, the text is uncredited.

Mad in its December 1959 number ran a page of bogus covers of merged titles, i.e. *The Saturday Evening Post High Fidelity*, with a promo for "Tugboat Annie Blows Her Woofer."

The year after that, another rival, *Sick*, ran a page of Hollywood caricatures and asked readers to identify them. Eighteen did. Tugboat Annie was one of the mob in the seashore/beach scene.

Bill Griffith's *Zippy Stories* No. 2 in 1977 includes a one-page story, "Tugboat Annie Meets Alan Watts." Watts was an English "philosophical entertainer." Annie's head pops out of a television screen.

In mainstream newspaper funnies, cartoonist Billy DeBeck was prescient in August 1930 in listing "Tugboat Annie" along with "Picklewagon Flannagan" and "Foozle Woozle" and other nags running in the Comic Strip Derby in his *Barney Google* cartoon.[362] (Raine's first short story didn't appear until the next year.)

Beery got more attention from cartoonists than Dressler. Feg Murray's Seein' Stars panel noted Beery was a licensed transport pilot and spelled out his name in a highlighted list of his films.[363]

Wiley Padan in his *It's True!* syndicated panel cartoon in 1939 noted: "The ancient tugboat which carried Marie Dressler and Wallace Beery to fame in 'Tugboat Annie' makes its farewell appearance in MGM's 'Thunder Afloat.'" The same panel added a different anecdote about Beery. Both were illustrated.[364]

A "Tugboat Annie" —Lillian Bunkers, the only woman tugboat dispatcher in the United States, based at Los Angeles harbor — was portrayed in John Hix's *Strange As It Seems* cartoon panel in 1940.[365] When she started 18 years prior, she used flags and megaphone; in 1940, radio telephones in 1940, radio telephones were available.

The Philadelphia manufacturer Budd in a 1946 magazine advertisement captioned cartoonist Helen Hokinson's depiction of a matronly woman with a feathered bonnet standing on a ladder and examining the one of the company's passenger rail cars. "She had the determination of Tugboat Annie," reads the caption, "and she wanted to know! She wanted to know how you can tell a Budd-built car when you see one. How can you know that it's built of stainless steel from end to end, from truck to roof, inside and out — the strongest, safest railroad car built."[366] The reader of course might assume the woman was Ms. Brennan.

John Padgett's *Carriers Who Clicked* panel for 24 November 1950 spotlighted motion picture producer and director Mervyn LeRoy — a one-time newspaper paperboy — noting one of his films was *Tugboat Annie*.

The 24 October 1948 Sunday episode of the Ken Ernst-drawn *Mary Worth* depicts a fading Hollywood actress, Angel Varden, berating her agent: "Okay, Lew! You wired me you had a part for Angel! What is it? ... 'Tugboat Annie?'" (No, actually, it's to play a white goddess of a savage tribe.)

A decade later, the title character and his pal Wash Tubbs listen as a Hollywood agent drones on about movie stars and a remake of *Tugboat Annie* in a panel of the *Captain Easy* newspaper comic strip for 14 December 1982 drawn by Bill Crooks. Writer Mick Casale had a good memory.

A backup feature in the two-issue comic book *Beanbags*, created by Ben Brown (stories and pencils) and David Gantz (inks) and distributed to newsstands by Ziff-Davis in 1952 featured Towline Tillie, skipper of the *Powderhorn*, an obvious facsimile of Tugboat Annie. The feisty pipe-smoking heroine hectors rival *Seacat* chief Bunce Burner.

" 'I'm not like Dressler, and if they had wanted me to imitate her I wouldn't have taken the part,' [Marjorie Rambeau] said. 'I can do my own characterization, and I certainly do feel in the character with these old seagoing clothes and this make-up … No, they haven't tried to age me — just to make me look weather-beaten."

— "Marjorie Rambeau To Create A New
Tugboat Annie," Lima News, 7 July 1940

Chapter 15

Marjorie Rambeau's *Tugboat Annie Sails Again*

Marjorie Rambeau plays Annie and Alan Hale Sr. is Bullwinkle — here bargaining with Charles Halton as Alec Severn — in *Tugboat Annie Sails Again*. (Publicity still)

A sequel to *Tugboat Annie* was nearly a decade in the making. Produced by Warner Brothers, *Tugboat Annie Sails Again* premiered at three theaters during a Tugboat Annie Day event 18 October 1940 in Tacoma.[367]

"Seattle Nixed Stunt" of hosting the premiere, according to *Variety*.[368] Seattle had hosted the 1933 film premiere. As Raine told the *Seattle Sunday Times,* his first Annie story was written in 1930 when he was a resident at the Washington Athletic Club in Seattle.

"Tugboat Annie belongs to no one city," Tacoma Mayor Harry P. Cain placated. "She typifies the indomitable spirit, the resourcefulness, the determination which has made Puget Sound shipping outstanding in the navigation world. While it is true that the character has been inspired by Thea Foss, founder of the Foss Towing Company in Tacoma, the issue involved is a broader one which reflects only credit upon other prominent Puget Sound ports."[369]

Attending the gala from Hollywood were stars Marjorie Rambeau (1889-1970),[370] who played Annie, Alan Hale Sr. (1892-1950) as Bullwinkle, and Ronald Reagan (1911-2004) as Eddie Kent, Annie's protégé. They made personal appearances at the Roxy, Music Box and Blue Mouse theaters.

Roxy manager Walter Feeney with the help of S.A. Perkins, Tacoma Boat Club commodore, organized a tugboat race. There were six entries and a large audience.[371]

Some 750 tugboats and other craft swarmed a water carnival.[372]

"There were 11 surprised convicts at Steilacoom[373] when they got off a northbound train for transfer to McNeil Island penitentiary Friday afternoon," the *Tacoma News Tribune* reported. "They detrained to face a blaring band, a huge crowd and mayor of Steilacoom, who was carrying a foot-long key to the city! A flotilla of yachts, tugs and sailboats was lying alongside the Steilacoom pier. So was the government launch that sped them to the McNeil Island prison.

"The convicts didn't know it, but the crowd was waiting to welcome five movie stars coming to Tacoma for the world premiere this Friday night of 'Tugboat Annie Sails Again.' Since the prisoners were locked in a chartered car since the train left southern California, they didn't know they rode the same train northward….

"Boats of all types from Everett, Olympia, Seattle, Bremerton and other Puget Sound ports were anchored in Commencement Bay here for the day's water carnival and races."[374]

Local celebrities appeared, as described by newspaper columnist Glen Carter: "Three women shared the limelight as 'Annies' at the 1940 Tacoma premiere. As honored guests they were introduced as Mrs. A.L. Walker of Everett, who managed three tugs, Mrs. Anna Grimson,[375] operator of three stern-wheelers out of the Skagit

River and Mrs. Chancey Wyman of Vashon Island who had piloted tugs until her retirement."[376]

Rambeau "signed autographs by the wholesale, posed with all the local dignitaries, received a dozen and one different presents, acted very pleased about the whole thing and carried on in a manner befitting a seasoned trooper," the *Seattle Star* said.[377]

Tacoma Mayor Cain announced "Tugboat Annie Day" would become an annual event[378] and a plaque would establish Tugboat Annie Brennan as "the patron saint of the Puget Sound waterfront."[379]

Rambeau, Reagan, Hale, Donald Crisp and Hedda Hopper posed for a photo op in front of the Roxy Theater, 901 Broadway, to unveil a plaque: "Dedicated to Tugboat Annie — 1940 — Pioneer Spirit of Puget Sound."[380]

Also in the film were Jane Wyman as Peggy Armstrong, Charles Halton as Severn, Victor Kilian as Sam, Paul Hurst as Peter and Chill Wills as Shiftless. James Burkett produced. Lewis Seiler directed.

The picture was released 26 October 1940.

Wedell, Henry and Arthur Foss attended an elaborate party at the Winthrop Hotel. "A highlight of the three-hour banquet and program was a salty talk by Oscar B. Brown, who for fifty years has been a lighthouse keeper, first at Tatoosh Head and later at Brown's Point Light," according to the *Seattle Post-Intelligencer*.

" 'I can remember the old days,' he said, 'when there would be as many as thirty-nine sailing vessels waiting off the straits for tugs to take them into Puget Sound ports.' "

Boat model-builder A.C. Garrison of Tacoma presented one of his sailing ship and tugboat creations to actress Rambeau, who declared them the nicest gifts ever.

The *Tacoma Times* commissioned Homrick artist Cy Simms to depict Rambeau, Hale, Reagan and Wyman in a drawing, which ran in its 17 October 1940 issue.

Rambeau and Hale as Brennan and Bullwinkle are in typical calm discussion in *Tugboat Annie Sails Again*, released in 1940. (Publicity photo)

Finding Annie

As reporter Paul Harrison explained: "Marie Dressler died almost six months ago, and the Tugboat Annie stories bought for her by Metro began to gather dust. For a while it was said that no other actress would replace her in the salty characterization, but the studio began looking around for a successor about the time Grauman's Chinese Theatre moved its box office onto the cement slab containing Miss Dressler's footprints.

"Then began a procession of doughty old dolls who either didn't quite look the part or couldn't act it. Metro sold the movie rights to Warner Brothers[381] and the search continued. Not long ago it almost culminated in the selection of Elsa Maxwell.[382] Then Louise Fazenda, wife of Warners executive producer Hal Wallace, appeared likely. With Beery maybe coming back.[383] Then Alan Hale Sr. was chosen.

Actress Marjorie Rambeau admires a ship model, the gift
of Tacoma's A.C. Garrison. (Richards Studio, 1940)

Former Seattle soprano and grand opera star Alice Gentle, who had appeared in some early Warner talkies, was mentioned as a candidate for the starring role.[384] Likewise Elsa Lancaster.[385] And May Robson.[386] And Elsie Robinson.[387] Hollywood Is Asking columnist Mayme Ober Peak wondered aloud:" "Will Sophie Tucker Take Marie's Place [as tugboat Annie]?"[388]

All were jilted. After a 13-month search the new Tugboat Annie was named: Marjorie Rambeau. "[389]

"I am taking the biggest tumble down the social ladder in history," Rambeau laughed to one interviewer. "From college dean to tugboat battleaxe. And to tell the truth, I like the role of Annie best… I'm the only woman in Hollywood with a legitimate excuse for being fat. If I lose any weight I'm liable to lose my job right along with it…

"But we're staying as close to the real Annie as possible. I'm crazy about the blustering old battle axe. The only thing in the world she really loves is the 'Narcissus,' her boat."[390]

"Hollywood thinks she's a good choice. [391] Seeing and hearing her on the set, you'd be sure of it. Miss Rambeau is a colorful and lusty character in her own right. She's a sort of feminine John Barrymore; there have been a lot of dips and peaks in her career; if she has missed theatrical immortality it's because she has been too busy having fun; but whenever she sets her mind to it she can do a bang-up job of acting."

"Once when she was playing in stock in Tacoma, Miss Rambeau knew the original Tugboat Annie [referring to Thea Foss] ...She also has known Raine for several years,' according to Paul Harrison.[392]

The author approved; he sent the actress a silver cigarette box and a note: "To Tugboat Annie in Grateful Appreciation. Norman Reilly Raine."[393]

"To get into shape for Tugboat Annie, perhaps shipshape is the word, I had to put on twenty-two pounds," Rambeau told reporter Charles Darnton. "Annie needed 'em to give her a wallop."[394]

Asked if she was a good sailor, the actress replied yes, and that she also knew the Northwest coast from when she was 11 and traveled to Alaska with her mother. She said she was the first white child to travel up the Snake River.

Hale during production took an unexpected leap into the San Pedro harbor. He and Rambeau were at the end of a wharf, waiting for a scene. A young woman approached and asked for their autographs. After they were signed, the fan "stepped back into thin air and, eventually water.

"Hale jumped in, sea boots, mackinaw and all, and towed the thrashing girl to a boat moored nearby."[395]

Rambeau fancied herself something of a self-taught expert on tugboating. She "learned the tugboat lore and handling from one of the tow captains, Frank Crandall. She can now warp a tug into a pier or nuzzle it against the side of a ship (in smooth water, at any rate) without tearing down the one or knocking a hole in the other.

She can steer fairly well, knows how to use speeds forward and in reverse to maneuver the shovel-nosed craft.

"And she knows all the signals," according to the *Montreal Gazette*, "can give orders to the deck hands and engine crews correctly and understands most of the harbor and navigation rules.

"Didn't have to do it for the picture at all, but it probably helped. I did it just because it was fun, and because the sea and tugboats and Annie's printed adventures have always intrigued me."[396]

Rambeau was no stranger to Seattle. In 1928 she appeared twice on the President Theater stage as a guest performer with the Henry Duffy Players — in *The Valley of Conflict* in July, in *The Torch Bearers* in September.[397]

•

Raine was head scenarist at Warner Brothers at the time[398] and *The New York Times* announced prematurely that he would prepare the script.[399] The assignment ultimately went to Walter DeLeon.

Production was nearly over when a fire at the Culver City studio destroyed $50,000 worth of sets and property including a city-block-size set.[400]

When filming was attempted in San Pedro, fog was lacking, so "a prop man raced off to a local ice cream factory and returned with a truckload of dry ice. The load was dumped into the sea all around the boats. The resulting fog took the place of capricious mother nature."[401]

The flotilla of tugboats used in making the picture consumed some 18,000 gallons of fuel oil during film production.[402]

"Tugboat Annie, senior captain of a touring company, mishandles a wealthy client, by being present when his daughter is spanked by a young man, and the client rolls into a fish-cart. She gets the contract when she offers to retire," explained *The Norwood News*. "The new skipper has to tow a valuable dry dock, but Annie takes over, as the skipper is drunk. The dry dock is beached after a crash in the fog, and a rival skipper tries to claim salvage. Annie is sacked and decides to become a lady, but the night before she leaves, she remembers a clause that will save the client a lot of money at the expense of the rival. Eventually she wins back her job."[403]

Reviewers such as Richard E. Hays gushed about the picture; "Under Lew Seiler's direction, the screenplay has action and suspense and a lot of slapstick fun."[404] Bosley Crowther in *The New York Times* wasn't smitten: "An invariable thing about hand-me-downs is that they never seem to fit the second-hand wearer quite as snugly as they did the original. And that goes for film roles too ... And Marjorie Rambeau is now giving out with little more than a broad imitation of the late and beloved Marie Dressler as the West Coast waterfront queen ... The attempt, to put it bluntly, is labored."[405]

Raine was Rambeau's table companion at the Tea Room when she was guest of honor at an Assistance League lunch; Joyce Raine was hostess at the luncheon in Hollywood. This was prelude to the film's release, *Boxoffice* reported.[406]

The New York Daily News noticed the *Narcissus* was called *Secoma* in the new picture.[407]

Warner Bros. optimistically announced the next movie in the series, *Tugboat Annie in Drydock*, would again feature Rambeau and Hale.[408] The idea was scuttled.

•

There were several challenges to filming the story. "The Tugboat Annie company has been working with real vessels lately, the story problem being hot to refloat a freighter which is supposed to have gone on a sandbar. Two tugs have been hired for Annie and her rival, Captain Bullwinkle, and a large Danish captain is in a vile humor and is being treated like a temperamental star. His ship is idle in the harbor as a result of Germany's conquest, and the hold is full of thousands of tons of soy beans which have got a little damp and are beginning to swell. The swelling is springing the freighter's plates, thus admitting more water to produce more swelling … One of these is going to crack open and sink, and not even Annie Brennan can do anything about it," said the *Wilmington Morning Star*.[409]

The Saturday Evening Post elaborated: "The vessel had been standing by the breakwater for five long weeks while the captain, his wife and a crew of twenty-two worried where the next pay check was coming from. They were sort of worried, too, about their cargo of 5000 tons of emotional Manchukuan soybeans, originally destined for Denmark, which couldn't be dumped over the tariff wall. If the beans got too damp and sprouted they would have sunk the ship; if they dried out too thoroughly they might explode and sink it. The movie offer of a hundred dollars a day not only allayed the crew's financial worries but also gave them something to think about besides those beans.

"So Tugboat Annie (Marjorie Rambeau) and the Narcissus pulled and yank the Nord Pol off mythical sand bars for a week, while Peter Bullwinkle (Alan Hale) and his Salamander made it as difficult as possible...."[410]

The studio snubbed maritime law in painting new names on the two borrowed tugs; the Coast Guard this was an old trick of pirates. "The Warners squared themselves by displaying small signs, invisible to the cameras, with the real names of the tugs," according to Frederick C. Othman.[411]

MGM created a four-acre pond on a Hollywood back lot for filming. "The harbor is filled with all types of ships from a 300-foot steamer to a five-foot dingy. Sails and nets are drying on the wharf, while along the busy street are fish peddlers, housewives, drunken sailors, urchins and merchants. Old men sit at sidewalk cafes, laughing, drinking and talking," the *Brooklyn Daily Eagle* said.[412]

The Danish freighter *Nordpol*, ship and crew temporarily stranded in the Pacific by U.S. immigration authorities, were pleased to make an arrangement for scene making and relieve the tedium.[413]

The *Narcissus*, embarrassingly, was transformed into a garbage transport for *Tugboat Annie Sails Again*. (Richards Studio, 1940)

Cinema Tidbits

Big Parade of Comedy (MGM, 1964) includes excerpts from *Tugboat Annie* (1933).

Raine narrated a trailer for *Tugboat Annie Sails Again* (1940).

The National Legion of Decency listed *Tugboat Annie Sails Again* as unobjectionable for adults.[414] It may have thought the death of one crew member was too much for children.

Tugboat Annie was parodied or loosely copied in animated and live-action comedies.

Tillie and Gus (Paramount, 1933), released two months after Dressler's *Tugboat Annie*, was called by a *Time* magazine reviewer "part parody of Tugboat Annie, part pure farce,"[415] though the picture may have taken broad strokes from the Raine stories or *Min and Bill*, rather than the Dressler/Beery shipboard depiction. W.C. Fields and Alison Skipworth, he on the run from a criminal trial, she just losing her waterfront saloon in Shanghai, are in Seattle, investigating the death of Tillie's brother, in hopes of nabbing his estate.

Tugboat Princess (Columbia, 1936), directed by David Selman, is about young "Princess" Judy (Edith Fellows), who is adopted by old Captain Zack (Walter C. Kelly) and brought to live on his tugboat.

Tugboat Mickey (Walt Disney, 1940) follows the cartoon mouse with Donald Duck and Goofy Dog as his hapless crew as they try to save a sinking ship in a cartoon.

Tugboat Granny (Warner Brothers, 1956), a Friz Freleng-directed Merrie Melodies animated short, finds Tweety Bird and Granny in charge of a tugboat when Sylvester cat tries to come aboard.

The year she played Tugboat Annie on radio, actress Marjorie Main appeared on movie screens in *The Harvey Girls* with Judy Garland and *Murder He Says* with Fred MacMurray.

Chapter 16

Marjorie Main, Betty Garde *&*
Others on the Airwaves

Marjorie Main, a prolific actress who shone as Ma Kettle in a
hillbilly film series with Percy Kilbride, voiced Tugboat Annie
in an episode for radio's *This Is My Best* in 1946.

Tugboat Annie appeared on radio.

"Tugboat Annie Fails Again" — the punning title of a sketch
on the *Rudy Vallee Show* 13 February 1941 — featured Marjorie
Rambeau, John Barrymore, Susan Miller and Lurene Tuttle at the
microphone along with Vallee as Rudy Brennan, Annie's son. Rudy
is in love with J. Ironsides Barrymore's daughter. Barrymore wants
to buy the *Narcissus*. The jokes fly.

The variety program was carried over NBC from 1929 to 1939.
Rambeau returned for the 20 March 1941 episode: "Tugboat Annie
Sails Into Society."

Fresh from a rustic portrayal as Ma Kettle[416] in *The Egg and I*
(1945) —with Percy Kilbride playing Pa Kettle — Marjorie Main

voiced Tugboat Annie on an episode of radio's *This Is My Best* that aired 14 May 1946. (Columnist Hedda Hopper in 1939 had ventured the actress would be an ideal performer for the in-the-works new Tugboat Annie film.[417])

Jane Darwell's cinema Annie was in movie theaters. Main was fresh from her own Annie picture, a role in *Gentle Annie.* Some newspapers were confused by the two seafaring women; the *Roanoke Times*, for example, captioned a photo: "Character actress Marjorie Main stars in her famous screen characterization of 'Tugboat Annie' on 'This Is My Best' over CBS and WDBJ at 8:30 p.m. Tuesday night."[418]

KNX in Wilmington, Calif., broadcast the show at 5:30 p.m., with this newspaper description: "Marjorie Maine [sic] popular rough-tough-and ready screen character actress, comes before the microphone in the radio dramatization of Norman Reilly Raine's 'Tugboat Annie Sails Again' on 'This Is My Best.'"[419]

A preview for WREC's 7:30 p.m. broadcast in Memphis, Tenn., said: "The sea story by Norman Reilly Raine begins with Annie being 'beached' because of trouble with an old enemy, Capt. Bullwinkle, and when she is permitted to resume her command the old feud blazes anew."[420] In other words, the usual plot.

One paper noted of the actress: "She may not be a pin-up girl, but Marjorie Main, Hollywood's 'Tugboat Annie,' is not without her citations by service men. Miss Main, who will play the title role in 'Tugboat Annie Sails Again' on tonight's CBS 'This Is My Best' series, has been designated as 'Occupation Girl' by the 96th Division station in the Philippines."[421]

Indiana-born Main (1890-1975) was born Mary Tomlinson. She gravitated to the stage and eventually became an MGM contract player. She appeared with Wallace Beery in another waterfront film, *Barnacle Bill* in 1941 and on a radio version that aired 1 April 1946 on *Lux Radio Theater.* Main never warmed to her co-star, but as MGM's designated successor to Dressler she was obliged to appear with Beery in six more pictures. Chemistry only clicked when she was partnered with Percy Kilbride in *The Egg and I*. The Kettles appeared in another eight pictures for Universal.

The CBS radio drama anthology *This Is My Best* first aired in 1944. Welles became producer-director-narrator-actor for 1945 and 1946. The program adapted the story from "Tugboat Annie Sails Again," sponsored by Cresta Blanca Wine.[422] Among pre-airing blurbs, the *Columbus Enquirer Sun* didn't quite get it right: "Marjorie Main, who is pretty well noted for her portrayals of the well-known character, Tugboat Annie, will do it again on This Is My Best at 8:30 p.m. The version is known as 'Tugboat Annie Sails Again.' "[423]

Another key voice for the live program was veteran actor Ray Collins (1889-1965), who began his career associated with Orson Welles' Mercury Theatre company. He appeared in *Citizen Kane* (1941), but is well-remembered in his role as Sgt. Arthur Tragg in the *Perry Mason* TV series. Collins voiced Bullwinkle. It was his last radio appearance.

This Is My Best ran for 75 episodes. "Tugboat Annie Sails Again" was third from last.[424]

Main never played Annie on film or television, though Damon Runyon's thumbnail description of her could have fit: "She has a dead pan, square shoulders, a stocky build, a voice like a file, and an uncurried aspect ... She has a stride like a section boss. She has little bright squinty eyes. It is her eyes that you want to watch when you see Miss Main in action. They are amazingly expressive. She generally starts off looking as if she had never smiled in her life, then suddenly she smiles from her eyes out, so to speak. The effect is as surprising as the glint of a diamond in a slag heap….."[425]

Main did have a role in a film based on one other *Saturday Evening Post* series character in 1942. She played Letitia "Tish" Carberry who with spinster friends of a like age Aggie Pilkinton (Zasu Pitts) and Lizzie Wilkins (Aline MacMahon) meddles in the affairs of others in 25 stories by Mary Roberts Rinehart (1910-1937), collected in seven books.

"Tugboat Annie Quotes the Law" was a comedy episode on the anthology show *Curtain Time*, which aired over CKCO radio in Ottawa and other ABC affiliates on 23 April 1947.[426]

"It wouldn't be Tugboat Annie, of course, if she didn't tangle with her ancient rival, Captain Horatio Bullwinkle ... and on this particular occasion he follow her out of port in answer to a distress signal from the British steamer, *Harrowgate*." Wrote At Radio Ringside columnist Charlie Walls. "Well the *Harrowgate's* skipper turns out to be even more dastardly than Bullwinkle ... but trust old Annie to pin back their respective ears and emerge from the fray ... well, listen and see for yourself."[427]

Captain Tugboat Annie was at the time playing in movie houses.

A Lewiston, Maine, radio station in 1939 aired a *Screen Guild* show over WABC-Columbia network featuring a Raine-written script, details not available.[428] On 19 August 1947 Raine copyrighted a "Tugboat Annie" radio script, described as "new matter" on the registration card.

Betty Garde (1905-1989) played the heroine in an Annie pilot for NBC[429] that ended up airing in 1950. The show wasn't picked up for a series. Hal Fimberg wrote the script. Garde had regular roles on *The Big Story, Perry Mason, The Fat Man* and other radio shows.

Author Raine had a limited experience with radio. He wrote a microphone drama, "Bridge of Mercy," for the *Screen Guild Show*, airing 5 March 1939 over ABC-Columbia.[430]

Raine stories were adapted for other programs:

"Glasgow Keelie," *Forty Fathom Trawlers*, WABC, 1930, adapted from the short story "The Glasgow Keelie"

"The Perfect Specimen," from Samuel Hopkins Adams story, *Lux Radio Theatre* (CBS), 1939

"The Life of Emile Zola," *Lux Radio Theatre*, 1939

"The Captains of the Clouds," *Cavalcade of America*, 1942

"The Fighting 69th," *Lux Radio Theatre,* 1942
"Each Dawn I Die," *Lux Radio Theatre,* 1943.

Fashion

It wasn't difficult to upgrade Annie's apparel; Marie Dressler was given the frumpiest of ankle-length dresses and raincoats. According to columnist Roscoe Fawcett, she wore "a grotesque costume and a great purse fastened to her belt and a tattered ostrich feather protrudes from her fearsome hat. The feather can depict any emotion just by the way Marie lets it stick up or hand down, she says. Bent down it droops in dejection and despair; sticking straight up it denotes triumph and braggadocio."[431]

Television's Minerva Urecal told one gossip columnist: "This role of Annie is not for a clothes horse. My wardrobe consists mainly of a turtle neck sweater, man's shirt, a tattered skirt, high boots and a captain's hat. I really look a sight." [432]

K.C. Bushnell's Brownbilt Shoe Store in Ventura, Calif., offered "Tug-Boat Annie" shoes, "The sensation in Sports Footwear for girls. Unsurpassed for wear and comfort." They were $4 a pair. How many teens were excited?[433]

It's not clear how it began, or why it was centered in Chicago, but that city's *Daily Tribune* in 1940-1941 fixated on redesigning Tugboat Annie's clothing.

In the 22 June 1940 issue, the *Tribune's* fashion editor Rea Seeger zeroed in on "sea-going shoppers": "With the salty name of 'Tugboat Annie,' These jacket coats [unpictured] are assured of an exciting fashion career. Instead of the famous Tugboat Annie millinery with the periscope father, there is a detachable hood also lined and quilted and padded The price is easy, the general effect just about the breeziest affair ever unpacked."

In the 14 July 1940 issue, "Smart Sports Models for Summer Treks Away from Routine," one of six drawn figures wears a " 'Tugboat Annie,' appropriately named swagger coat of red sailcloth lined with navy printed bandana kerchiefs. Worn over navy slacks and matching flannel shirt."

"For the Discriminating Sportswoman," in the 12 March 1941 issue, included among seven drawings one of a model in a wheelhouse wearing a " 'Tugboat Annie' jacket of drill cotton, quilted and padded… lined with red bandana handkerchiefs in hood and jacket …."

Ed Randall of Rochester, N.Y., in a letter in the *Post* observed that the 16 April 1955 issue mentioned women wearing toreador pants in three separate stories and wondered: "Can we expect to see Hazel and Tugboat Annie decked out in something similar soon?" The editor replied: "Hazel almost gets away with it… but Tugboat Annie — never!"[434]

The women who portrayed Annie in pictures and TV shows may not have picked up on these fashions; they were stylish in their own ways. Urecal, for example, off-camera "looks more like the type who'd disembark from a Rolls-Royce than a tugboat. Without her battered yachting cap, pea jacket and gusty waterfront language you'd never recognize here," wrote Bill Fiset. But she reveled in Annie's attitude: "I'm never happier during filming than when I'm beating the stuffing out of Bullwinkle," she said in a husky character voice.[435] She said her husband, Max Holtzer, a retired businessman, got a kick out watching her slap Bullwinkle with a dead fish.

Since 2011, British ITV has broadcast a series of crime stories featuring novelist Ann Cleeves' Detective Chief Inspector Vera Stanhope. As depicted by actress Brenda Blethyn, Stanhope in her slouch hat and droopy raincoat is a modern-day manifestation of Tugboat Annie. In fact, with an Irish instead of Northumberland accent, she'd make a marvelous Tugboat Annie, should the series again be brought to screen.

•

Raine himself? Wilkes-Barre columnist Katy Dangerfield thought him pretty spiff when he visited his hometown in 1939: "Just in case you had pictured the Tugboat Annie author as a rough 'n ready waterfront individual, Raine is an English-Irish American, is a red-haired, red-mustached man of husky though not overly-tall build who wears impeccably tailored casual clothes, and speaks with a slight, pleasing British accent. His blue eyes are both alert, as he studies his fellow-conversationalist with an author's observing eyes, and friendly. He inspires easy conversation, bouncing it around like a be brightly colored rubber ball, because to really enjoy either talking or listening."[436]

Raine was in Wilkes-Barre to visit relatives before moving on to see his brother Malcolm in Buffalo then to New York City on business.

"Foremost among the visiting vessels [at the premiere of *Tugboat Annie Sails* Again in Tacoma] is the tug 'Arthur Foss' of Seattle. Used for the 'Narcissus' in the first Tugboat Annie picture, the 'Arthur Foss' will relive the moments of glory when it serves as the official boat bringing the stars to Tacoma."

— "City Opening Arms For 'Tugboat Annie,'"
Tacoma News Tribune, 19 October 1940

Chapter 17

The *Arthur Foss*

The *Arthur Foss*, launched in Portland in 1889, had several
name changes. It was the *Narcissus* in the motion picture
with Marie Dressler. (Bernard A. Drew photo)

"The historic tugboat Arthur Foss is coming…," Suzi Sarna told readers in the *Anacortes American* in 1998. "Launched in Portland in 1889, she was built to tow sailing ships over the Columbia River bar. During Gold Rush fever in 1898 she made several trips to Alaska, towing barges and ships full of supplies and gold prospectors.

"In World War II, she was the last American ship to escape Wake Island before it fell to the Japanese invasion. Most of her years of work were spent towing log booms. She was even in the 1933 movie Tugboat Annie!"[437]

If ever it had a non-speaking star, that film's *Narcissus* was it.

The *Arthur Foss* was minimally verbal — it tooted on cue. Vessels communicated in early years with their steam whistles; direction per the United States Brotherhood of the American Association of Masters and Pilots of Steam Vessels, were spelled out in a rhyme:

If one whistle you should blow
To starboard then your bow should go.
And speeding on across the tide
She'll pass along her starboard side.
If two whistles you should blow
Why then to port your bow must go,
And if the space is far and wide
You'll pass along her starboard side.
From three short blasts 'tis yours to learn
That she is going full speed astern[438]

One long blast, one short one, then another long one and another short one is a distress signal.

Three toots is a goodbye to a sinking ship.

•

The *Arthur Foss*, the oldest surviving wooden-hulled tugboat, is home-docked at the Northwest Seaport Maritime Heritage Center at Lake Union Park in Seattle. (Bernard A. Drew photo, 2018)

The tugboat — the oldest floating wooden vessel in the Pacific Northwest — was constructed in Portland in 1889 for Oregon Railway & Navigation.

"Heavily built, the hull planking and ceiling were four-inch Douglas fir," according to Norman R. Knutsen,[439] "and the sheathing laid on the outside of the hull was one-inch-thick iron bark. The power plant installed, driving an eight-foot-diameter wheel, was a double compound steam engine of 122 horsepower built by Union Iron Works in 1887. This machinery had been salvaged from the California tug *Donald*, brought north to the Columbia River in 1877 to work for Oregon Railway and Navigation Company before being retired in 1889."

Christened the *Wallowa*, the tug worked for the railway for nine years, then sold and served a route between Puget Sound and Gold Rush Alaska first for the White Star Line then for the Pacific Clipper Line. Beginning in 1903 it spent 25 years towing logs for Puget Sound Mill & Timber Co., during which time its original engine was replaced with a compound engine, according to Knutsen.

A National Park Service National Register of Historic Places provides a few more vital statistics. The tug is 111.6 feet long with a 23.9-foot beam, a 11.6-foot depth of hold, and a 16-foot draft…

"The 15-inch thick keel was built with a 2 12-inch thick ironbark shoe, and the hull above the turn of the bilge is sheathed with 1-inch thick ironbark…."

The original coal-burning engine was replaced in 1907 and again in 1937 following an engine room and deckhouse fire.[440] It was towing logs to Everett and Seattle. Rescue craft raced to the scene from Port Angeles and Port Townsend.

Its next owner was Merrill & Ring Logging, which used it to tow logs from the Pysht River on the northern Olympic Peninsula and along the Strait of Juan de Fuca.

Foss Launch & Tug acquired the vessel in 1929, renamed it the *Arthur Foss* and continued to use it for log tows until leasing it to

MGM in 1933, where it became the *Narcissus*. The movie producers in 1934, paid to have an 80-ton, 700-horsepower Washington Iron Works direct-lubricating diesel engine installed at the Smith Cove terminals in Seattle (about a decade before the fictional *Narcissus* was converted). That may have been when a 120-volt generator was installed for the towing winch, windlass and quadrant-cable steering system. Knutsen said this was when the deckhouse was removed and replaced with a new one.

The boat was re-outfitted for *Tough Guy,* a 1936 film featuring Joseph Calleia, Rin Tin Tin Jr. and Jackie Cooper.[441]

The *Arthur Foss* at work in 1945.

Briefly mothballed after *Tugboat Annie,* it was brought out of drydock on MGM's back lot — where it narrowly avoided an engine room fire[442] — to appear in another Wallace Beery film, *Thunder Afloat,* in 1939. Set in New England, Beery plays tugboat captain Pop Thorson who joins the Navy. The *Wallowa/Narcissus* was renamed the *Susan H.*[443] A second tugboat set was built for Beery's film rival Rocky Blake played by Chester Morris.[444]

Conscripted for duty in 1941, the craft supported the World War II effort by, among other things, taking a drydock gate to Pearl Harbor. Chartered by Contractors Pacific Naval Air Bases, it continued service until Wake Island alongside the smaller *Justine Foss*. The *Arthur Foss* left to tow two barges to Honolulu when Pearl Harbor was attacked. The tug was repainted to disguise it. It was rechristened the *Dohasan* in 1942 and for three years became a yard tug for the U.S. Navy. It floated idle for two years then in 1947 returned to the Foss fleet, becoming the company's first tug homeported in Tacoma. It was given necessary maintenance and renamed the *Theodore Foss*, it served coastal trade with a cruising range of 1,000 hours or 10,000 miles.[445] Its service speed was 13 knots. It plied the Juan de Fuca Strait until 1971.

The *Arthur Foss* left regular service with a bit of grandstanding. As recounted by *Seattle Times* seaport columnist Glen Carter,[446] it made what was perhaps the longest-distance and largest-ever ship tow accomplished by a single Foss Launch & Tug craft, guiding the Essex-class ex-U.S. Navy aircraft carrier *Philippine Sea* some 1,244 miles from San Diego to Zidell Dismantling in Tacoma for scrapping.

The *Arthur Foss* captain for the trip was Guy H. Johnson Jr., the mate Charles Finley. Jack Gilden was chief engineer, Erling Johnson first engineer, Bill Reese second engineer, Ken Martin oiler, Jim Amudson cook and Bob Jefferson, Cliff Gaddis and Bruce Pulley seamen.

The 796-foot, 38,500-ton *Philippine Sea,* nicknamed the "Flippy," was towed with a 2,000-foot 2¼-inch cable.

The carrier had entered service in 1945. Some 7,243 combat sorties were made from its decks. It was decommissioned in 1959.

"Ya, it was a big tow," Johnson told Carter, "But we had 5,000 horsepower. Weather was good, and we had no mechanical trouble. In the old days we had only 100 horsepower and sometimes bad weather. So a record depends on how you look at it."[447]

The *Arthur Foss* glossed this with an even larger haul, delivering to the same scrap yard another Korean War-era carrier, the 888-foot, 33,00-ton *Princeton*, from Long Beach.[448] That vessel had logged 137,844 aircraft landings during its career.

The *Arthur Foss* engine room. (Todd A. Corteau, 2009;
Historic American Engineering Record, Library of Congress)

Donated by Foss Maritime to Northwest Seaport — it was open for the museum's season in May 1971[449] — the *Arthur Foss* occasionally makes excursions to Olympia, Gig Harbor, Port Townsend and Anacortes — and in 1984, to Juneau[450] for Alaska's 25th anniversary of statehood. It sported a renovated smoke stack, gleaming brass bell and repaired deck. It was received as a celebrity; "It's been a real part of the transportation linkage between the histories of the two states [Alaska and Washington]," said Don Dickey, director of the Alaska Division of Tourism.

Carter in 1981 credited restoration work by Neil O'Shea, Al Rees, Harold Aus, William "Woody" Wood and others with keeping the "old gal" throbbing.[451]

"Arthur Foss is the only known wooden-hulled 19th century tugboat left afloat and in operating condition in the United States," according to the National Park Service.

In the hull, a large chain locker is forward, then an engine room, galley, ward room and crew's quarters. On the first level of the deck are two quarters for four crew members. On the upper level, reached by stairs, there are a Texas deck, sing head, cabins for captain, mate and engineer. The pilothouse has all-original equipment including a large wooden manual wheel and smaller brass power wheel, telegraph, binnacle and steam radiators.

Historic American Engineering Record (HAER WA-190) indexed some 42 black-and-white photographs of the ship plus two color transparencies, taken by Todd A. Croteau in 2009.

The boat earned a seven-page spread in Austin Dwyer's book *Tugboats to Remember* (2023).

That's a lot to digest — but there's no Annie without a *Narcissus*, and the craft's appearance in the 1933 motion picture makes it a national treasure.[452]

•

C. Arthur Foss (1885-1964), for whom the ship was named, became prominent in the Puget Sound area when the family moved west from Minnesota in 1889. "Mr. Foss literally grew up on the waterfront. As a boy he piloted launches of the Foss Launch & Tug Co., which was started in Tacoma 75 years ago by his parents, Andrew and Thea Foss," according to the *Seattle Daily Times*.[453]

Foss described his family's business at a Kiwanis Club meeting at the White Swan Café in Isaquah in 1941 and showed film footage of the floating bridge on the Duwamiso.[454] Guests came from that community, Cle Elum, Snoqualmie and Renton.

His brother, Wedell (1888-1955), a friend of author Raine, practiced maritime law before joining the Navy during World War I and serving on the battleship *South Dakota*.

A third brother, Henry, was also active in the company. He provided a recipe for flapjacks to an American Weekly feature in the *San Francisco Examiner* in 1940. He recalled, "I remember many times when I helped my mother with her cooking and all of the old bread went into a large stone crock, there to soak and be on hand when it was necessary to make hot cakes, which might be any time of the twenty-four hours but particularly in the morning."[455]

All three brothers were featured in a *Saturday Evening Post* article in 1940, "The Sons of Tugboat Annie."[456]

Theodore Foss was Thea Foss's oldest brother-in-law.

The Foss Family sold the business in 1969. It is now part of the Saltchuk Resources group based in Seattle.

•

The *Arthur Foss* may be seen at the Northwest Seaport Maritime Heritage Center at Lake Union Park in Seattle. Also preserved as floating museums are the 60-foot wooden-hulled *Sandman* at Percival Landing in Olympia, built in 1910 by Crawford & Reid Shipyard in Tacoma and employed primarily in towing sand and gravel barges for Olympia Sand & Gravel, and the 117.5-foot wooden-hulled *Dominion*, designated the *LT-366* when built for the U.S. Army at Grays Harbor Shipbuilding in Aberdeen in 1944. One of 61 Miki-class tugboats, it is now a floating museum at Dominion Historical Workboat Association in Bremerton. During the war the latter was the *Pvt. Romeo LeClair*, to honor a World War II Army medic. In private service with Foss Maritime, it was called the *Patricia Foss* and made runs from Seattle to Alaska. It took its present name in 1980, after retirement.

•

Piling Busters

A venture that began as something of a lark in 1950 grew into a modest social organization then evaporated after four years. Piling Busters was the inspiration of food distributor (later Chrysler-Plymouth salesman and real estate agent) Jack P. Shipley.[457] A native of Helena, Mont., Shipley (1914-1976) spent most of his life in Tacoma.[458]

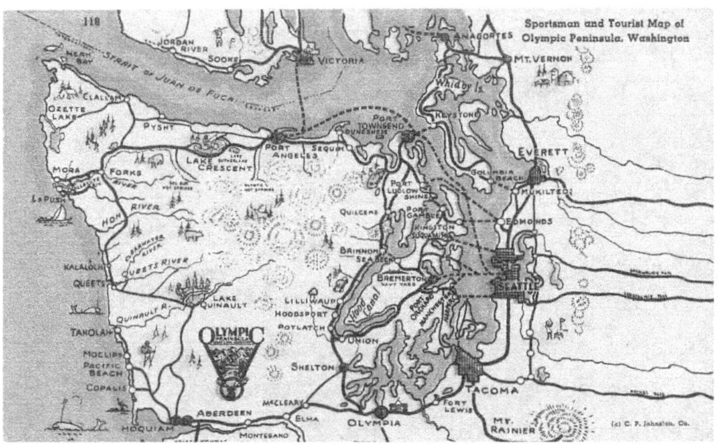

This vintage postcard depicts many of the communities along Puget Sound.

Raine was the only professional to submit a tall tale to Piling Busters' story-telling contest in 1952, though he was out of the running for a prize — meant for amateurs. His friend Shipley steered the competition.[459]

According to Along Tacoma's Waterfront columnist Ed Garrison, writing in the *News Tribune*, "It started when a tug crew began razzing Jack Shipley, owner of the cruiser Silver Spray, about being a 'bologna peddler' (which he is, incidentally, if you can call a distributor of sausages, bologna, wieners, etc., by such a name), Shipley answered that he had heard quite a bit o bologna 'peddled' by tug crews.

"Then Shipley, who collects tales of the waterfront, offered a prize or two for the best stories Tacoma tugboat men could tell."

Shipley thought that was it. But sailors up and down the Sound expressed interest in the contest. Other prize sponsors ditto.[460] Contest rules emerged. There would be three divisions, and cartoons as well as prose would be accepted.[461] Oh, and each entry should be accompanied by a 500-lb. anchor. (Ha ha.) Piling Busters Story Telling Contest entries (without ironwork) rolled in. Judges were to be Shipley, Garrison and Leo Livingston of *Pacific Motorboating.* Fifty-one entrants vied for 30 prizes for comical, tallest tale, sharp tugboating and cartoons.[462]

Raine gravitated to the group for obvious reasons, among them to hear stories — potential fodder for his *Post* work — and bask in the camaraderie. From Hollywood he let Shipley know he would write a special story for the contest.

Warren Larson, mate on Tacoma Tug & Barge Co.'s *Edward A. Young,* won the Tugboat Annie Oscar, co-presented by Raine. "Larson won the Oscar with a yarn about how doughnuts made by a tugboat cook were used as axles to get the boat and its tow of logs into downtown Tacoma," according to a news story.[463] Davis had a real-life experience when he lost a barge [*Foss No. 16* in 1941] with 26,000 gallons of aviation gasoline in a gale off Destruction Island, retrieved after a harrowing 11 hours.

Shipley self-published spiral-bound yearbooks of stories and cartoons in 1950 and 1951 and collected material in 1952 but never published a third issue. Given the material in 1978, Retired Tugboat Association assembled an omnibus and published it through Peninsula Gateway in Gig Harbor. Though subtitled "Stories of Towboating by Towboat Men," three entries are by women — one recalling being a novice cook at age 18, another being a cook on her husband's vessel and the third an offspring of a mate. The anecdotes and stories are of the sort Raine would have heard in his roaming the waterfront and gabbing with the towboaters.

Piling Busters faded and Shipley went on to other activities.

Writers Take Liberties

Raine appears as a character in his writer friend Brett Halliday's Mike Shayne detective novel, *The Blonde Cried Murder* (1956).[464] In the story, yachtsman Norman Raine discovers a body in the water and reports it to the police and to Shayne.

Perhaps the earliest reference to the *Narcissus* master, oddly enough, is in William Heyliger's juvenile adventure novel *Steve Merrill Engineer*, published in 1935. A woman is described as "short, broad and competent looking." Merrill, interviewing her for a job, "snapped his fingers and chuckled. … Tugboat Annie Brennan, if Tugboat Annie had been Polish. All Anna Kovic lacked was a shore-going hat with a feather."[465] This reference would have gone over the heads of most of its readers.

Secoma provides a setting for adventure writer John Scott Douglas's "Afloat!," about the perils of finding a body in the ocean. It's in the March 1943 issue of the pulp *Mammoth Detective*.

Our Puget Sound heroine is mentioned in a *10 Detective Aces* story from 1947, "Midnight's Deadly Threat" by Rex Whitechurch. The main character, night watchman Fred Stryker, tells a friend: "I hope you marry her, Lou, before she gets big and fat and becomes another Tugboat Annie."[466]

Ships, a Truck, a Train and a Flying Fortress

There have been several tugboats named Annie.

One 1864 *Annie* sank in London. One 1883 *Annie* was active in Baltimore. And one 130-foot *Annie* sank at the foot of 7th Street in New York in the 1970s.

The screw steamer *Narcissus* was launched in Albany, N.Y., in 1863 and was purchased by the Union navy, only to sink in 1866. Another *Narcissus*, a bay and sound tender, was launched from Camden, N.J., in 1939.

There was a U.S. Air Force B-17 Flying Fortress known as the *Tugboat Annie* —financed by the residents of Portland, Ore., and manufactured in Seattle. It flew bombing missions before sinking in 1943 "to her death in the waves of the South Pacific after numerous victories over the Japanese," according to the *Chicago Daily Tribune*. The nine-member crew survived.

The British named a new suburban express engine on the London, Midland and Scottish Railway in 1934 (running from Euston Station to Glasgow) "Tugboat Annie" because of its deep resonant siren/whistle, like an ocean liner's.[467]

Rocketfin Hobbies in 1950 marketed a hobby kit, the Trian Penguin clockwork *Annie* river tug.

Miller Motors, a Plymouth and DeSoto dealership in Mankato, Minn., added a wrecker truck to its fleet in 1937. It was a cab-over-engine International 1½-ton chassis with streamlined body. They called it *Tugboat Annie*. R&R Vacuumcraft in 1950 issued a resin model kit for the vehicle.

Tugboat Annie Barge & Construction Services, based in Franklin, N.Y., incorporated in 2020. Its stated purpose: "Any lawful activity."[468]

The Hangman's Whip opened 24 February 1933 at the St. James Theatre in New York City. It closed 1 March.

— Playbill

Chapter 18

Stage Plays

Raine had dramatic aspirations.

As the film *Tugboat Annie* crept toward release, he was busy with *Hangman's Whip*,[469] a play written with Frank Butler based on the story "The Sixth Man" by Raine. It mildly interested critics — " 'Hangman's House' [sic] left e frigid, but not shivery," barbed critic Burns Mantle[470] —but had a short run on Broadway in 1933 and a decade later was renamed *Man Alone* in a London production.[471]

While in New York for the opening, Raine was alerted to a pending bank holiday but brushed it off. He traveled to Toronto, arriving with $7 in his pocket and unable to cash a check. He needed funds to purchase transportation to Seattle and for food and lodging.'

"So he dropped into the office of Maclean's Magazine, where he used to be an assistant editor.

" 'How about a little advance on those two stories I'm going to write you?' asked Raine.

" 'Right-o!' said the editor, and that's how Raine got the money to come home on, and that's why he had to tarry here a couple of days longer than he expected in order to finish the two 'I.O.U.' stories," according to the *Seattle Daily Times*.[472]

Hedda Hopper reported cryptically in 1943 that "John Wildberg may do Raine's play, 'White Orchid,' on Broadway this fall."[473] Nothing further could be found about a play of that name.

The Norman Reilly Raine Collection at Boston University includes outlines for a musical in two acts, "Bonanza," and a stage play in three acts, "Wild Grapes."

Margaret Blanchat flew her one-woman characterization of Tugboat Annie by Kurtzer Flying Service seaplane from Lake Union to

Portland, Phoenix, El Paso, Dallas, New Orleans, Jacksonville, Key West and Havana in winter 1950 on behalf of Seattle Salts, that city's equivalent of a chamber of commerce.[474]

Robin Hood the Musical aka *Hi, Ho, Robin Hood* (1990), with book by Tim Kelly, music by Arne Christiansen and lyrics by Ole Kittleson, was adapted in part from the screenplay by Raine and Seton I. Miller and new music inserted by Director Colin Wilson for a Cayman Drama Society production in 2001,

The Tacoma Art League and Tacoma Junior League in 1957 entertained with a puppet play, *Tugboat Annie & Captain Tarpenny*, performed at College of Puget Sound.

Tugboat Annie was put on by Word for Word/National Maritime Museum Association at Fisherman's Wharf, San Francisco, in 1996 featuring Linda Hoy as the star.

Dick Corn adapted "Tugboat Annie Quotes the Law" in 1998 for a Lemon Bay Playhouse staged reading fund-raiser in Sarasota, Fla.[475]

Music

Several popular songs mention Tugboat Annie.

Irving Bibo crafted music and lyrics for a song, "Tugboat Annie," for the film *Captain Tugboat Annie* (1945).

Detroit-based songwriter/singer/musician Lori Jacobs[476] was responsible for music and lyrics for "Tugboat Annie," a 45 rpm disc released on the Neostat Music label (1978). The song refers to a female hobo.

Robert "Sailor Bob" Griggs (1933-2019),[477] host of a children's television show aired by WRVA in Richmond, Va., from 1959 to the mid-1970s, released a 45 rpm disc on the Juke Box label in 1980: "Tug Boat Annie's" ("Top to the Bottom" on the flip side).

The Music Tree series of piano instruction included a short Jon George tune, "Tugboat Annie," to a Chugging along" tempo.[478]

Bob Kotta, then director of Northwest Seaport, and Mariide Widmann, a member of the folk group Victory at Sea, wrote "A Hundred Years Ago," relating the history of the *Arthur Foss* including a verse: "In Tugboat Annie when Hollywood came — Oy, aye oy; The tug Narcissus was her name — A hundred years ago…" The song appears on the LP *Victory Sings at Sea*, released by Victory Music, and is collected on *Northwest Tugboat Tales* CD (2010).[479] The disc's last track is "The Arthur Foss Leaves the Dock," three horn blows-engine chug-telegraph jingle-engine start jig recorded live by Chris Glanister.

An alt-rock musical group called Tugboat Annie formed in Buffalo in 1990, moved to Boston and issued several CDs.

"CAPTAIN TUGBOAT ANNIE… the blustering salt of the briny deep in the year's laughingest, seafaring comedy!"
— Advertisement for *Captain Tugboat Annie*

Chapter 19

Jane Darwell's *Captain Tugboat Annie*

Jane Darwell and Edgar Kennedy step into Annie's and
Horatio's boots for *Captain Tugboat Annie*. (Publicity still)

Phil Rosen directed *Captain Tugboat Annie*, released by Republic Pictures in November 1945. Featured were Jane Darwell (1879-1967)[480] as Annie, Mantan Moreland as Pinto, Jack Norton as Shiftless and Joe Crehan as Alec Severn. New crew members were Missouri Jones (Barton Yarborough) and Johnny Webb (Hardie Albright).

World War II is over, the U.S. government has released tugboats back to their owners and Severn wants to reinvigorate his Secoma Towing & Salvage. Annie Brennan lines up a crew, some old members, some new. It's the same old rivalry, however, with Edgar Kennedy (1890-1948), as Bullwinkle, and Anthony Ward as Jake.

Annie has another challenge: a newly adopted delinquent young man (played by Charles Gordon as Terry Jordan), an angry probationer who romances a judge's secretary (Pamela Blake as Marion Graves). At the same time, Annie facilitates the Severns taking in an 11-year-old girl musical prodigy.

Republic Pictures released *Captain Tugboat Annie* in 1945. (Publicity still)

Narcissus crew members await an important radio message. (Publicity still)

There's a bittersweet ending, with one crewman lost to fire. Annie tries to reconcile with Bullwinkle — but he dives over the pier to avoid a kiss.

Of course it's the usual Brennan-Bullwinkle rivalry in *Captain Tugboat Annie*. Note the feather in Annie's bonnet. (Publicity still)

It's a quiet moment in the *Narcissus* wheelhouse. (Publicity still)

A bank manager refuses a loan to Severn, largely because of Annie's constant bickering with Bullwinkle. "Severn leaves her in charge during his absence on a business trip. In an effort to raise the 25,000 dollars [needed for repairs], Annie contacts Armstrong, a shipyard owner but Armstrong's spoiled daughter Peggy has an encounter with Edie Kent, a young man Annie is helping through college who works on the tug during holidays, as a result of which Annie pushes Armstrong into a fish cart, which wrecks her chances of getting more work from him," teased the *Shepton Mallet Journal* in U.K.[481]

The screenplay was by George Callahan. The budget was $300,000. Considered as a title but rejected was *Tugboat Annie's Son*. (The title was used, however, in at least one fan magazine.)

Film Daily advised readers the picture is "packed with hokum and sentimentality. With due regard for comedy, the picture continues the feud between Tugboat Annie and Captain Bullwinkle to the satisfaction of those who may have lost memory of the flavor that Marie Dressler and Wallace Beery brought to the roles years ago."[482]

The low-budget picture relied heavily on a fake waterfront built on a back lot — a pool of water with models floating back and forth. No obvious tugboats to be seen, even during a raging fire scene.

When Republic took on the project in 1944,[483] the expectation was that at least two more pictures would be made. James B. Burkett, producer, secured the rights from Raine and Warner Brothers (which had taken over some of them from MGM) for 21 short stories. *Showmen's Trade Review* reported he planned to feature Rambeau in a series, with Charles Winninger possibly playing Bullwinkle.[484]

Who should play Annie? Columnist Louella O. Parsons made a guess it would be Rambeau again.[485] Marjorie Main and comic actress Lulu McConnell were considered.[486] Wisecracking Winnie Lightner was approached.

The starring role went to Darwell,[487] who was born Patti Woodward in Palymira, Mo., attended school in Chicago, Boston and Louisville then studied at Dana Hall in New York. Her father, W.R. Woodward, was a railroad executive. A veteran performer, she won an Academy Award for best supporting actress playing Ma Joad in *The Grapes of Wrath* released in 1939.

Raine wrote a 1954 episode of the syndicated television series *Waterfront*, which featured Preston Foster as Captain John Foster of the tugboat *Cheryl Ann* and Ann Robinson as his wife, May. (Publicity photo)

She told a *Capitol Hill Beacon* reporter she liked both stage and screen, but for different reasons. "She likes pictures because she can have a permanent residence in California which she loves, particularly the San Fernando Valley where she has a ranch home. She also likes San Francisco because she said San Francisco was so gay an exciting. At her ranch home in the valley she raises chickens, ducks, turkeys, a garden and has dogs. She likes dogs and at the present time has seven…."

She also had a home in Van Nuys she shared with her nephew, Winston Ogden, and a poodle named Mike. Darwell never married.

"Miss Darwell said she occasionally liked to do a stage show 'just for a change' and there was also the added zest of appearing before an audience in person. She played in 'Suds in Your Eyes,' a New York stage comedy, recently...," the *Beacon* added.

"She said she hoped her fans would like her in the role [of Tugboat Annie] and that she hoped to do more of them in the series her studio is planning to make."[488]

Charles Winninger was eyed for the part of Bullwinkle that went to Kennedy.

Calling it a "palatable mixture of homespun matter and slapstick comedy plus a smattering of sentiment," *Motion Picture Daily* gave a nod to the secondary characters: "Satisfactory in incidental comedy and straight dramatic roles are Mantan Moreland, Hardie Albright, H.B. Warner, Jack Norton, Barton Yarborough and many others."[489]

Film Daily's critic said "Director Phil Rosen has managed to give the picture considerable action and some excitement, although his work is haphazard and uninspired... The performers do the best they can with the material at their disposal."[490]

The eight-reeler was released 17 November 1945.

It turned out to be a movie series of one.[491]

Mr. Gallup discovers his cargo doesn't match what it says on the manifest.

— *Schlitz Playhouse of the Stars* episode

Chapter 20

Teleplays 1954-1957

Raine migrated to television in the 1950s. He maintained a familiar pattern in his research, "going around with the Los Angeles Homicide Squad, studying crime investigation. He told [the Toronto *Financial Post*] that the police department of that city is completely frustrated by an ingenious gambling device; has offered a reward to any patrolman who can think of a solution to the problem."[492]

These are his television projects:

"Sea Bells," episode of Emmy-nominated syndicated *Waterfront*, 1954, based on characters created by M. Bernard Fox. Preston Foster appeared as Captain John Herrick of the *Cheryl Ann* in 78 half-hour black-and-white episodes that first aired in 1954-1955.[493] Fox and Jesse L. Lasky Jr. wrote the first teleplay. Filming was in Los Angeles Harbor and at Hal Roach Studios by Roland Reed Productions.

"The Life of Emile Zola," *Lux Video Theatre* (1955), adaption of Raine, Herald & Herczeg screenplay, reshaped by S.H. Barnett.

"Wild Call," *Schlitz Playhouse* (1955), based on a Gordon Gaskill story.

"The Argonauts," *Schlitz Playhouse* (1955), based on a Kenneth Grahame story.

"The Mysterious Cargo," *Schlitz Playhouse of the Stars* (1956), featuring J. Carrol Naish, based on his story featuring Mr. Gallup, aired 20 April 1956.

"A Fork in the Road," *Policewoman* (1956). This premiere episode is about a policewoman who works with homicide detectives.

Tramp Steamer (1957), pilot script, never filmed. The producers of *Douglas Fairbanks Presents* chartered a freighter for a proposed series.[494]

The program "may not be the greatest TV series ever produced, but like the original model [the 1933 film], it's loud funny and it has managed to retain that intangible TV quality called 'heart.'"

— Steve N. Scheuer, "Tugboat Annie Sails On Again," *Herald Statesman*, 19 April 1958

Chapter 21

Minerva Urecal's *Adventures of Tugboat Annie*

Minerva Urecal takes the helm for the made-in-Canada television series,
singing along with the Sailor's Hornpipe. (Publicity photo)

A deal to sell Tugboat Annie rights to Paramount didn't materialize, but Raine in 1950 said he was entertaining several television
offers.[495] He signed with CBS in 1950[496] for a project that apparently
came to naught. He signed with Television Programs of America's chairman Ed Small in 1954.[497] TPA inked an arrangement with
Chertok Television of Hollywood (which headquartered with General Services Studios) to produce the series.[498] Both *Broadcasting
Telecasting*[499] and *Variety* said rights were obtained from the "estate
of Norman Reilly Raine, author," suggesting erroneously he was no
longer alive.

Film comedienne Winnie Lightner, Broadway's "Song-a-Minute
Girl," was considered for the top role. So was Verna Felton, who was
in the cast of *December Bride*.[500]

As early as 1943, six-foot-tall Broadway, vaudeville, radio and film actress Charlotte Greenwood and "Ma Kettle" herself, Marjorie Main, were considered for the title role.[501] Verna Felton wouldn't have minded playing the role, but figured a television series would cast a younger woman and call it 'Tugboat Anne."[502] Edna Mae Oliver and Alice Brady were suggested.[503] Producer Dory Shary was intrigued by Helen Traubel.[504] Victor McLaglen was given the once-over and signed to play Bullwinkle.[505] Edgar Kennedy got a look-see. So did Las Vegas comedian Hank Henry was also considered[506].

But announcement came in 1956 of *The Adventures of Tugboat Annie* featuring Minerva Urecal (1894-1966), radio's Mrs. Pasquale, as the heroine. Character actor Walter Sande (1906-1971), who appeared in such other TV shows as *The Lone Ranger, Johnny Ringo* and *The Farmer's Daughter*, was Bullwinkle. Don Orlando was Pinto the cook, Eric Clavering played Shiftless, Don Baker was Whitey, Stan Francis was Severn and James Barrow was Jake on the *Salamander*.

Urecal — Florence Dunnuck, who performed using her middle name (Minerva, the Greek goddess of flute players) and a last name compacted from "Eureka, Cal."[507] — described herself as "the poor man's Marjorie Main. For years producers would have me do that type role when they couldn't afford her."[508]

Her scenes were with one exception filmed dockside. "I only went to sea once. That was when we were making the pilot film and I got seasick," the actress said.[509]

Normandie Productions, a subsidiary of Television Pictures of America (TPA), syndicated the series 1957-58.[510] The company previously distributed *Lassie, Captain Gallant* and *The Last of the Mohicans*. A major sponsor and part owner was Lever of Canada, through the Walter J. Thompson Toronto office.[511] Associated Rediffusion Ltd had distribution rights in the United Kingdom. Milton Gordon acquired Small's share in the undertaking.[512]

Walter Sande is Minerva Urecal's nemesis in *The Adventures of Tugboat Annie*, syndicated beginning in 1958. (Publicity still)

Episodes were filmed at Lakeshore Studio in Toronto. Executive producers were Leon Fromkess and Anthunt Veiler. Sig Neufeld was producer. Leslie Goodins directed. Thirty-nine half-hour, black-and-white episodes were made.[513]

Except for the principals, the cast was Canadian.

"Neufeld is shooting each film in an average of two to three days," *Canadian Broadcaster & Telescreen* reported.[514]

Urecal chuckled at audience reaction to her much-altered persona for the production. "You won't believe it, but off camera, Minerva Urecal looks more like the type who'd disembark from a Rolls-Royce than a tugboat," said a writer in the *Calgary Herald*. "Without her battered yachting cap, pea jacket and gusty waterfront language you'd never recognize her."[515]

" I'm taking the biggest tumble down the social ladder in history," she joked to journalist Vernon Scott, "from college dean [in the CBS-TV situation comedy *Meet Mr. McNutley*, 1953-54] to Tugboat Battle-Axe. And to tell you the truth, I like the role of Annie best."

Terming herself "a poor man's Marjorie Main," she went on: "This role of Annie is not for a clothes horse. My wardrobe consists mainly of a turtleneck sweater, man's shirt, a tattered skirt, high boot and a captain's cap. I really look a sight."

"But we're staying as close to the real Annie as possible. I'm crazy about the blustering old battle-axe. The only thing in the world she really loves is the 'Narcissus,' her boat...."[516]

" 'I read some of the stories in a book,' she said, 'and I could tell that Norman Reilly Raine intended Tugboat Annie to have a tough exterior and a heart of gold... I can see why the original stories were so funny... I'm never happier during filming than when I'm beating the stuffing out of Bullwinkle.'"[517]

Urecal the next year took over from Hope Emerson in the role of Mother in the *Peter Gunn* TV series.[518] She said that role allowed her to wear better clothes. "Both of them can take care of themselves in their tough waterfront environments," she said. "We did Annie on location in Toronto and it got so cold the camera froze. Of course, it wasn't a very good one to begin with.

"I had to wear quilted nylon underwear — made me look like a Chinee communist general — and 'death to romance' stockings. They are those heavy woolen leggings like they wore at Valley Forge."[519]

To save on costs, they worked with a single tugboat, Urecal said in another interview. " 'We had signs for the 'Narcissus' and the 'Salamander' and it seemed like every time they changed camera angles they'd change the signs on the tugs.'"

The 71-foot, steel-hulled U.S. tugboat *J.C. Stewart* owned by Canadian Stewart Co. Ltd. played the part of the *Narcissus* during Toronto filming according to one authority, the Canadian vessel *H.J.D. No. 1* became the *Salamander*. That wooden-hulled tug was built in 1925 at Port Stanley, Ontario, for Finlay Fish & Storage Co. It was acquired by Toronto Drydock Co. Ltd. in 1939 and rebuilt as a harbor tug, remaining in service until about 1961, when it was dismantled.[520]

The *Stewart* was built by Johnston Brothers of Ferrysburg, Minn., in 1915. It was called the *Col. M.J. McDonough* when serving the U.S. Army Corps of Engineers after 1924, then again the *Stewart* when acquired by Toronto Dry Dock and converted to harbor tug and passenger ferry in 1946. It was scrapped in 1965.[521]

Regular production in Toronto began in July 1957 under director Lee Goodwins. As CP reported: "Monday, Annie had to shout to be heard, and stood with eyes skyward and skirts billowing while a seaplane buzzed overhead and a police launch cruised by. Then production resumed.

"Noise is their most serious problem so far, Goodwins says. Horns toot at the wrong time, airplanes fly over the harbor, and trucks tangle in the camera cables along the pier.

"Five Canadians have running parts with the Hollywood crew. They are: Stan Francis, who plays Alex Severn, owner of Annie's tug; James Barron, first mate on Bullwinkle's tug and Hugh Watson, who plays the tug's owner; Eric Clavering, who plays Shiftless, a deckhand; and John Vernon as Big Sam, a grease monkey on the Narcissus."[522]

Seven other Canadians had smaller parts.

Why Toronto? Actor Walter Sande, aka Bullwinkle, said, "People are getting used to seeing San Francisco Bay, it is used so much. Besides, this is a nice spot."

" 'We had to work eight straight months on the series,' Urecal told Ron Tepper. 'I never worked so hard or had so much fun. I play the part of a real down-to-earth person.'"[523]

She often had to row herself to the filming set, according to the *Montreal Gazette*, which ran a photo as proof.[524] The paper carried another photo of actor Sande, entertaining the singing Hames Sisters, Marjorie, Norma and Jean, who were featured in CBC-TV's *Country Hoedown*.[525]

The pilot, with a script by Lou Derman, was made in San Pedro Bay.[526] It cost $128,000, a record at the time for a half-hour show.[527]

The pilot was filmed in San Francisco, the rest of the shows in Canada. Urecal wasn't keen on relocating to Toronto to do the series, but it was a contractual requirement. "We worked from dawn until dark, six days a week, and I had to sit up late every night learning about 9,000 line for the next day's shooting ..." she told reporter Robert Anderson. "A lot of folks think I should dress like a deckhand on a garbage scow and swill beer the way Marie Dressler did in the part. But you can't do that on TV where you go into the living room in front of the kiddies."[528]

The series was produced on film. Chicagoans were given a sneak preview of the pilot in February 1957 at the Lake Theatre in Oak Park.[529]

Raine reportedly earned $1,000 for each episode filmed.[530] TPA boasted in a *Variety* advertisement 19 February 1958: "Winnipeg — outrates Gunsmoke, December Bride! Montreal — outrates Disneyland, Climax! Vancouver — outrates Dragnet, Alfred Hitchcock! Regina — outrates Perry Como, Gunsmoke! Toronto — brings in a 33.7% share within one month (six stations divide share of market)!"

Montreal Star & Herald reporter and photographer Bill Brown and Walter Curtin in a two-page feature story said of the production: "On Toronto's busy waterfront, some of the best-known and best-liked characters in North American fiction have been coming back to life. Tugboat Annie, the rough-tongued, soft-hearted captain of the tug Narcissus is once more in fierce and funny rivalry for the best jobs and towing contracts with her old enemy, Capt. Horatio Bullwinkle, of the Salamander. Canadians are currently seeing them in action in a series of 39 half-hour episodes on the CBC-TV network."[531]

Star Urecal confided: "I psychoanalyze my parts. I take them apart, figure out which emotions they'd express and which ones they'd repress and why. I know Annie pretty darn well now, and I think she's one of the best."

Her co-star Sande said, "This Bullwinkle is a good fat part, but more than that, he's a lot of fun."

Producer Stan Neufeld said Toronto had a rich pool of actors and first-class film facilities. "Another reason is economic, since Canadian production will facilitate distribution throughout the Commonwealth. Still another is sentimental rather than practical, since author Raine was living and working in Toronto, in sight of the harbor, when he first began writing and thinking about Tugboat Annie. [That's not quite the story, as we know.] But filming a tugboat story on the waterfront has one big disadvantage. Time and again scenes have to be halted and re-shot — mostly because of sound interference from the tooting and splashing of ferries and tugboats in the harbor."

The theme song was the traditional "Sailor's Hornpipe."

The show title lettering resembles a ship's hawser.

Directors included Les Goodwins and Sam Newfield.

By December 1957, when the cast took a Christmas break, 30 episodes were in the can. Filming resumed in January for the final nine. It premiered in the United Kingdom on New Year's Eve.[532]

Syndication

Television Programs of America advertised the TV show as pre-tested; "Over 650,00,000 readers of Norman Reilly Raine's 65 Tugboat Annie stories' 27-year run continues by popular demand."[533] It quoted R.B. Collet, advertising director for Lever Brothers, who said the show drew more viewers than *Perry Como, Gunsmoke, Wyatt Earp, Dragnet, Climax* and *Disneyland* on Canadian network markets.

WBZ to publicize the program engaged a Navy tug and took the press on an hour-long tour of Boston harbor, then treated for a seafood dinner at the union Oyster House.[534]

The shows found syndication markets in Los Angeles, Cleveland, Detroit and Philadelphia.[535] New York's WAB-TV dialed in.

An advertisement in *Variety* boasted: "The Adventures of Tugboat Annie outrates all competition combined improves the time slot by 27.1% increases audience share 45.2%."[536]

WBZ-TV in Boston "wrangled a Navy tug, base at Charlestown Navy Yard, and took the tv scribes out into the briny" to promote its broadcasts of *The Adventures of Tugboat Annie,* not expecting to encounter other ships such as WNAC-TV's touting *Robin Hood* and another plugging *Lucy* and then a tug marked with a big "T." WBZ's producer distracted reporters by allowing them to take the wheel to the Union Oyster House.[537]

A handful of scriptwriters have been identified: Jack Roche, "Commodore Bullwinkle"; Earl Baldwin, "Annie's Retirement" and "Getting Annie's Pig"; Maurice Richlin, Fred S. Fox and Joel Rapp, "The Romance of Horatio Bullwinkle"; and Bill Freedman and Larry Rhine, "Operation Hotcake" aka "Pinto's Pancake Heaven."[538] The two were credited with writing "Hero Without Halo," which may have had a change of title.[539] *The International Television Almanac Who's Who* for 1959 identifies Baldwin, Edward Chandler and Elwood Ullman. *Single Season Sitcoms, 1948-1979* also lists Milton Pascal.[540] *Writer's Digest* credits Bill Derman with "Annie's Wedding."

Scripter Rhine, who also wrote for *Life of Riley, Mr. Ed, I Love Lucy, Brady Bunch* and *Odd Couple,* told an interviewer: " 'Tugboat Annie' was a weird one. Anthony Veiller, whose father, I believe was a famous New York dramatic, produced these, but they were filmed in Canada and the quality was horrible. It was like they were shot through a dirty window."[541]

No matter. *The Saturday Evening Post* editors were proud the see the magazine represented in television broadcasts. "Already showing are two series, Phil Wylie's Crunch and Des stories, presenting Forrest Tucker as Crunch,[542] and Earle Stanley Gardner's Perry Mason, with Raymond Burr as the famed mystery solver. And in preparation are Bill Upson's Alexander Botts, with Don Adams selling the tractors...."[543]

Half-Hour Shows

In a typical exchange, "Hi, Bullwinkle, you old baboon," greets Annie." "Annie Brennan, I'll get even with you if it takes the rest of my natural life," snorts Bullwinkle.

These are the episodes:

"Home is the Sailor." The pilot, co-written by Ben Starr, was filmed in California. Annie intervenes when the miserly owner puts an old sailors' home on the market.

"Queen Annie." Assassins stalk the sovereign of a small European country who is visiting North America. Talked into acting as her double, Annie lures the villains into a trap.

"Tugboat Annie's Chicken Farm." This was the first episode filmed entirely in Toronto. It's the annual seamen's carnival. Bullwinkle, who has just lost a contract to Annie, bribes a fortune teller to give the *Narcissus* skipper a dire prediction. Annie takes up another career, raising hens.[544]

"Sophisticated Annie." A niece is coming for a visit and Annie wants to make good impression. She borrows use of a nice home of a rich friend and sets about learning good manners in a hurry.

"Tugboat Annie Psychologist." Annie helps Pinto stand up to bully Bullwinkle.

"Stowaway." Bullwinkle eyes a reward for turning in a runaway boy who has taken refuge on the *Narcissus*.

"Tugboat Annie Meets the Texan." Annie intervenes when Bullwinkle plans to take advantage of a Texan whose oil tanker has run ground near Secoma. She pretends to be a fellow Texan.

"Pizza Romance." Pinto falls in love with the daughter of the owner of Louie's Pizza Palace.

"Commodore Bullwinkle." Annie is energized when Bullwinkle's friend Murdoch McArdle assumes ownership of the *Narcissus*.

"Annie's Race Horse." Annie takes an unusual payment for a tow job and turns it into an asset.

"Annie's Retirement." Suffering a severe toothache, Annie decides it's time to take it easy. Until she learns Bullwinkle will take over command if the *Narcissus* in her place.

"Tugboat Annie and the Admiral." Annie tangles with a retired admiral when she broaches the idea of converting her tugboat into a replica of the *USS Missouri*.

"Annie Is a Lady." Lumberman Harding doubts a woman can handle his company's big job.

"Ballots and Ballast." Annie competes against Bullwinkle to be treasurer of the Dock Benevolent Association.

"Happy Birthday." Annie throws Bullwinkle a birthday party, but doesn't invite him. When the police arrive, the *Salamander* skipper is taken away for disturbing the peace.

"Annie Finds a Baby." Bullwinkle babysits a foundling abandoned aboard the *Narcissus*.

"The Romance of Horatio Bullwinkle." Annie helps Bullwinkle evade a wily woman named Lydia, who has a boyfriend and wants to ship stolen goods.

"Annie's Cold Cargo." Annie decides to raise a sunken boat to make enough money for a new engine.

"Annie and the Smuggler." A thief hides stolen diamonds in Terry Brennan's old marbles bag.

"Annie Plays Cupid." Annie tries to settle a family's feud so a young couple can marry.

"Getting Annie's Pig." Loretta the pig comes into Annie's reluctant ownership as payment for a towing bill.

"The Chinese Formula." Annie is conned into buying a phony formula from Bullwinkle that he promises will convert salt water into fresh water.

"The Butler Did It." Annie and Bullwinkle have to deal with an efficiency expert.

"Operation Hotcake." Annie's advice to Pinto to get a raise from Alec Severn backfires. So he falls for a con and acquires Fogarty's debt-ridden café.

"Community Chest Drive." Annie and Bullwinkle both want the Secoma Community Chest award for raising the most money.

"High Blonde Pressure." Annie's interest in a manicure jeopardizes a lucrative tow.

"Annie's Inheritance." Annie can inherit a ship if she has a son. So she adopts Bullwinkle.

"Delinquent." Annie takes a young thug under her wing.

"Golden Fleece." Annie grits her teeth and hires Bullwinkle for a tow when the *Narcissus* breaks down.

"Bullwinkle's Folly." Bullwinkle feigns amnesia to wrangle out of a contract with Annie to take over one of his tows while his engine is repaired.

"The Reformation of Horatio Bullwinkle." Annie uses a seamen's mission band to get back at Bullwinkle when he cheats her out of a job.

"Smoke Screen." Annie plots revenge when she loses a towing arrangement.

"Annie's Big Deal." After Bullwinkle kidnaps her cook, the heroine must prepare a meal for a gourmet in order to secure a contract.

"Lord Horatio Bullwinkle." The *Salamander* skipper believes he has inherited a British estate — until Annie reveals the advising lawyer is a confidence man.

"Annie's Treasure Hunt." Again a salvage job is key to paying for engine repairs.

"A Medal for Annie." Bullwinkle makes false claims in order to win a city medal for the seafaring hero of the year. Annie is determined to expose him.

"A Matter of Principle." Racing to Secoma, Annie and Bullwinkle crash their tugs into a yacht.

"The Sixth Santa." "There really is a Santa Claus," Annie tells a brokenhearted young orphan, Georgie Moore.

"Annie's Wedding." Losing a contract, Bullwinkle frames Annie for rum smuggling.

Della Reese and Ernest Borgnine appear as a boarding house owner and one of her tenants, captain of a salvage tugboat in "Twice in a Lifetime," which aired over NBC in 1974. The storyline was revamped for an unsold pilot, "Flo's Place" (without Borgnine) in 1976. (NBC publicity photo)

'Flo's Place' Didn't Flow

An MGM Television half-hour pilot show featuring Della Reese (1931-2017) as the proprietor of a waterfront lunchroom and boarding house in San Pedro, Calif., didn't appeal to NBC but was included in the network's *Comedy Theater* — a home for foundling episodes — in August 1976.

Media columnist Percy Shain called it "a Tugboat Annie variation."[545] The producers didn't mention Raine's heroine, but the storylines had the Puget Sound flavor.

"Flo's Place" features the singer/actress as "the owner of a modest dockside hotel whose newly acquired (by bequest) tugboat brings unexpected woes to her and her son." Eric Laneuville plays the son, Lewis." Don Weis directed.[546]

This pilot reworked an earlier, 90-minute TV movie, "Twice in a Lifetime," which aired on *NBC Double Feature Night at the Movies* in March 1974. Ernest Borgnine played Vince Boselli, a former Navy cook who now helms a salvage tug, the *Rosa*. He boards at Flo Harrison's Snug Harbor and is responsible for a chair-busting melee. Vince and Flo clash with a dock foreman, Pete Lazich (played by Slim Pickins). Herschel Daugherty directed for Martin Rackin Productions.[547]

In response to fan A.C. McDonald sending him a Confederate bill in thanks for an autograph in 1932, the author replied he couldn't tell if a simple signature was desired, or a letter, so he sent both, as he was "particularly pleased to do so in view of the fact that you are a resident of the north-west, where I have many friends, and in which I spent some delightful months last year."

— Raine to McDonald, 22 April 1932

Chapter 22

Raine Keeps Busy

Joyce Raine performed with the Opera Reading Club Juniors
for various USO centers in 1943. (*Daily News*, 14 June 1943)

The Raines weekended on their Seattle-based cruiser in summer 1934. It was a working vacation as they explored the Sound "gathering new material for his salty sea tales," according to the *Spokane Chronicle*.[548]

The author traveled to Toronto in 1936 to deliver his story "Mr. Gallup is a Terror to Snakes," leading the editor of *Maclean's* to comment: "Norman Reilly Raine … cares naught for weather at all. He was in Toronto during the spring, and plowed through snow and slush in a pair of thin shoes and no rubbers. He did have a scarf around his neck. He usually has. Scarves are his weakness. He buys a selection wherever he goes and is constantly having to move into more commodious premises in order to get space for them...."[549]

Raine in 1938 purchased two buildings lots in a new subdivision on Castilian Drive in the Outpost residential park in Los Angeles, with the expectation of building a new home. It was close to Warner Bros. Studios.[550]

Raine revisited Buffalo in 1939, the city where "as a copy boy [he] once toted black coffee for newspapermen on the old Morning Express."

"Smoking a stubby pipe, the red-haired creator of 'Tugboat Annie' took a few hours from a visit to his brother, Malcolm Raine of 184 St. James Pl., and renewed acquaintances" at the *Evening News*.[551]

Joyce Raine found a social niche in Hollywood. Among close friends were actor Montague love and comedienne Marie Wilson. [552] In 1940 welcomed opera fans to her home for a presentation of *Gianni Schicchi* by the Hollywood Opera Reading club.[553] She was elected vice president that year.[554] In 1941 she sang several songs in a short program for the Assistance League's British Day.[555] The audience included a Sherlockian quartet: the Basil Rathbones and the Nigel Bruces.

The writer's circle of friends included Sir Francis Evans when the latter was British Consul in Los Angeles.[556]

Roger, the maître d'hotel of the Sunset strip's swankiest night club, offered some of his "bests" of guests. Ginger Rogers, for example, was his best dressed girl, John Carroll his smoothest wolf. His favorite customer was Raine.[557]

Raine's income in 1942 was $76,000, according to *Motion Picture Herald*[558]; in 1946 it was $102,375, *Motion Picture Daily* reported.[559]

The Raines lived at 70560 LaPress Dr. in Los Angeles in 1945.

•

Norman and Joyce divorced in 1946. She asserted cruelty as justification: "For some time before we separated, he kept extremely irregular hours. He rarely came home to dinner, and was noncommittal when he did come home.

"We discussed it, and he said he didn't want to be tied. He wanted to be free. He didn't want to have set times to do things," she testified. Her nephew was a corroborating witness. [560]

Raine "liked to call himself 'The Bachelor Type,' his wife testified…."[561]

Joyce Raine married Columbia actor George E. Eldridge (ca1891-1968) in 1951.[562]

Raine's name was for a time linked romantically to dancer Nova Dale, who divorced night club operator Vincent Chalone.[563] Her real name was Mary Dorothy Lynch.[564]

Weds Betty Prudhomme

Raine quietly remarried. His bride was Elizabeth "Betty" (1931-2016), one of the Prudhomme twins. The other was Beverly (1931-2023).

The sisters —from a family of 10 siblings, Los Angeles-born offsprings of William W. and Edna Mae (Ducloslange) Prud'homme (to use the traditional spelling) — wrote songs recorded by Sam Cooke, Fats Domino, Elvis Presley, Tina Turner, Michael Jackson and Aretha Franklin, among others. They also recorded and performed, sometimes billed as the Creole Twins. Their first song, "Ring, Phone, Ring," was recorded by Marion Marlowe. Other Twins compositions were "Cobra Eye," "Earthly Heaven," "Love's Torture." "Love and Life," "Love's Torture Chamber," "I Don't Need a Diary" and "Sugar, Sugar, Sugar Babe." They co-wrote "Rome (Wasn't Built In A Day)" with Cooke. The pair also had independent careers as background singers and stage performers.

Magazine photographers sought the twins for cheesecake poses, such as "Pretty Good 'Bet' " in the *Pittsburgh Courier* in 1952, when Betty was a contender for "Miss Bronze L.A.[565]

Divorced from Joyce Pett, Raine married Elizabeth "Betty" Prudhomme in 1958. (*Los Angeles Times*, 7 January 1959).

Jet magazine carried a beach pinup of the sisters, "Double Exposure," in November 1957.

Raine acknowledged the 30 December 1958 marriage to the 26-year-old entertainer six months after the fact. He was 64. She had two previous marriages. He had one.[566]

"It was kept a secret because I was so tied up with writing commitments," was his explanation.[567]

Prudhomme had recently appeared in the films *Rains of Ranchipur* and *The Ten Commandments*.

"As a writer, Raine has been figuring whether to use his new black-haired, black-eyed actress-singer-songwriter wife as a central character," reported the *Los Angeles Times*.[568]

The new Mrs. Raine, though her film career ended, continued writing songs with her sister. Betty kept active after her husband's death; in 1979 she produced "Tut Tut Twins," Parts 1 and 2 on either side of a 7-inch 331/3 rpm vinyl for the Cobra Eye. In 2014 the sisters took part in a Mixcloud podcast interview, discussing their career.

Double Exposure: Frolicking on the beach at Santa Monica, alluring Beverly and Betty Prudhomme almost give viewers an illusion of seeing double. The identical Los Angeles twins are singing, dancing and acting stars with identical height, weight and physiques.

The Prudhomme Twins — Betty and her sister Beverly — were songwriters as well as performers and occasional pinup gals. (Howard Morehead, *Jet*, 21 November 1957)

Normans Mixup

Fame goes only so far.

"One morning, while breakfasting in a Hollywood café," *The Saturday Evening Post* related in 1952, "he observed three young marines conversing impetuously with Virginia, a waitress who is delectable even that early in the morning. This seemed normal until Raine realized that they kept glancing at him. *What ails me now?* He thought, *An attack of dandruff? Necktie tied in a wad?*"

Virginia approached Raine and told him the young men were from the East Coast and were on the lookout for movie stars. She gave them his name.

"Raine delightedly resigned himself to the annoyance. Leisurely finishing his breakfast as fast as he could bolt it down, he rushed slowly outside, and hurried with dragging feet past the waiting boys. Just as he decided, with horror, that he had got by them without being plagued, one grabbed his arm with a diffident, crushing grip, and ventured, his eyes shining, 'Please may I have your autograph, Mr. Rockwell?'"[569]

Raine in fact knew the popular illustrator Norman Rockwell.

Nancy Joyce (Pett) Princehorn (1936-2018) of Massillon, Ohio, "was partly raised by her Great Aunt Joyce, who was married to the famous Oscar winner [for screenwriting], Norman Reilly Raine. She lived a grand adventure there in a home just beneath the Hollywood sign. Her neighbor was Norman Rockwell, who would come to draw and visit on their patio."[570]

Rockwell (1894-1978) was in Hollywood in 1930, staying with his cartoonist friend Clyde Forsythe. Through Forsythe's neighbor, attorney Alfred Barstow. Rockwell met and married Mary Barstow, a teacher.[571]

Time to Retire

Raine served as a member of Screen Writers Guild and California Writers and became a governor of the Academy of Motion Picture Arts & Sciences in 1941.[572]

His prose writing career which began with "Heritage" in 1924 closed out with "The Karimata Ghost" in 1963. His screenwriting which began with *Tugboat Annie* in 1933 ended in 1960 with *The American Doctor*.

It was time to retire.

" 'All I do is go to one of the greasy spoons on the waterfront, take a seat and listen,' NRR said. 'I get ideas and plots and all. And if I've pulled some boner the guys give me plenty of hell.' "

— Glen Carter, "He gave us 'Tugboat Annie,' "
Seattle Times, 30 July 1971

Chapter 23

Ashes Scattered

"He wrote many screenplays and won an Oscar for 'The Life of Emile Zola,' but Norman Reilly Raine was known to millions of Americans only as the creator of Tugboat Annie," said the *Tacoma News* in announcing the author's death.[573]

"To those who struggled through the Depression," Ed Meagher wrote in the *Los Angeles Times*, "there were few things to laugh about — but high among them were the Tugboat Annie stories and films."[574]

Raine died 19 July 1971 at the Motion Picture Country Hospital in Woodland Hills. A memorial service was held at the Little Country Chapel in North Hollywood.

Survivors included his wife Betty and his brother James B. Raine, who came from England for the funeral.

The writer's ashes fittingly were scattered at sea, to commemorate his love of saltwater lore and maritime traditions. [575]

James in 1981 donated his brother's papers to Boston University's Howard Gottlieb Research Center.

Lee Harris of LMHS Entertainment represented Betty Raine, who retained ownership of her late husband's literary output.[576] Many of the stories' copyrights were renewed in Elizabeth Raine's name in the early 1980s.

The final exchange between Annie and Bullwinkle in the final story has the latter receiving a broad kick in the seat of the pants from the former.

" 'What the hell was that fer, ya cow-bellied old dugong?' he roared.

" 'Remember me bellerin' an' cussin' at ye that day when we was headed for Port Tundra?' she demanded belligerantly.

" 'What of it?' he snarled.

" 'Well, that kick in the tail,' said Annie, complacently now, 'was to l'arn ye that next time a leddy cusses ye out, ye'll cuss her back, like a genelman should!' "

— "Annie and the Killer Ship"

Chapter 24

Tugboat Annie's Legacy

Canada issued a Marie Dressler commemorative postage
stamp in 2008. The *Narcissus* is in the background.

Scholar Fred Erisman sees Annie as a feminist. "Woman she is and woman she remains, but it is as towboat master that she insists on being judged, making her one of the earliest of modern feminist advocates in American popular fiction." [577]

He notes: "If she conventionally speaks of herself as "a towboat man," she nevertheless defends the capabilities of her sex with all the passion of which she is capable."

He says one of her best demonstrations of her ability are found in "If The Cap Fits," when she succinctly puts a ship owner in his place: "If a god in pants like yerself had been in command o' the Narcissus, ye'd ha' called it a act o' providence or peril o' the sea, and made the best of it. But because a woman was skipper, ye call it poor seamanship and bad judgment, and ye cancel Alec's contract and git me the sack! But don't you forget, me fine-feathered friend ... that it was a woman what l'arned you to eat, and talk, and walk, and blow yer nose, and put yer little britches on!"

•

Dear Dr. Eisenberg:

It gives me pleasure to send you greetings from *Tugboat Annie* and *Horatio Bullwinkle*

Sincerely yours --

Norman Reilly Raine

Did Annie and Horatio exist? They signed this card for a fan, didn't they?

The last new Tugboat Annie story appeared in 1961.

All told print and visual presentations totaled 120, by Raine and assorted screenwriter partners. The books have gone out of print. Two of the three black-and-white films air from time to time but the television shows except for one available on YouTube are out of circulation.

It's hard for the old woman to maintain her profile.

The *Kennewick Courier-Reporter* in 1949 reported: "A Memorial plaque to a fiction character 'Tugboat Annie' rests on a traffic island in downtown Tacoma Wash."[578]

According to another newspaper, Tacoma in 1951 installed a memorial plaque to "Tugboat Annie" on a traffic island downtown.[579] Later the same year, it designated East F. St. north of the 11th Street bridge over the Puyallup Waterway as Tugboat Annie Street. Because the name was so long, private funds had to be solicited to cover the cost of a sign.[580]

Restaurateurs have done their best. There have been Tugboat Annie restaurants in Olympia, Wash.; Richmond, British Columbia; Dania Beach, Fla.; Oklahoma City, Okla.; Claremont, Calif. (built in the shape of a tugboat); and Baltimore, Md. Towboat Annie Floating Café launched in Jefferson, Ind., and relocated to Louisville, Ky., in 1997.[581]

In 1983, the Downtown Tacoma Association won the Queen's Trophy for its float in the 50th annual Puyallup Valley Daffodil Festival, its theme the filming of the movie *Tugboat Annie*.[582]

Tacoma's Maritime Fest 2009 included a "Miss Tugboat Annie" contest.[583]

In the printing industry, Agfa Monotype announced a "Tugboat Annie" font in 2001.[584]

Canada Post in 2008 issued a 52¢ commemorative postage stamp for Marie Dressler, a tugboat *Narcissus* in the background.[585]

In 2019, Olympia Harbor Days featured a vintage tugboat show and races.[586] The near-annual tradition had begun in 1991.

Puget Sound hasn't forgotten its maritime history or its famous literary heroine, and neither have the rest of us.

"The fictional stories of Annie were so vivid that even now some old-timers are reluctant to say there was no real Annie… Real or not, Annie quickened the hearts of men. Seattle was an old-tradition port city. In her floppy hat and bulky peacoat, Annie shouted above wind in a foghorn voice. She battled storms, tides, a balky engine and old Bullwinkle and won. Her heart was big and solid gold…."

— Glen Carter, *My Waterfront* (1977)

Afterword

'Woman Tugboat Skipper Dies At Age 80'

The *Bremerton Sun* ran this lead obituary in its 25 June 1977 issue:

"Anna Flynn Brennan, 80, former captain of the tugboat 'Narcissus' and recipient of the Navy Cross, died Friday at the family home in Anacortes.

"In 1945 Mrs. Brennan received the Navy Cross and her boat and crew received a Presidential Unit Citation for their efforts, under fire, in towing off Kamikaze-damaged destroyers during the invasion of Okinawa.

"She was born in 1897 in Friday Harbor, daughter of Captain John P. Flynn, a skipper in the Mosquito Fleet.[587] She married Captain Terence F.Q. Brennan of the tugboat 'Narcissus' in 1917. Soon after her marriage she began accompanying her husband on his trips, acting as mate. Upon her husband's death in 1923,[588] the Seacoma Deep-Deep-Sea Towing and Salvage Company asked her to become captain of the 'Narcissus.' She accepted and for the next 29 years managed the tugboat until 1952,[589] when she was elected chairman of the board of Seacoma. In 1942 she spent several months helping the United States Coast Guard to revise 'The Rules of The Road for Inland Waters.' She retired from active participation in company affairs in 1972, saying at the time that she felt that, 'three quarters of a century is enough for any old seadog.'

"At the time of her death she was chairman emeritus of the Seacoma Deep-Sea Towing and Salvage Company.

"Services and cremation are private."

The notice, accompanied by a photo of Anna Flynn Brennan,[590] appeared without preamble or explanation in the newspaper. It was cleverly written by one quite familiar with the dearly departed. The daily Kitsap County paper's editor was Gene Gisley.

So, was Tugboat Annie a real person after all?

We'd ask her daughter, if we knew more about her.

Acknowledgements

I have been a weekly newspaper reporter, editor, columnist and/or page designer. I've been a freelance writer of too many magazine and newspaper articles and op-ed pieces to count and nearly 60 books, about evenly split between popular literature references and Berkshire County, Massachusetts, local histories.

Researching this dual biography was largely a solitary endeavor. However, daughter Jessie Drew of Olympia, Wash., a staff member at the Lacey Timberland Library, connected me with valuable Northwest resources and with her husband Jo Élan helped me and my wife, Donna, explore the South Puget Sound a few years back. The two Olympians enjoy an occasional Irish night at Tugboat Annie's.

Younger daughter Darcie Drew of Portland, Maine, a high school history teacher, apprised me of maritime matters on Casco Bay and was a general cheerleader.

Donna, a veteran elementary art teacher, accompanied me on several research excursions. And she read some of the Tugboat Annie stories.

Endnotes

Face and obverse of a souvenir Marie Dressler token issued by
MGM when the film *Tugboat Annie* was released in 1933.

1   "Specialization Necessary for Story Writing," *Seattle Post-Intelligencer*, 2 April 1930.

2   Raine, "Author Reveals 'Annie's' Origin," wire story, *Bakersfield Californian*, 17 August 1933.

3   "Arts Editor of Journal Retiring," *Lansing State Journal*, 30 May 1965, and "Retired Editor Dies at 72," same source, 25 November 1970. Also Phil M. Daly, Along the Rialto, *Film Daily*, 8 September 1933.

4   Raine, "That's How Tugboat Annie Was Born," *Pacific Motor Boat*, November 1934. Reprinted in *The Sea Chest*, Puget Sound Maritime Historical Society, September 1969, and in part in "The Genesis of Tugboat Annie," *Sea History*, autumn 1982.

5   "How 'Tugboat Annie' Was Born," *Warren Times Mirror*, 26 August 1933.

6   Martin Sheridan, "Seventy-year-Old Woman Manages Tugboat Company," *Springfield Sunday Union*, 14 January 1940; "Mrs. Catherine Sutton, 82, 'Tugboat Annie' Prototype," *Washington Evening Star*, 3 January 1959; and "Kate Sutton; Prototype of Fictional Tugboat Annie Dies," *Daily Boston Globe*, 4 January 1959.

7   Providence reporter James S. Hart provided information.

8   Death notice, 4 January 1959. Also "Mrs. N.H. Sutton Dead," *New York Times*, 4 January 1959. See Jillian Fulda, Ed Spinney & Brent Dibner, "The Providence Steamboat Company: Still a Family Business," *PowerShips*, Summer 2012.

9   "Only Woman Boss of Tugboat Fleet," *Daily Boston Globe*, 14 January 1940.

10   Among other sources, Sarah Laskow, "How the Original 'Tugboat Annie' Turned a $5 Rowboat Into an Empire," *Atlas Obscura*, 15 July 2015.

11   Lynn Bragg, *More Than Petticoats: Remarkable Washington Women* (Globe Pequot Press, 2010). See also Marta Brooks, "The daughters of Tugboat Annie," *The Dispatcher*, March 2004.

12   "Tugboat Annie's Origin Revealed," *Oregonian*, 15 September 1940. See also R.H. "Skipper" Calkins, "Towboating on Puget Sound," *Marine Digest*, 7 February 1951.

13   "Rites Being Arranged for Wedell Foss," *Seattle Times*, 7 January 1955.

14   " 'Tugboat Annie's' Son Visits Here," *Cleveland Plain Dealer*, 16 September 1941.

15   " 'Tugboat Annie' Founded On Fact, Writer Reveals," 23 July 1933.

16   Michael E. Tollaksen death notice, *Seattle Times*, 3 October 1928, and "Mrs. Tollaksen, Widow of Tug Skipper, Dies," *Seattle Daily Times*, 6 June 1961. Also *Evening Star*, 5 June 1961.

17   Left Hand Corner, 29 January 1934.

18   The Pulse of the West. When the Washington legislature dithered over renaming Mt. Tacoma (favored in Senate) or Mt. Rainier (representatives preferred) in 1924, a suggestion was made to take letters from Seattle and Tacoma and call it Mt. Tattle. "Seacoma, Rainoma, Spokane; These and Tattle are Suggested as Compromise Names for West Side Mountain," *Spokane Press*, 28 April 1924.

19   Lee Side o' L.A., "Personal Glimpses of Famous Folks" *Los Angeles Times*, 11 December 1932.

20   Power With Words syndicated column, *Reno Gazette Journal*, 21 February 1952.

21   Keeping Posted, 17 October 1959.

22   Her full name was only revealed in *Glencannon Meets Tugboat Annie*, when the novel's two main characters are called before a district court judge and are fined for disturbing the peace.

23   "Creator of Tugboat Annie Back in Buffalo for Visit," *Buffalo Evening News*, 1 July 1939.

24   Bernard A. Drew, "Scattergood Baines, Tugboat Annie and Friends," *Million*, November-December 1992.

25   "The Short Story Grows Up," *Saturday Evening Post*, 1 January 2011. See Jan Cohn, *Creating America: George Horace Lorimer and The Saturday Evening Post* (University of Pittsburgh Press, 1989)

26   Tish would appear in four films, Botts in one, Scattergood in six and Slappy in four.

27   Periodical Reading Room, *Journal of Marketing*, January 1998.

28   Published by Literary America, 1935.

29   "Don't Go Near the Water," *Oakland Tribune*, 31 December 1958.

30   "Famed Film Writer Was City Native," Wilke Barre *Times Leader*, 4 August 1971. City directories listed John W. Raine living variously at 24 Madison St., 219 Madison St., 156 Blackman St. and finally 219 Fell St. He then relocated to Boston, per the 1896 directory.

31   1 May 1928.

32   Ruth Ellis, "Buffalonians in Hollywood," *Buffalo Evening News*, 24 July 1935.

33   As he was born in 1894, he would have been 21.

34   Attestation Papers, No. 527637, viewed on Ancestry.com. and MyLife.com.

35   "We Can Hold Anything Fritz Puts Across; Buffalo Boy With Canadians Writes of Life at Front," 17 April 1918.

36   Regimental record.

37   See also Harry Bossin, "Norman Reilly Raine," *Maclean's*, 1 July 1938.

38   Leeside, *Los Angeles Times*, 17 March 1944.

39   Norman Riley [sic] Raine, "Buffalo's 74th Over There, Eager for Blow at Boche," *Buffalo Evening News*, 5 August 1918.

40   "In the Trenches," 13 October 1918.

41   Last Pay Certificate, signed by paymaster, No. 2 District, Toronto.

42   Medical Examination Upon Leaving the Service of Officers and Other Ranks Who Have No Disability, 6 March 1919.

43   Discharge Card, 21 October 1918.

44   " 'Exchange Street Looked Better Than Monte Carlo,' " *Buffalo Evening News*, 27 February 1919.

45   Issue of 1 May 1928.

46   In the Editor's Confidence, *Maclean's*, 1 February 1924.

47   Advertisements, *Montreal Gazette*, 16 October 1922, and *Ottawa Citizen*, 4 January 1927.

48   "A Layman's Study of the Hospital," Ontario Sessional Papers, 1923.

49   "Corps, Band Will Greet Raine at Station Tonight," 30 July 1942.

50   "Priceless Relics From Regiment," *Spokesman Review*, 21 August 1938. The unit was also known as John Graves Simcoe's American Rangers in Canada.

51   In the Editor's Confidence, *Maclean's*, 15 April 1933.

52   "Not Many Authors Can Do This Much," 22 March 1930.

53   "Born On Same Day As Prince," *Montclair Times*, 16 August 1924, repeating information from *Everybody's Magazine*.

54   In the Editor's Confidence, *Maclean's*, 15 April 1933.

55   Everybody's Chimney Corner, September 1924.

56   In the Editor's Confidence, *Maclean's*, 15 May 1926.

57   "Tugboat Annie, Colin Glencannon Join Forces as Authors Collaborate Here," 12 February 1950.

58   Raine, "Contemporary Writers and Their Work," 25 October 1924.

59   "Publicity Work For Vancouver in Orient," *Vancouver Province*, 29 February 1924.

60   "To Marry Prominent Author," *Montreal Daily Star*, 21 April 1928; "Miss Joyce Pett Will Wed Writer Of Sea Stories," *San Antonio Light*, 11 October 1932; "Soldier to Wed Canadian Beauty," *Windsor Star*, 2 April 1928; "Toronto Girl To Wed Well-Known Writer," *Toronto Star Weekly*, 24 March 1928; and "Writer Will Marry Miss Pett in Toronto, *Windsor Star*, 4 April 1928.

61 In the Editor's Confidence, *Mclean's,* 1 February 1932.

62 He is misidentified as Raine's son in "Wife Said Attentive To Men in Services," *San Bernardino Sun,* 26 July 1944, which described Pett's divorce action. See also "Mother Loses Custody of Two in Divorce Suit," *Los Angeles Times,* 26 August 1943.

63 December 1927.

64 November 1928, the byline "Captain N.R. Raine."

65 "Now on the News Stands," advertisement, *Montreal Gazette,* 27 February 1928.

66 "Name This Child," 30 November 1955. Not to mention other tri-named contemporaries William Hazlett Upson, Octavus Roy Cohen, George Harmon Coxe, Samuel Hopkins Adams, Clarence Budington Kelland or Mary Roberts Rinehart.

67 "Brilliant Editor," *Vancouver Sun,* 17 August 1928.

68 "Maclean's Editor Visits Edmonton," *Edmonton Journal,* 7 August 1928.

69 Succeeded by Napier Moore, Mackenzie was born in New York, educated in Canada and served as a pilot in the Royal Flying Corps. "Fit as a Commando," *Evening Standard,* 16 August 1944.

70 Mackenzie became an Associated Press war correspondent in the 1940s.

71 "Author Raine Is Displayed Like Goldfish at 'U' School," 2 April 1930.

72 McKenzie gave himself credit for correcting a mistake that brought Raine's early manuscripts sailing back from publishers. "I found the reason for rejection slips — he had been making the same mistake each time. It gives me pleasure to know that he is now a writer." He didn't say what that mistake was. And it wasn't as if Raine wasn't making sales. Christine Neergard, "A Reason for Traveling," *The Town Crier,* 1 December 1934.

73 Society, *Medicine Hat News,* 27 August 1928.

74 "Short Story Club Meets," *Seattle Daily Times,* 7 May 1930.

75 "Modeling for Charity Is Success to Society," *Seattle Sunday Times,* 14 September 1930.

76 Joan Arnold, "Women Credited With Good Taste in Masculine Gifts," *Seattle Daily Times,* 18 December 1930.

77 Personals, *Wrangell Sentinel*, 10 July 1930.

78 Robert M. McBride & Co, 1935. Reviewed in The Book Beat, *The Quill*, September 1935.

79 Obituary, *Bellingham Herald*, 27 June 2010.

80 June Burn, Puget Soundings, *Bellingham Herald*, 10 December 1930, and Strolling Around the Town, 31 December 1940 & 18 August 1942; Anne Hellickson, "Local Novel Features Phoebe and Her In-Laws," *Star Tribune*, 7 April 1946; & "San Juan Island Novel Due This Week," *Seattle Daily Times*, 2 September 1951, and other sources.

81 "Strained Ankles, New Pencils Start Seattle Woman on Literary Career," *Seattle Daily Times*, 19 June 1930.

82 "Author Hunting Material in N.W.," 9 April 1930.

83 Personal Mention, *Vancouver Evening Columbian*, 28 April 1930.

84 "Impresario May Rush In Where Boy Friend Hesitates," *Seattle Daily Times*, 18 January 1931.

85 "Interesting Speaker," *Seattle Star*, 25 April 1931.

86 P.D.S., "Writes Sagas of the Sea; Raine Likes Seattle; Nationally-Known Author Originates New Northwest Character; to Live in Sound Country," 19 July 1931.

87 *Film Daily*, 19 July1931. Also Hubbard Keavy, "Role of Actress In 'Anna Christie' Inspires Another," *Indianapolis Star*, 21 December 1932.

88 Raine, "That's How Tugboat Annie Was Born," *op cit*, and "Puget Sound Is Good Enough For Tugboat Annie, She Says," *Seattle Daily Times*, 29 October 1934.

89 Gwen Cash, The Passing Parade, Vancouver *Province*, 28 May 1938.

90 "Last Meeting Told," *Seattle Daily Times*, 22 April 1931, and "Norman Raine To Be Guest," *Seattle Post-Intelligencer*, 26 April 1931.

91 "Free Lances," *Seattle Daily Times*, 30 April 1931. The writers' group organized in 1921. "More Than 1000 Washingtonians In Organized Writing Groups," *Seattle Daily Times*, 23 June 1956. Other guests included Betty MacDonald, James H. Stevens, Beatrice Cook, Kenneth Gilbert and Frank Richardson Pierce.

92 "Marie Dressler Inspires Raine, Sea-Tale Author," *Seattle Times*, 21 August 1932. See also "Author Is Here," *Seattle Post-Intelligencer*, 14 August 1932.

93 "Raine, Author, To Help Film 'Annie,' " *Seattle Daily Times*, 24 October 1932.

94 " 'Tugboat Annie' Author Is Here," *Seattle Post*-Intelligencer, 14 August 1932.

95 Lee Side o' L.A., "Personal Glimpses of Famous Folks," *Los Angeles Times*, 11 December 1932.

96 "Pink Tulle Curves Latest Fad in Film City, Collette Is Told," 5 September 1932.

97 "Norman Reilly Raine To Be in City Saturday," *Province*, 12 March 1933.

98 "Brilliant Writer Edmonton Visitor," *Edmonton Journal*, 17 March 1933.

99 "Raine Stops In 'Tugboat Annie's' Port," *Seattle Daily Times*, 23 March 1933.

100 New York Day by Day, *Nebraska State Journal*, 5 April 1934, syndicated.

101 "Entre Nous, *Seattle Daily Times*, 30 June 1934, and "Ewings on Sound at Summer Home," *Spokane Chronicle*, 5 July 1934.

102 Society, *Seattle Daily Times*, 1 July 1934.

103 "Gay Tables Are Filled At The Olympic," *Seattle Daily Times*, 1 May 1934.

104 "Save 4 Ways with Triton!," *Seattle Post-Intelligencer*, 30 My 1937.

105 Gwen Cash, The Passing Parade, *The Province*, 28 May 1938.

106 "Pow! Cowboy, 8, 'Hoists' Pierce With His Own 'Pistol,' " *Seattle Daily Times*, 28 May 1938.

107 "Students and Faculty Tell Vacation Thrills," *Seattle Daily Times*, 4 October 1938.

108 "Opera Club to Give 'Tales From Hoffman,'" *Los Angeles Times*, 3 December 1939.

109 "Opera Club Will Gather Presents for Servicemen," *Los Angeles Times*, 7 December 1942.

110 See Carl Abbott, *Imagined Frontiers: Contemporary America and Beyond* (University of Oklahoma Press, 2015).

111 This paragraph was spurred by John J. Kucich, "The Understory: Henry Thoreau, Richard Powers and the Cultural Edge, *The Concord Saunterer: A Journal of Thoreau Studies*, New Series Vol. 31, 2023.

112 On the Columbia River; population 192,000. Not to be confused with Vancouver at Burrard Inlet, the ethnically diverse city of 675,000, the most populous in British Columbia. Both are named for Dutch explorer George Vancouver.

113 "Coast Offers Much Color For Story Writers," *Times Colonist*, 21 July 1931.

114 "Anacortes Shipping," *Bellingham Herald*, 27 March 1928.

115 "Fifty Years of Service," 2 April 1942.

116 "The Sea-Tac Airport," *News Tribune*, 3 January 1943.

117 Tasha Anderson, Northwest Seaport Alliance special section, *Alaska Business Monthly*, June 2016.

118 See also his *Puget's Sound: A Narrative of Early Tacoma and the Southern Sound* (2018) and Ronald Magden and A.D. Martinson's *The Working Waterfront: The Story of Tacoma's Ships and Men* (International Longshoremen's and Warehousemen's Union, Local 23, of Tacoma and Washington Commission for the Humanities, 1982) and Joy Keniston-Longrie's *Seattle's Waterfront* (Arcadia, 2014).

119 *Cruising Guide to Puget Sound and the San Juan Islands Olympia to Port Angeles* (International Marine/Ragged Mountain Press, 2005). See also Caroline Gallacci and Ron Karabaich's *Tacoma's Waterfront* (Arcadia, 2006).

120 J.W., Chartroom Chatter, " 'Tugboat Annie Scores Again," *Seattle Sunday Times*, 14 November 1954.

121 This writer followed travels of the *Narcissus* on a U.S. Department of Commerce National Oceanic and Atmospheric Administration National Ocean Service Coast Survey of Puget Sound, scale 1:150,000, 30th edition, 2010, corrected through 2016.

122 Possibly a nod to Henry O. Foss of the Foss Launch & Tow Co.

123 "Hunting the Issue, *Daily Boston Globe*, 22 June 1934.

124 Down the Hatch, "People Of Waterfront Know 'Tugboat Annie,'" *Seattle Post-Intelligencer*, 26 February 1953.

125 Wonder how dangerous these waters really are? See John M. MacFarlane's *Shipwreck! A Chronicle of Marine Accidents & Disasters in British Columbia* (MacFarlane, 2021).

126 Richard W. Blumenthal, *Maritime Place Names: Inland Washington Waters* (Bellevue, Wash.: Inland Waters Publishing, 2012).

127 "Capt. Nat. Sutton Dead; Well Known Bay Pilot," *Fall River Evening Herald*, 23 July 1915.

128 See Norman H. Clark, *Mill Town* (University of Washington Press, 1970) and M.L. Dehm's *Downtown Everett* (Arcadia, 2005).

129 See Erich R. Ebel with Chuck Fowler, *Exploring Maritime Washington: A History and Guide* (History Press, 2023).

130 "Author Honors Local Oil Man!," *Wilmington Daily Press Journal*, 10 may 1934.

131 See Jefferson County Historical Society's *Port Townsend* (Arcadia, 2008).

132 See Jill Bullock's *Olympia* (Arcadia, 2010) and Les Eldridge and John W. Hough's *Maritime Olympia and South Puget Sound* (Arcadia, 2017).

133 Tacoma Public Library digital Place Name archive.

134 For a general overview, see Chuck Fowler and Capt. Mark Freeman's *Tugboats on Puget Sound* (Arcadia, 2009).

135 There is a meaning for each steam or compressed-air horn/police whistle signal. Droll Yankees of Providence, R.I., in 1960 recorded on DY104 of Captain Leon Nickerson at work in the pilothouse of the *Gaspee* and on DY105 exchanges between the pilothouses of the tugs *Maurania II* and the *King Philip* as they docked a British tanker and of the *Gaspee* approaching an Egyptian tramp steamer.

136 Of All Things, Keeping Posted, 9 January 1937.

137 Of All Things, Keeping Posted, 17 April 1938.

138 11 June 1938.

139 Keeping Posted, 11 June 1938.

140 "Enjoy The Post Tonight," *Daily Utah Chronicle*, 29 September 1938.

141 *New of Norway* would on 9 September 1954 publish" 'Tugboat Annie' Based on Life of Norwegian Immigrant."

142 Among Other Things, 22 October 1938.

143 Tacoma Public Library digital Place Name archive.

144 "Screen Tugboat Annie Approved by Author," 1 January 1941.

145 "Senhora Annie," Keeping Posted, 23 March 1940.

146 "Annie Rides Again," Keeping Posted, 19 October 1940.

147 "Writer May Leave 'Annie' to Posterity," 29 September 1940.

148 Letters, Raine, 16 December 1940; replies, 6 January 1941.

149 "The Position of Eire," 17 December 1940.

150 Among Other Things, 7 March 1942.

151 "Ahoy There, Annie!" Keeping Posted, 18 May 1943.

152 "Tugboat Annie Picture to be Sold," *Seattle Times*, 4 April 1986.

153 "The Long Absence of Tugboat Annie," 15 June 1946.

154 A port for ferries.

155 Richard W. Blumenthal, *Maritime Place Names: Inland Washington Waters* (Bellevue, Wash.: Inland Waters Publishing, 2012).

156 Weber Studies, Spring 1991.

157 "Beef About Bullwinkle," 17 May 1947.

158 See also Tacoma Public Library's digital resource, Place Name Index.

159 There was a signaling code of bells and jingles between the wheelhouse and the engine room. One source of information about their meanings, as well as descriptions of rigging and other tugboat methods, is in Robin Sheret's *Tugs Booms & Barges: The Story of the Tugs and Crews in British Columbia and Puget Sound* (Victoria: Western Isles Cruise & Dive Co., Ltd., 1999)

160 Tacoma Public Library's digital resource, Place Name Index.

161 "Tugboat Annie to Meet Mr. Gallup, Says Raine," *Times Colonist*, 25 May 1938.

162 "Man From Nova Scotia," *Saturday Evening Post*, 31 January 14948.

163 Tacoma Public Library digital Place Name archive.

164 "We See by the Papers ….," *Classics Journal*, December 1948.

165 *Saturday Evening Post*, 9 October 1948.

166 Blumenthal, *Maritime Place Names.*

167 The popular spelling of the old French name is Prud'homme.

168 Tacoma Public Library digital Place Name archive.

169 Tacoma Public Library digital Place Name archive.

170 Blumenthal, *Maritime Place Names.*

171 Keeping Posted, "Farewell to Glencannon," 26 August 1950.

172 *Guy Gilpatric's Flying Stories* (1946) collects many of these tales.

173 IMDb and other sources.

174 G.B. Lal, "It Was All So Useless," *San Francisco Examiner*, 10 September 1950.

175 "A Salty Affair," Letters to the Editor, *Saturday Evening Post*, 30 September 1950.

176 "An Historic Meeting," 3 March 1951.

177 "When Glencannon Meets Tugboat Annie," 25 February 1951. The fictional seaman had a legion of fans. He inspired a two-volume *The Glencannon Encyclopedia* by Walter W. Jaffee (Glencannon Press, 2003).

178 "Hilton, Raine, Stern, Innes," 3 March 1951.

179 "Books; Sagas of the Sea Top Navy's Library List," March 1951.

180 "Laughter Rocks This Tale," *Independent Press Telegram*, 4 February 1951.

181 "Wrong Boat," To the Editor, *Saturday Evening Post*, 7 October 1950.

182 "Not So Fast," *Saturday Evening Post*, 9 June 1951.

183 "Annie Explains," To the Editor, *Saturday Evening Post*, 21 July 1951.

184 "A Weary Old Ship," Keeping Posted, 17 March 1951.

185 Blumenthal, *Maritime Place Names.*

186 Beatrice Cook, "How to Cook — And Like It!," *Seattle Times*, 10 February 1952.

187 T.V. In Review, "Stay on your tugboat, Annie," 17 October 1957.

188 Keeping Posted," Tugboat Annie Has a Nostalgic Meeting," *Saturday Evening Post*, 12 January 1957.

189 "First in the Post, Then on Television," 26 October 1957.

190 Letters to the Editor, September 1981.

191 Tacoma Public Library digital Place Name archive.

192 "Admiral Hornblower," 31 May 1958.

193 Blumenthal, *Maritime Place Names.*

194 Letters, 18 February 1961.

195 Blumenthal, *Maritime Place Names.*

196 Sherrie A. Inness, ed. (University of Pennsylvania Press, 1998).

197 Wife of Sigmund and mother of Sigurd in Norse mythology.

198 A beautiful Valkyrie German and Icelandic in heroic literature who defies chief god Odin and spurns would-be savior Siegfried.

199 "Cash or Credit" by McCandless and "Flowers for Violet" by Adams are reprinted in Drew, ed., *Hard-Boiled Dames* (New York: St. Martin's Press, 1986). *The Big Book of Female Detectives* (New York: Vintage Crime/Black Lizard, 2018), Otto Penzler, ed., contains a McCandless story, "Too Many Clients."

200 "Fischer Does 'Annie' Press Book Drawings," *Motion Picture Daily*, 17 September 1940.

201 All in Fun, "Media," Peter Puget Jr., *Tacoma News Tribune*, 12 October 1932.

202 Kathrine Sigsbee Fischer and Alex A. Hurst (Mill Hill Press, 1984).

203 Sterling Publishing, 1964.

204 Keeping Posted, 12 January 1957.

205 Peacock Press/Bantam Books 1976.

206 "From 'Tugboat Annie's' Pappy," February 1949.

207 The letter appeared in the February Issue.

208 Compiled by Ian Ballantine. (New York: Simon & Schuster)

209 *Tow Line,* March 1959.

210 "Rec'd Too Late for X'mas Issue," March 1961.

211 The Lee Side o' L.A., 4 December 1934.

212 "The Daughters of Tugboat Annie," March 2004 issue of the International Longshore & Warehouse Union publication.

213 "Dressler And Beery 2nd Week at Loew's," *Reading (Pa.) Times*, 18 August 1933.

214 Louis Arthur Cunningham, "Kool is the Word for Molly," *Toronto Star Weekly,* 3 June 1939. Paul Morden, "Great Lakes shipping group calls for more icebreakers," *Windsor Star*, 5 June 2019.

215 "Pt. Alberni Has Tugboat Annie," *Windsor Star*, 18 February 1942.

216 "Eve Gulliford celebrates her 70th birthday," *Salmon Arm Observer*,28 January 1987.

217 *Congressional Record*, House of Representatives, 1 October 1969.

218 Edward Rowe Snow devoted an entire chapter to "Tugboat Annies" in his *Women of the Sea* (Commonwealth Editions, 1962).

219 "Columbia River Now Has 'Tugboat Jennie," *Corvallis Gazette Times*, 24 December 1938, and "Port of Secoma Has Rival In Portland Now," *Eugene Register Guard*, 26 December 1938.

220 "Another Tugboat Annie," *Toronto Star Weekly*, 23 March 1935.

221 Drew, "In the Wheelhouse of the Russell I," Berkshire Edge, 18 January 2020.

222 A device that measures a vessel's speed through water.

223 "Canadian Author Sells Movie Rights," 28 July 1931. Also "Writer Paid $10,000 For Picture Rights," *Toronto Daily Star*, 14 July 1931.

224 "Author's Inspiration Is People Around Him," 12 March 1932.

225 "Marie Dressler, Noted Actress, Dies," *New York Times*, 29 December 1934.

226 "Wallace Beery, 64, Screen Star, Dies," *New York Times*, 17 April 1949.

227 Entertainment, *Indianapolis Star*, 12 November 1932.

228 "Mervyn LeRoy, 86, Dies; Director and Producer," *New York Times*, 14 September 1987.

229 David L. Goodrich, *The Real Nick and Nora: Frances Goodrich and Albert Hackett, Writers of Stage and Screen Classics* (Southern Illinois University Press, 2001)

230 Lewis Jarrard, "Hoosier in Hollywood," *Angola (Ind.) Herald*, 20- May 1932.

231 "Troupe Is Like Little Family," *Detroit Free Press*, 20 September 1932.

232 George Shaffer, "Colleen Moore Finds Her Comeback Chance in 'Lost,' " New York *Daily News*, 13 January 1933.

233 New Films Reviewed, 5 August 1933.

234 James Bawden & Ron Miller, *You Ain't Heard Nothin' Yet: Interviews with Stars From Hollywood's Golden Era* (University of Kentucky Press, 2017)

235 "Marie Dressler Explains Perilous Pitfalls of The 'Tailor-Made' Role," *Southtown Economist*, 16 November 1933.

236 "Marie Solves a Problem," 28 May 1933.

237 "Actress Good Cook," *Tacoma News Tribune*, 26 August 1933.

238 "Joan's Eyes O.K.? Sure! They Make Writer Blink," *Daily News*, 13 October 1932.

239 "Beery Is Forced To Forget Tricks," *Daily Olympian*, 27 August 1933.

240 "Thrills, Laughs, Perils, Pathos in 'Tugboat Annie,' " 1 August 1933. For an overview of films made in the Puget Sound region, see Zachary Keeler, "When Hollywood Went to Washington: Film's Golden Age in the Evergreen State," The Great Depression in Washington State, https://depts.washington.edu/depress/when_hollywood_went_to_washington.shtml (viewed 9 November 2022).

241 "London's Haunts Shown at Fifth," *Seattle Post-Intelligencer*, 1 August 1933.

242 Theatres, 23 October 1933.

243 " 'Tugboat Annie' Cameras Get Tough Workout in Making This Film," *Arnold (Neb.) Sentinel*, 8 March 1934.

244 *My Own Story*, As told to Mildred Harrington (Little, Brown, 1934). The anecdote also appears in "Life Begins at 60," by Dressler as told to Harrington, *Redbook*, December 1934.

245 "Storm at Sea Adds Thrills In 'Tugboat Annie'," 2 August 1933. See also "Tugboat Moved South for Film," *Seattle Post-Intelligencer*, 3 August 1933.

246 Screen Oddities, Washington *Evening Star*, 24 June 1933.

247 *The Record*, 31 July 1933.

248 "Film Players Due in City for Shots," *Bellingham Herald*, 18 April 1933.

249 " 'Tugboat Annie' Needs Seattle Crew of 5,000," *Seattle Daily Times*, 14 April 1933 & "Welcome Flags Going Up For Annie's Son," *Seattle Daily Times*, 19 April 1933.

250 Kunte Berger & Stephen Hegg, "How Tugboat Annie pulled Seattle onto the silver screen" *Norwegian American*, 28 January 2021.

251 "Tug Boat Annie, Ahoy!" *Seattle Daily Times*, 11 April 1933.

252 "Movie Staff In Seattle To film 'Tugboat Annie,'" *Seattle Post-Intelligencer*, 10 April 1933.

253 " 'Ah! Ha!' Hisses 'Villain' Hubbard to Tugboat Annie," *Seattle Daily Times*, 24 April 1933.

254 "Tugboat Annie's Fleet Likely To Escape Wrath," *Seattle Times*, 25 April 1933.

255 "Prima Donna Tugs! Annie's Boats Won't Smoke Up; So Raine Puffs, LeRoy Fumes," *Seattle Daily Times*, 13 April 1933.

256 Mainly About People, *Daily Olympian*, 5 September 1933.

257 https://entertainment.ha.com/itm/movie-tv-memorabilia/tugboat-model-miniature-from-tugboat-annie/a/997049-1131.s

258 11 April 1933. Also "Hizzoner Gives Advice," *Los Angeles Times*, 27 April 1933.

259 "U. of W. Coed Crashes Aboard Film Tugboat," 20 June 1933.

260 " 'Old-Timer' Talks On Okanogan-Cariboo Trail," *Bellingham Herald*, 14 August 1933.

261 Andy Lytle, "Andy Visits Land of Make-Believe," *Vancouver Sun*, 29 May 1933.

262 "Housewife Doubles For Marie Dressler," *Evening Sun*, 25 April 1933.

263 Mike Foster, "What, No Sea Gulls? Director Must Have Them For Real Nautical Picture," 11 April 1933.

264 From the Crow's Nest by The Skipper, 26 December 1941.

265 "Old 'Tugboat Annie' Ship Has North Sea War Job," *New York Times*, 8 November 1941. See also "Reminiscent of Seven-Mast Schooner," *Seattle Star*, 8 May 1936.

266 Hollywood Notes, *Morning Sentinel*, 22 February 1944.

267 " 'Celebrity' tugboat taken up the Tyne," *Evening Chronicle*, 11 January 2012.

268 Keeping Posted, "A Weary Old Ship," 17 March 1951.

269 " 'Celebrity' tugboat taken up the Tyne," *Newcastle Evening Chronicle*, 11 January 2012.

270 "At M-G-M," *Silver Screen*, April 1934.

271 Richard E. Hays, " 'Tugboat Annie' World Premiere of Wide Interest," *Seattle Daily Times*, 28 July 1933.

272 "Tugboat Annie Here; Governor, Mayor to Honor Film; Ships in Harbor Blow Whistles," *Seattle Daily Times*, 28 July 1933.

273 Eleanor Boba, "Tugboat Annie: Seattle's First Movie," HistoryLInk.org, 10 November 2015.

274 " 'Tugboat Annie' Evokes Cheers," 29 July 1933.

275 "Marie Dressler and Wallace Beery in a Picture of Life Aboard a Pacific Coast Tugboat," 12 August 1933.

276 " 'Tugboat Annie' Scores as Box-Office Hit of Season," 12 August 1933.

277 "Pu-lenty of 'Tugboat' in Troy Showing," *Motion Picture Herald*, 21 October 1933.

278 "Vehicle Advertising the Film 'Tugboat Annie' ...", 10 August 1933, Library of Congress.

279 "It's an Idea," *Variety*, 13 February 1934.

280 *Motion Picture Herald*, 30 September 1933.

281 "Box Office Champions of 1933," 3 February 1934.

282 "Radio Broadcast Features 'Tugboat Annie' Campaign" 30 September 1933.

283 "No Swank as Movie Stars Eat Little and Talk Much," *Toronto Daily Star*, 27 January 1933.

284 Raine, "A Writer Looks at Hollywood," *Maclean's*, 15 April 1933.

285 Norman soon took a break and booked into San Ysidro Ranch in Santa Barbara to get away from Hollywood for a few weeks. *Santa Barbara News Press*, 4 December 1938.

286 "Canadian Writer Weds This Month," *Brantford Exposition*, 4 April 1928.

287 "Park's Advantages Induce Warners To Shoot More Scenes," *Chico Record Sun*, 3 October 1937.

288 H. Katherine Smith, A Good Listener, *Buffalo Courier Express*, 11 December 1938.

289 Strolling Around the Town, 25 March 1933.

290 "Peter B. Kyne, 77, Novelist Is Dead; Creator of Cappy Ricks Had Written 25 Books and 1,000 Stories and Articles," *New York Times*, 26 November 1957.

291 Coincidentally, in *Cappy Ricks; or, the Subjugation of Matt Peasley* (1916), a Glasgow-built, London-based steamer *Narcissus* figures. In *Cappy Ricks Retires* (1922), passing reference is made to another freighter belonging to the Oriental Steamship Co., the *Narcissus*.

292 Cappy Ricks may have been based on Captain Robert Dollar of the Dollar Steamship Line, or on newspaper publisher Sam Perkins. "Peter B. Kyne Is Gone, But Others Spin Northwest Yarns," *Bellingham Herald*, 5 January 1958.

293 "Buffalonians in Hollywood: Norman Reilly Raine Finds Writing for Movies Is Not Real Work, But Just Recreation," 24 July 1935.

294 O.O. McIntyre, New York Day by Day, *Grand Island Daily Independent*, 5 April 1934.

295 "Get Out Where Story Is Urges Norman Reilly Raine," 23 March 1936.

296 "Author's Inspiration Is People Around Him," 12 March 1932.

297 "Creator of Tugboat Annie Back in Buffalo for Visit," *Buffalo Evening News*, 1 July 1939.

298 Fergus Hoffman, "Gen. Wood et al Go North; Heaven Help Wild Animals," *Seattle Daily Times*, 8 August 1939.

299 Simon Willmetts, *In Secrecy's Shadow: The OSS and CIA in Hollywood Cinema 1941-1979* (Cambridge University Press, 2016)

300 "Birth Of Idea For Film In Hollywood Described," *Charlotte Observer*, 7 January 1940.

301 Cinemarks, *Boxoffice*, 13 May 1939.

302 Card serial number 2956, Ancestry.com.

303 "St. Patrick's Program" and "Opera Reading Club Juniors," *Los Angeles Daily News,* 16 March and 14 June.

304 "Screen Life in Hollywood, *Standard Sentinel*, 22 January 1940. Coons replied in her column for 20 February 1940.

305 "Norman Reilly Raine, Film Author, in Ottawa," *Ottawa Citizen*, 21 March 1941.

306 Jessica Leonora Whitehead, "Hollywood Goes North: The Making of a 'Canadian' War Epic, Captains of the Clouds," *Canadian Journal of Film Studies*, autumn 2018.

307 Raine's nephew later donated it to the Marie Dressler Foundation in Cobourg, Ontario, according to Betty Lee in *Marie Dressler: The Unlikeliest Star* (Univeristy of Kentucky Press, 1997).

308 "Boy Meets Girl Theme Leads as in Fiction Mart, Agent Says," *Charleston Daily Mail*, 27 April 1937.

309 "H.N. Swanson, 91, An Agent for Writers in Hollywood," *New York Times*, 3 June 1991.

310 "Can the Hollywood Agent Save the Movies?," *Writer's Digest*, January 1951.

311 The contracts in the Drew collection are only ones with Warner Brothers and are from the Swanson years as Raine's agent.

312 The Swanson agency by now is located at 8523 Sunset Blvd., West Hollywood.

313 *Eagle Squadron*, about American pilots who volunteered for the Royal Air Force before the United States entered World War II.

314 Omitted from this list are the original "Tugboat Annie" plus the next four stories, "Passage to Secoma," "Nickel-or-Million," "Spareribs and Sauerkraut" and "No Cure, No Pay." No conclusions can be reached without seeing the M-G-M contract, other than a Variety mention that it was for three stories.

315 "Muni's Zola a Masterpiece," 17 July 1937.

316 "Norman Reilly Raine: A writing career launched in Maclean's leads to an Academy award for the best screen play of the year," *Maclean's*, 1 July 1938.

317 *Walter Wanger Hollywood Independent* (University of Minnesota Press, 2000). The writer misidentifies Raine as a former pilot.

318 *Canadian Film Weekly*, 5 June 1957.

319 *Canadian Film Weekly*, 26 June 1957.

320 From the Editor's Easy Chair, "Norman Reilly Raine Tilts His Lance At Some of Editor's Opinions," 1 October 1938.

321 "Maple Leaf in the Hollywoods," 3 July 1941.

322 "Writing's a Grind," *Cinema Progress*, January 1939.

323 "Five Who Help the Stars Shine," *Cinema Progress: The Life in Film*, January 1939. Los Angeles: Cinema Appreciation League/American Institute of Cinematography.

324 Lexington, Ky.: University of Kentucky Press, 2006.

325 Raine to Wallis, letter, 28 September 1939, Elizabeth and Essex File, Warner Archive of Performing Arts, University of Southern California Archive.

326 Warner Archive, University of Southern California Archive, reproduced in Rudy Behlmer, ed., *Inside Warner Bros. (1935-1951)* (New York: Simon & Schuster1985).

327 Warner Archive, University of Southern California Archive. See also Alan K. Rode, *Michael Curtiz: A Life in Film* (University of Kentucky Press, 2017).

328 Vida Hills Shepard, "Author of Picture Here to Rewrite Part of Film," *Chico Record Sun*, 3 October 1937.

329 Warner Archive, University of Southern California Archive, reproduced in Behlmer.

330 Looking at Hollywood, *Burlington Daily News*, 18 January 1945.

331 "New Orleans Locale," *Buffalo News*, 27 November 1936.

332 "Secretaries Asked to Get Confidential," *Scrantonian Sun*, 9 January 1938.

333 "Norman Raine Is writing Biography Of Bernhardt For Bette Davis To Screen," *Fresno Bee*, 14 March 1938.

334 H. Katherine Smith, A Good Listener, *Buffalo Courier Express*, 11 December 1938.

335 Screen Notes, *Brooklyn Citizen*, 26 May 1938.

336 Reviews and Previews, *Harrisburg Telegraph*, 15 February 1939.

337 Kay Dangerfield, Palette Vignettes of the Valley, *Wilkes-Barre Times Leader*, 5 July 1939.

338 Advertisement, *Times Tribune*, 1 November 1940.

339 Louella O. Parsons, Mary Pickford May Return To Films For Biography," *Fresno Bee*, 26 Mach 1939).

340 "Warner Bros. Report Leigh, Olivier Set For 'Hornblower' Leads," *Los Angeles Evening Citizen News*, 15 July 1940.

341 Edwin Schallert, "Two Studios Propose Franklin Biographies," *Los Angeles Times*, 9 October 1939.

342 Screen News Here and in Hollywood, *New York Times*, 21 December 1939.

343 "Wanger to Europe," *Journal Herald*, 26 October 1941.

344 "Norman Raine To Speak to Future Writers Tonight," *The Battalion*, 4 August 1942.

345 "Disneyish Idea … for New Screen 'Follies,'" *Salt Lake Tribune*, 15 November 1944.

346 Edwin Schallert, "Dickens' Christ Story Highlights Life Saga," *Los Angeles Times*, 17 May 1945.

347 Looking at Hollywood," *Los Gatos Times*, 16 March 1945.

348 Edwin Schallert, " 'Package' Aimed at Roz; Bromfield tale Bought, *Los Angeles Times*, 2 August 1946.

349 Looking at Hollywood, *Los Angeles Times*, 20 June 1946.

350 " 'Free Agent' Leslie Will Do Independent Picture," *Los Angeles Times*, 28 May 1946.

351 "Try and Stop Me," *Burlington Free Press*, 20 November 1954.

352 Hye Bossin, managing editor, *Canadian Film Weekly*, 1960.

353 Glen Carter, "He gave us 'Tugboat Annie,' *Seattle Daily Times*, 30 July 1971.

354 In the Editor's Confidence, 1 February 1932.

355 1 November 1925.

356 "Thesis Presented Through Character," *The Editor*, 25 October 1924.

357 *Nieman Reports*, January 1958. Threnody is a lament.

358 "Berkeleyans Play Major Role in Writers' Parley," *Berkeley Daily Gazette*, 28 April 1960.

359 Al Martinez, "Writers in Parley Here Told to Set Sights on TV Market," *Oakland Tribune*, 15 May 1960.

360 Unrelated, *The Adventures of Tessie the Tugboat* by Eunice Pearl MacDougall is a children's book published in 2014.

361 It was reprinted in *More Trash From Mad* No. 2 (1959). See also "'Tugboat Annie' Takes Helm Today in Tacoma," *Seattle Post-Intelligencer*, 18 October 1940.

362 King Features Syndicate, *Lancaster New Era*, 4 August 1930.

363 *Oakland Post Enquirer,* 31 May 1935.

364 *Nanaimo Daily News*, 23 September 1939.

365 *Salt Lake Telegram*, 30 March 1940.

366 "Woman With a Whim of Iron," *Saturday Evening Post*, 30 November 1946. Hokinson was a staff cartoonist for *The New Yorker.*

367 "Three in Tacoma Will Premiere 'Tugboat,'" *Boxoffice*, 12 October 1940.

368 " 'Tugboat Annie' Sails Its Preem Into Tacoma; Seattle Nixed Stunt," 18 September 1940. See also " 'Tugboat Annie' Gets Official Tacoma Toga," 16 October 1940, and " 'Tugboat Annie' Gets Big Tacoma Sendoff," 23 October 1940.

369 "Tacoma Set To Premiere New Annie Picture," 13 October 1940.

370 "Film actress Marjorie Rambeau, 78," *Boston Globe*, 8 July 1970.

371 "Walter Feeney Puts Over a Tugboat Race," *Motion Picture Herald*, 7 October 1933.

372 " 'North West Mounted' Snatches Limelight," *Boxoffice*, 19 October 1940.

373 A town in Pierce County.

374 "City Opening Arms For 'Tugboat Annie,'" *Tacoma News Tribune*, 19 October 1940.

375 Often labeled by the press as "Tugboat Annie," Anna G. Grimson was head of the Skagit River Navigation & Trading Co., with help from five sisters. The company had been started by their father, Captain H.H. McDonald. In 1934, Grimson was charged by the Washington Department of Public Works with violating shipping regulations by offering cut rates and failing to follow schedules. ("Files Suit to Force Action," *Vancouver News,* 28 April 1934) Columnist Frank Jenkins mused" "Back in war time, they arrested people for raising prices. Now they are arresting them for cutting prices." (*Medford Mail Tribune*, 8 May 1934) The state Supreme Court absolved Grimson, any crime,

accepting her version of scheduling errors. ("Woman Defeats State in Marine Rate Suit," *Spokesman Review*, 3 May 1935). Her *Skagit Belle* was taken over by the U.S. Army during World War II, then returned to her small fleet to carry cargo between Seattle and Mount Vernon, Grimson's brother Capt. Harry H. McDonald on the bridge. Her *Skagit Chief*, launched at Lake Union in Seattle in 1935, was retired in 1960 after it was punctured by a log. A third boat was the *Harvester*. ("Sternwheeler to Be Junked," *Spokane Chronicle*, 29 March 1960).

376 Glen Carter's Carrousel, "Tugboat Annie, *Seattle Times*, 14 June 1970.)

377 "Tacoma Welcomes 'Annie,'" 19 October 1940.

378 " 'Tugboat Annie' Day Made Annual Event," *Boxoffice*, 19 October 1940. See also "Big Tacoma Premiere for 'Tugboat Annie,' " 26 October 1940 and "Proclamation," *Tacoma Times*, 10 October 1940.

379 "Plan to Honor Tugboat Annie," *Tacoma Times*, 10 October 1940. Also Len Higgins, Moovie Memos, "To Name Patron Saint," *News Tribune*, 11 October 1940.

380 "Looking Back at South Sound History Through Words and Pictures," *Tacoma News Tribune*, 18 October 2015. The plaque was later moved to the theater's south wall, then went into storage when the theater was remodeled to become the Broadway Center for the Performing Arts.

381 M-G-M had acquired rights to film four stories; the number was later expanded.

382 "Elsa Maxwell Likely for 'Tugboat Annie' Role," *Los Angeles Times*, 24 January 1940, and Jimmie Fidler, In Hollywood, *Monroe Morning World*, 24 March 1940.

383 Edwin Shallert, "Louise Faenda Named to Play Tugboat Annie," *Los Angeles Times*, 2 November 1939, and "Wally Beery May Team With Louise Fazenda," 11 November 1939.

384 Richard E. Hays, Along Film Row, *Seattle Daily Times*, 10 May 1940.

385 Sheila Graham in Hollywood, *Montreal Star*, 13 May 1955.

386 Philip K. Scheuer, "Warners Scour Town for New Tugboat Annie," *Los Angele Times*, 5 September 1939.

387 "Elsie Robinso Began Brilliant Newspaper Career at Age of 35," *Editor & Pnublisher*, 11 May 1940.

388 *Daily Boston Globe*, 30 April 1937.

389 Hollywood Chatter, "Marjorie Rambeau To Create A New Tugboat Annie," *Lima News*, 7 July 1940.

390 "Tugboat Annie, Sea Heroine, Set for TV in New Series, *Montreal Star*, 27 March 1956.

391 Harold W. Cohen, Cinema Desk, *Pittsburgh Post-Gazette,* 31 January 1940.

392 "A Brand New Tugboat Annie," *Lowell (Mass.) Sun*, 29 June 1940.

393 "Actress Is Annie In Author's Eyes," *Pittsburgh Press*, 30 August 1940.

394 "Woman with a Wallop, *Screenland*, April 1941.

395 "Life-Saver Hale Didn't Like Job," *Spokane Chronicle*, 12 July 1940.

396 "Tugboat Lore Expert Plays Tugboat Annie," 6 January 1941.

397 Covers of *Town Crier*, 14 July and 1 September 1928.

398 " 'Tugboat Annie' Set To Sail Once More," *Evening Star*, 18 September 1939.

399 "Screen News Here and in Hollywood; Warners Buy 'Tugboat Annie' From MGM — N.R. Raine, the Author, to Prepare Script," 2 September 1939.

400 "Fire Rages at Film Studio: 'Tugboat Annie' Set Among Property Lost in $50,000 M.G,M. Blaze," *Los Angeles Times*, 23 November 1940; "Fire in Studio Causes Damage Totaling $50,000," *Santa Maria Daily Times*, 23 November 1940; and "M.G.M. Blaze Cost $350000," *Lost Angeles Times*, 24 November 1940.

401 "Studio Men Make Their Own Fog," *Seattle Post-Intelligencer*, 8 August 1940.

402 "18,000 Gals.," *Tacoma Times*, 3 August 1940.

403 "Tugboat Annie Sails Again," 5 September 1941.

404 " 'Tugboat Annie' Has Laugh Cargo," *Seattle Daily Times*, 25 October 1940.

405 "Tugboat Annie Found Bucking Strong Currents in Warner Film at the Strand," 9 November 1940.

406 Cinemarks, 17 August 1940 and "Actress, Writer and Wife To Visit Tea Room," *Hollywood Citizen News*, 12 August 1940.

407 John Chapman, Hollywood, 7 September 1940.

408 Hollywood Personalities, *Boxoffice*, 24 August 1940, and "Fall Production Pattern Taking Shape, With Prospects Bright," same publication, 14 September 1940.

409 In Hollywood, 16 July 1940.

410 "Beans," Keeping Posted, 3 August 1940.

411 "War Does One Movie Big Favor; Interred Danish Steamer 'Saves' New Tugboat Annie Picture," *Pittsburgh Post-Gazette*, 28 June 1940.

412 "Four-Acre Lake," 31 July 1938.

413 Preview Postscripts, *Modern Screen*, January 1941.

414 "National Legion of Decency List," *Catholic Northwest Progress*, 8 November 1940.

415 Cinema, 23 October 1933.

416 In an amusing switch, Peter Kenter in *TV North: Everything You Wanted to Know About Canadian Television* (Vancouver: Whitecap, 2001) said "crusty skipper Tugboat Annie, [was] the Ma Kettle of the Pacific Northwest sea lanes...."

417 Hedda Hopper's Hollywood, *Los Angeles Times*, 8 September 1939.

418 "Marjorie Main," 5 May 1946.

419 Dial-Lites, *Daily Press Journal*, 14 May 1946.

420 The Listener, " 'Tugboat Annie' On WREC at 7:30," *Press-Scimitar*, 14 May 1946. See also "Tugboat Annie," *Circleville Herald*, 14 May 1946. Other stations in that city that same Tuesday timeslot aired *Date With Judy*, *Jack Armstrong*, *Captain Midnight* and *Whoa Bill Club*. WCAU in Camden, N.J., ran *This Is My Best* at 9:30 p.m. against *American Forum*, *Doctor Talks It Over* and *Fibber McGee and Molly*.

421 Jean M. Miller, Daily Dialings, *Latrobe (Penn.) Bulletin*, 14 May 1946.

422 On the Beam, *Boston Globe*, 14 May 1946, and "Tugboat Annie," *Circleville Herald*, same date.

423 "Hollywood Night," 12 May 1946.

424 Jerry Haendiges Vintage Radio Log.

425 The Brighter Side, *Chillicothe Gazette*, 19 September 1940.

426 "Two New Programs Debut Tonight," *Ottawa Citizen*, 23 April 1947, and Charlie Walls, At Radio Ringside, *St. Catherines Standard*, 23 April 1947.

427 *St. Catherines Standard*, 23 April 1947.

428 Radio Programs Saturday, *Sun Journal*, 4 March 1939.

429 Mark Barron, On Broadway With Barron, *Lancaster Eagle-Gazette*, 10 April 1950; C.D. Butterfield, Radio-TV Day by Day, Long Branch, N.J., *Daily Record*, 10 February 1950; Danton Walker, Broadway, *New York Daily News*, 24 February 1950; and Radio-TV Sidelights, *Kansas City Star*, 18 June 1950. Also "'Tugboat Annie' for Air," *Fort Worth Star-Telegram*, 12 February 1950.

430 Radio Column, *Logansport Pharos Tribune*, 3 March 1939.

431 Captain Roscoe Fawcett, Screen Oddities, *Dayton Daily News*, 6 June 1933.

432 "Tugboat Annie, Sea Heroine, Set for TV in New Series," *Montreal Star*, 27 March 1956.

433 Advertisement, *Ventura County Star Free Press*, 23 November 1940.

434 "Toreador Pants," 21 May 1955.

435 "Fashionable 'Tugboat Annie,'" *Buffalo Evening News*, 9 May 1959.

436 Palette Vignettes of the Valley, *Times-Leader*, 5 July 1939.

437 I Cover the Waterfront, "Historic Foss tug arriving for visit," 2 September 1998.

438 "Talk by Toots: How Harbor Tugs Communicate," St. John, New Brunswick, *Daily Sun*, 11 November 1903, reprinted from the *New York Sun*.

439 *Tugs and Other Hard-Working Vessels of Puget Sound: A Scrapbook from the Earlier Days* (Bothell, Wash.: Book Publishers Network, 2010).

440 "Famed Tug On Fire in Stormy Sea," *Seattle Star*, 18 February 1937 &"Blaze in Foss Tug Quelled," *Tacoma Daily Ledger*, 19 February 1937.

441 Wiley Padan, It's True, *Culver Citizen*, 13 May 1936.

442 "Salvage Planned for 'Tugboat Annie' Craft," *Hollywood Citizen News*, 19 February 1937.

443 "Same Tugboat Wally Beery Used in 'Tugboat Annie,'" *Tacoma Times*, 25 October 1939. Also "Dressler's Tugboat Again Faces Camera," *Spokesman-Review*, 2 July 1939.

444 " 'Thunder Afloat' Uses Old Tugboat," *Tacoma Times*, 28 December 1939.

445 "Ocean Going Tug Nearly Finished," *Tacoma Daily Ledger*, 25 April 1934. See also "Boat Building Shows Upturn," same newspaper, 29 May 1934.

446 Glen Carter's My Waterfront columns were collected in a book from Seagull Books in 1977. See Carter, "Red Stack to haul Bristol Bay fish," *Seattle Daily Times*, 9 April 1971. Carter discussed Tugboat Annie several times, including "Funny you should ask about 'Tugboat Annie,'" *Seattle Times*, 3 September 1976, and "He gave us 'Tugboat Annie,'" 30 July 1971. Carter (1923-2002) covered the seaport for the *Times* beginning in 1969, retiring in the early 1980s.

447 Glen Carter's Carrousel, *Seattle Sunday Times*, 16 May 1971.

448 "Mighty Foss Tug Tackling A Leviathan," *Tacoma News Tribune*, 4 April 1971 & Michael J. Sweeney, "Famed Carrier Here for Dismantling," same newspaper, 28 June 1971.

449 Glen Carter, "Stand by for a big week," *Seattle Daily Times*, 16 May 1971.

450 Chuck Kleeschulte, "History Afloat," *Juneau Empire*, 28 August 1984.

451 "Tugboat gets top billing," 16 May 1981.

452 See also Mike Stork, *Foss Maritime Company* (Arcadia, 2007) and Michael R. Skalley's *Foss: Ninety Years of Towboating* (1981).

453 "Arthur Foss, of Tug Company, Dies," 19 October 1964.

454 "Kiwanians Hear Tugboat History," *Issaquah Press*, 20 March 1941.

455 "Hotcakes for the 'Cowboys of the Deep,'" 21 April 1940.

456 Written by Alfred L. Gehri, 20 January 1940. *Marine Digest* for 12 August 1944 carried the article "House of Foss Has Added Brilliance To Colorful History of Pacific Northwest."

457 G. Franklin Shirbroun and Susan Eggleton, proprietors respectively of Live Oak Booksellers in Langley, Wash., and Timbuktu Books in Seattle, provided copies of elusive *Piling Busters* and *My Waterfront* books.

Collins Books supplied a copy of *Seafair Cook Book*, which brims with Northwest recipes.

458 Obituary, Tacoma *Sunday News Tribune*, 3 October 1976.

459 "Norman Raine To Write For Piling Busters," Tacoma *Sunday News Tribune*, 19 October 1952.

460 13 August 1950.

461 Garrison, "Piling Busters Rules Issued," *News Tribune*, 20 August 1950.

462 Garrison, "Piling Busters Results Near," *News Tribune*, 17 September 1950.

463 Jay Wells, Marine News, "Capt. Noel Davis Wins Work Boat Service Trophy," *Seattle Sunday Times*, 1 March 1953. G Also "Piling Buster Dinner Feb, 28," *Tacoma News Sun*, 1 February 1953, and "Pick Tacoman's Very Tall Tale," *News Tribune*, 1 March 1953.

464 The novel was serialized by NEA in the *Lubbock Morning Avalanche* and other newspapers and featured in the crime fiction digests *Manhunt*. The author's real name was Davis Dresser.

465 New York: D. Appleton Century.

466 March 1946.

467 "On L.M.S.," *Derby Evening Telegraph*, 22 May 1934, and " 'Tugboat Annie' of the Rails; How an Engine Was Named," Gloucester *Citizen*, 22 May 1934. Also " 'Tugbot Annie' How New Railway Engine Got Its Name," (Dundee, Scotland) *Evening Telegraph*, 21 May 1934.

468 Public Notice, *Adirondack Daily Enterprise*, 25 November 2020.

469 Also erroneously called "Hangman's Noose" and "Hangman's Wit." "Shuberts, Busy at Last, Making Tryout Bookings," *New York Daily News*, 31 July 1932.

470 " 'Hangman's Whip' Is a Tough Melodrama," *New York Daily News*, 25 February 1933.

471 Edwin Schallert, "Women Revolt Against Screen War Horrors," *Los Angeles Times*, 14 April 1943.

472 "Raine Stops In 'Tugboat Annie's Port," 23 March 1933.

473 Looking at Hollywood," *Harrisburg Telegraph*, 26 July 1943.

474 "Tugboat Annie On Deck," *Marine Digest*, 4 February 1950.

475 Community Notes, *Sarasota Herald Tribune*, 29 January 1998.

476 Suzanne Chessler, "Multi-Talented," *Jewish News*, 16 December 1994.

477 Frances Clark et al, *Music Tree Book One* (Sunny-Birchard, 2000).

478 Bill Lohmann, "Beloved host of 'Sailor Bob' children's show dies," *Richmond Times-Dispatch*, 22 February 2019.

479 Maritime Folknet: Celebrating the Maritime Music of the Pacific Northwest. Maritime Folknet.com (viewed 14 December 2018).

480 "Actress Jane Darwell, 87, Won Oscar in 1939 Film," *Boston Globe*, 15 August 1967.

481 "The Regal, Shepton Mallet," 19 December 1941.

482 "Captain Tugboat Annie," 28 December 1945.

483 It was reported that Poverty Row studio Monogram had acquired the screen rights; Monogram had become a Republic affiliate. "News of the Screen," *Elizabethtown Echo*, 27 April 1944. The *Los Angeles Times* reported James S. Barkett had acquired rights to 21 Annie stories. "Buys Many Annie Stories," 11 July 1944.

484 "James S Burkett Plans Series Based on 'Tugboat Annie' Stories," 14 April 1944.

485 "Marjorie Rambeau to Star in Tugboat Annie," *Seattle Post-Intelligencer*, 8 April 1944.

486 Actress Kathy Staff (1928-2008), who played frumpy, no-nonsense Nora Batty in British television's very-long-running comedy *Last of the Summer Wine*, would have been an apt Annie, albeit with a North Yorkshire accent.

487 "Tugboat Annie Resumes Career," *Rocky Mountain Telegram*, 9 March 1946.

488 "Jane Darwell, Screen and Stage Star Is Neighborly Type Person," 5 January 1945.

489 "Captain Tugboat Annie," 17 December 1945.

490 "Captain Tugboat Annie: Combination of Hoke and Sentiment Should Go Over with the Family Trade," 28 December 1945.

491 *The Daily Boston Globe* for 15 September 1946 ran a non-story about Marian "Tugboat Annie" McKaye of Miami, "who tips the scales at

250 pounds," in New York Harbor with a cargo of good-will cigars for United Nations delegates, "underwent a screen test to determine if she can replace Marie Dressler in her famous role."

492 "Gambling By T.V.," Vancouver *Province*, 2 August 1950.

493 "Waterfront: Program of the Week," *TV Guide*, 5 February 1955.

494 Richard Irwin, *Film Stars' Television Projects* (2017).

495 Entertainment news, *Seattle Post-Intelligencer*, 31 October 1950.

496 Whitney Bolton, Looking Sideways, *Monitor*, 26 December 1950.

497 " 'Tugboat Annie' Rights to TPA," *Variety*, 16 June 1954.

498 "Chertok Producing 'Tugboat' For TPA, *Variety*, 26 October 1955.

499 "Film Production," 12 October 1955.

500 "$500-A-Word Star," *TV Guide*, 4 June 1955.

501 Erskine Johnson, Hollywood Today, *Bridgeport Telegram*, 5 November 1943, and In Hollywood, *Blytheville Courier*, 22 October 1954. "Charlotte Greenwood's 'Tugboat Annie' Vidpix," *Variety*, 23 August 1954, indicate the producer, was Edward Small. Jack Chertok was the next producer. "Chertok Producing 'Tugboat' For TPA," *Variety*, 26 October 1955. See also Dan Jenkins, Hollywood, *TV Guide Washington-Baltimore*, 23 October 1954.

502 "$500-A-Word Star," *TV Guide*, Chicago edition, 4 June 1955.

503 Best Bets of the Week, *Salt Lake Tribune*, 15 October 1939.

504 Louella Parsons, "Talk to Helen Traubel About Marie Dressler 'Tugboat Annie' Role," *Toronto Daily Star*, 2 July 1954.

505 Video Notes, *Daily Review*, 3 November 1954.

506 Jack Cortez, That's For Sure, *Fabulous Las Vegas Magazine*, 24 December 1955.

507 "Her Yacht Is Battered; TV's Tugboat Annie Is No Slattern While Ashore," *Chattanooga Daily Times*, 10 May 1959.

508 "Quilted Undies Keep Miss Nail-up Warm," *Toronto Daily Star*, 24 March 1959. "Miss Nail-Up" is a name Urecal gave herself, presumably referring to a pinup.

509 Robert Anderson, "No Beer for Annie Now on TV," *Chicago Daily Tribune*, 23 December 1958.

510 Associated-Rediffusion Ltd. of London handled United Kingdom airing. Advertisement, *Variety*, 31 July 1957.

511 "Lever of Canada Buys Interest in 'Tugboat,'" *Billboard*, 17 May 1957. The company was independent of Lever Brothers in the United States.

512 Sponsor Backstage, *Sponsor*, 24 May 1957.

513 Among other sources, "TPA's '56 Budget Tops $10,000,000; Four New Shows," *Variety*, 18 January 1956, and "TPA's $10,500,000 '57 Prod. Budget; Six New Shows," same publication, 9 January 1957.

514 Dick Lewis, "Sponsor Is Co-Producer of Adventures of Tugboat Annie," 8 August 1957.

515 More Theatre News, " 'Tugboat Annie' Found Fashionable On Land," 14 May 1959.

516 "Her Voice Resembles a *Cincinnati Enquirer* Hog Caller's And She Is Built Along Lines of Scow,", 27 March 1956.

517 More Theatre News, op cit.

518 "Minerva Urecal To Portray 'Mother' in 'Peter Gunn' Series," NBC-New York press release, 30 July 1959.

519 Robert Anderson, "TV's Tugboat Annie Takes 'Mother' Role," *Chicago Daily Tribune*, 23 August 1959.

520 "Toronto Drydock Company Ltd.: A Short Corporate History and Fleet List," *Scanner Monthly Bulletin of the Toronto Marine Historical Society*, March 1976.

521 Registry and Rig Information, Historical Collections of the Great Lakes, Bowling Green State University. Also, "Ship of the Month No. 266: J.C. Stewart," *The Scanner: Monthly News Bulletin of the Toronto Marine Historical Society*, January 2002.

522 "Tugboat Annie Is Back — This Time In Toronto," *Ottawa Citizen*, 17 July 1957, and "Tugboat Annie, Bulwinkle Are at Towing War Again," *Sault Star*, 16 July 1957.

523 "Minerva Urecal, a Character Actress, and a Character On or Off Stage!" *Los Angeles Times*, 22 March 1959.

524 "Tugboat Annie," *Montreal Gazette*, 21 September 1957.

525 "Visiting Ladies," 7 September 1957.

526 UCLA Library Special Collections, Performing Arts, holds a copy of the script.

527 " 'Tugboat Annie's' 128G Pilot," *Variety*, 14 March 1956. See also Milton A. Gordon, "In Highly-Competitive Era, Strong Syndicated Product is Proving A Major Weapon," same magazine, 19 March 1958.

528 "Minerva Urecal Didn't Want to Travel, But the Fine Print Said 'Anywhere'!" *Chicago Tribune*, 14 February 1959.

529 "Hold Theatre 'Sneak' Of New TV Program," *Motion Picture Daily*, 4 February 1957; " 'Tugboat' in Theatre 'Sneak,'" *Variety*, 6 February 1957; and "Pre-Tested" advertisement, 19 February1958.

530 Bill Fiset, The TV People, "A Lady All at Sea" and "Cheaper Than Chartering Two," *Oakland Tribune*, 14 April 1959.

531 "Tugboat Annie's On TV Now," 26 October 1957.

532 Entertainment, *Ottawa Journal,* 21 December 1957.

533 *Broadcasting,* 24 February 1958.

534 George A. and Edith Ann Burke, Looking at T-V, *Dallas (Pa.) Post*, 8 August 1958.

535 " 'Honeymooners' Spark a Trend," *Variety*, 5 March 1958.

536 12 March 1958.

537 "WBZ Drowned in Sea of Rival Plugs in Bally For 'Tugboat Annie,'" *Variety*, 6 August 1958.

538 Classic TV Archive — Canadian Series.

539 *Writer's Digest*, September 1957.

540 Bob Leszczak (McFarland, 2012).

541 Steven Vern Reddicliffe, *Voices of Comedy Conversations With Writers of Television's Most Enduring Shows*, master's thesis, University of Texas, Austin, 2010.

542 Philip Wylie's 69 stories about Captain Crunch Adams and his wife Sari and his partner Des Smith center on deep-sea fishing aboard the *Poseidon* from Gulf Stream Dock in Miami. The TV series aired 1956-1957.

543 "First in the Post, Then on Television," 26 October 1957.

544 Les Wedman, T.V. in Review, "News and Views," *Vancouver Province*, 19 October 1957.

545 Night Watch, "August a dumping ground for pilot shows that failed," *Boston Globe*, 22 July 1976.

546 "Television's audience scales Olympic heights," *Journal Herald*, 27 July 1976.

547 Vincent Terrace, *Encyclopedia of Television Shows 1925 Through 2010*, second edition (McFarland, 2011). Also "Double Feature Night," *News Pilot*, 9 March 1974, and "Good Friends," *The Republic*, 9 March 1974.

548 "Ewings on Sound at Summer Home," 5 July 1934.

549 "In the Editor's Confidence," *Maclean's*, 1 June 1936.

550 " 'Tugboat Annie' Author Buys," *Hollywood Citizen News*, 5 November 1938, and "New Dwellings Rising in Outpost Area," 27 January 1940. The Raines had previously built a house at Sherwood Lake. Public Records, *Oxnard Daily Courier*, 7 May 1937.

551 "Creator of Tugboat Annie Back in Buffalo for Visit," *Buffalo Evening News*, 1 July 1939; "Dancer Injured in Skid Crash," *Lost Angeles Times*, 21 December 1952; "Dancer Dies of Injuries in Auto Crash," *Los Angeles Times*, 29 December 1952. See also "Artist Home After 25 Years, Finds 2 Left in Family," *Scrantonian Sun*, 9 July 1939.

552 Kay Dangerfield, Palette Vignettes of the Valley, *Wilkes-Barre Times Leader*, 5 July 1939.

553 "Club Junior to Advance Plans for Puccini Opera," *Los Angeles Times*, 21 January 1940. See also Memo Pad, *Los Angeles Times*, 24 April 1940.

554 "Opera Group Elects Staff," *Los Angeles Times*, 24 April 1940.

555 "Assistants Will Hold British Day," *Los Angeles Times*, 10 March 1941.

556 Napier Moore's Scratch Pad, *National Post*, 9 June 1956.

557 Philip Scheuer, This Town Called Hollywood, *Chicago Daily Tribune*, 24 September 1944.

558 "U.S. Lists Top Salaries," 19 September 1942.

559 "U.S. Lists Salaries of Para., Warner, 20th Top Earners," 17 June 1946.

560 "Joyce R. Raine Divorces Writer," *Los Angeles Times*, 12 February 1946. Also "Norman R. Raine Sued for Divorce," *Los Angeles Times*, 10 January 1946.

561 "Norman R. Raine Divorced as Cruel," *Los Angeles Citizen News,* 11 February 1946.

562 News items, *Seattle Daily Times,* 23 March 1939, and *Eldridge Daily News,* 31 March 1951.

563 Harrison Carroll, Behind the Scenes in Hollywood, *Wilkes-Barre Times Leader,* 18 September 1950.

564 She died following an auto-pedestrian accident in 1952.

565 10 May 1952.

566 Betty divorced claiming her husband spent too much time flirting with her sister. "No Harmony in Home, Song Writing Twin Says," *Los Angeles Times,* 10 April 1957, and "Husband Flirts With Her Twin, Wife Declares," *San Bernardino County Sun,* 10 April 1957. 10 May 1952. "Dancer Granted Divorce From 'Run-Out' Mate," *Mirror News,* 10 April 1957. "Pretty Los Angeles Wife Says Husband Refuses To Contest Divorce Suit," *Jet,* 2 May 1957.

567 "Author Reveals Secret Wedding," *Albany Democrat Herald,* 8 January 1959; "Writer Reveals Actress Wife," *Corsicana Daily,* 7 January 1959; "Tugboat Annie Creator Reveals His Marriage," *Los Angeles Times,* 7 January 1959; " 'Tugboat Annie' Writer Discloses Secret Marriage," *Appeal Democrat,* 7 January 1959; "Raine Bares Marriage to Actress," *Press Telegram,* 7 January 1959, and others.

568 "Tugboat Annie Creator Reveals His Marriage," 7 January 1959.

569 Keeping Posted, 4 October 1952.

570 https://www.legacy.com/us/obituaries/indeonline/name/nancy-princehorn-obituary?id=14411442

571 Al Martinez, "Writers in Parley Here Told To Set Sights on TV Market," *Oakland Tribune,* 15 May 1960.

572 "Film Academy Board Elected," *Los Angeles Times,* 7 October 1941.

573 "Tugboat Annie Creator, Dies," 28 July 1971.

574 "Norman Reilly Raine, 76; Services Held for Creator of Tugboat Annie," 28 July 1981.

575 "Service Held for Creator of Tugboat Annie," *Los Angeles Times,* 28 July 1971. Same date, "Screen Writer Buried," *Oxnard Press-Courier.*

576 Lee Harris, Linked-in, viewed 11 November 2022.

577 Weber Studies, Spring 1991.

578 14 January 1949.

579 News item, Albany, Ore., *Democrat-Herald*, 16 May 1951.

580 "Street Named for Tugboat Annie," *Tacoma News-Tribune*, 26 September 1951; "Name Taconic Street For Tugboat Annie," *Amarillo Daily News*, 26 September 1951; "Want Street Renamed For Tugboat Annie," *Tacoma Daily Ledger*, 21 August 1951; "Tugboat Annie Street," *Fresno Bee*, 27 September 1951.

581 "Towboat Annie's Café Moving to Louisville," *Courier- Journal*, 26 February 1997, and "Owners told to move closed, floating eatery," same publication, 6 August 2004. By 2004, Towboat Annie's River Café, plagued by high water and other issues, closed

582 "50th daffodil festival draws throng," *Olympian*, 10 April 1983.

583 Advertisement, *News Tribune*, 26 August 2009.

584 "New Font from Agfa," *Printing World*, 4 March 2002.

585 "Canada Adds to Hollywood Stars Series," *Mekeel's Stamps Magazine*, 11 July 2008.

586 Advertisement, *News Tribune*, 1 September 2019.

587 Small, steam-powered passenger and freight vessels that plied Puget Sound and its various tributaries. Peak years were between the world wars.

588 According to the first short story, published in 1931, Terry had died the year before.

589 More likely in 1962, when the last *Post* story was published.

590 Aka Jane Darwell.